STANDING UNDER THE CROSS

T&T Clark New Studies in Bonhoeffer's Theology and Ethics

Series editors
Jennifer McBride
Michael Mawson
Philip G. Ziegler

STANDING UNDER THE CROSS

Essays on Bonhoeffer's Theology

Michael Mawson

LONDON • NEW YORK • OXFORD • NEW DELHI • SYDNEY

T&T CLARK

Bloomsbury Publishing Plc

50 Bedford Square, London, WC1B 3DP, UK
1385 Broadway, New York, NY 10018, USA
29 Earlsfort Terrace, Dublin 2, Ireland

BLOOMSBURY, T&T CLARK and the T&T Clark logo are trademarks
of Bloomsbury Publishing Plc

First published in Great Britain 2023
Paperback edition published 2025

Copyright © Michael Mawson, 2023

Michael Mawson has asserted his right under the Copyright, Designs and Patents Act, 1988, to be identified as Author of this work.

For legal purposes the Acknowledgements on pp. ix–x constitute an extension of this copyright page.

Cover image: Dietrich Bonhoeffer (1906–45) photographed in the late 1930s.
Photo by ullstein bild via Getty Images

All rights reserved. No part of this publication may be reproduced or transmitted in any form or by any means, electronic or mechanical, including photocopying, recording, or any information storage or retrieval system, without prior permission in writing from the publishers.

Bloomsbury Publishing Plc does not have any control over, or responsibility for, any third-party websites referred to or in this book. All internet addresses given in this book were correct at the time of going to press. The author and publisher regret any inconvenience caused if addresses have changed or sites have ceased to exist, but can accept no responsibility for any such changes.

A catalogue record for this book is available from the British Library.

Library of Congress Control Number: 2023939230

ISBN: HB: 978-0-5677-0946-2
PB: 978-0-5677-0951-6
ePDF: 978-0-5677-0947-9
eBook: 978-0-5677-0950-9

Series: T&T Clark New Studies in Bonhoeffer's Theology and Ethics

Typeset by Newgen KnowledgeWorks Pvt. Ltd., Chennai, India

To find out more about our authors and books visit www.bloomsbury.com and sign up for our newsletters.

For Ruth Wivell
Always ready to light a fire

CONTENTS

Acknowledgements ix
List of Abbreviations xi

INTRODUCTION 1

Chapter 1
STUDYING THEOLOGY IN A TIME OF CRISIS: BONHOEFFERIAN
INSIGHTS FOR THEOLOGICAL THINKING TODAY 10

Part I
THE FORMS OF THE WORD

Chapter 2
'AS A WHOLE AND IN ITS PARTS': BONHOEFFER'S APPROACH TO
SCRIPTURE 21

Chapter 3
LIVING IN THE FORMS OF THE WORD: BONHOEFFER AND FRANZ
ROSENZWEIG ON THE APOCALYPTIC MATERIALITY OF SCRIPTURE 37

Chapter 4
THE WEAKNESS OF THE WORD AND THE REALITY OF
GOD: BONHOEFFER'S GRAMMAR OF WORLDLY LIVING 49

Chapter 5
LUTHERAN OR LUTHERISH? ENGAGING MICHAEL DEJONGE ON
BONHOEFFER'S RECEPTION OF LUTHER 61

Part II
THE VULNERABILITIES OF BODILY LIFE

Chapter 6
CREATURES *CORAM DEO*: BONHOEFFER, DISABILITY AND
THEOLOGICAL ANTHROPOLOGY 73

Chapter 7
ENCOUNTERING GRACE AFTER THE FALL: BONHOEFFER'S 'NATURAL LIFE' AS A RESPONSE TO GERALD MCKENNY ON BIOTECHNOLOGY   91

Chapter 8
SHOULD WE LIVE FOREVER? REFLECTING ON LIFE EXTENSION TECHNOLOGIES WITH BONHOEFFER AND KARL BARTH   109

Part III
A COMMUNITY OF THE CROSS

Chapter 9
'ONLY THE SUFFERING GOD CAN HELP': BONHOEFFER AND JÜRGEN MOLTMANN ON DIVINE PASSIBILITY   119

Chapter 10
THE SPIRIT AND THE COMMUNITY: PNEUMATOLOGY AND ECCLESIOLOGY IN ROBERT JENSON, REINHARD HÜTTER AND BONHOEFFER   135

Chapter 11
THE POLITICS OF JESUS AND THE ETHICS OF CHRIST: ON WHY BONHOEFFER IS NOT AN ANABAPTIST   153

Chapter 12
THE STUMBLING BLOCK AND THE LYNCHING TREE: READING BONHOEFFER'S 'LECTURES ON CHRISTOLOGY' WITH JAMES CONE   172

Bibliography   183
Index   197

ACKNOWLEDGEMENTS

The essays that have been collected and revised for this book were written while I worked at the University of Aberdeen, Charles Sturt University and the University of Auckland. A number of friends listened to me present papers or commented on earlier drafts. Some of those who deserve mention are Claire Hein Blanton, Brian Brock, Andrew Clark-Howard, Amy Erickson, Brandin Francabandera, Tom Greggs, Ross Halbach, Cole Jodon, Caireen Likely, Gerald McKenny, Sue McIntyre, Ockert Meyer, Liam Miller, Kevin O'Farrell, Joel Pierce, Justin Pritchett, Di Rayson, John Swinton, Peter Walker and Philip Ziegler.

Other friends in Australia and Aotearoa New Zealand have more recently helped me to expand and deepen my understanding of theology as such: Tau'alofa Anga'aelangi, Sathianathan Clarke, Emily Colgan, Jione Havea, Brian Kolia, Chin Ming Stephen Lim, Janice McRandal, Andrew Picard, Maina Talia and Geoff Thompson. Your work and friendship have challenged and changed me. Thank you.

I appreciate the support of the Maclaurin Goodfellow Trust, which funds my current position and work at the University of Auckland. The Centre for Religion and Ethics and Society at Charles Sturt University provided financial assistance for proofreading and the construction of the index. Thank you to Andrew Clark-Howard for meticulously carrying out these tasks, as well as providing insightful comments that pressed me to clarify and deepen my thinking.

I am grateful to Jennifer McBride and Philip Ziegler, my wonderful co-editors for the T&T Clark Bloomsbury series, 'New Studies in Bonhoeffer's Theology and Ethics'. I appreciate your openness to considering this book for inclusion in the series. It has been a privilege to work with you. As always, it is also wonderful to work with Anna Turton and the team at T&T Clark Bloomsbury.

Finally, I acknowledge and appreciate Lars and Silas, who have regularly been dragged along to seminars and conferences over the last decade, and who complain less than they should. And thank you to my partner, best friend and co-conspirator, Ruth Wivell, to whom I dedicate this book.

Unless otherwise indicated, all Bible quotations are taken from the New Revised Standard Version. The following essays have been revised and updated for this volume with permission:

'Studying Theology in a Time of Crisis.' In *Letters to a Young Theologian*, ed. Henco van der Westhuizen, 234–44. Minneapolis: Fortress Press, 2022.

'Scripture.' *The Oxford Handbook of Dietrich Bonhoeffer*, ed. Michael Mawson and Philip Ziegler, 123–36. Oxford: Oxford University Press, 2019.

'Living in the Forms of the Word: Bonhoeffer and Rosenzweig on the Apocalyptic Materiality of Scripture.' *Studies in Christian Ethics* 34, no. 4 (2021): 455–66.

'The Weakness of the Word and the Reality of God.' *Studies in Christian Ethics* 31, no. 4 (2018): 452–62.

'Lutheran or Lutherish? Framing Bonhoeffer's Reception of Luther', *Modern Theology* 35, no. 2 (2019): 352–9.

'How God Suffers: Bonhoeffer, Moltmann and Theological Language', in *Bonhoeffer and Christology: Revisiting Chalcedon*, ed. Matthias Grebe, Nadine Hamilton, and Christian Schlenker, 154–69. London: T&T Clark Bloomsbury, 2023.

'Encountering Grace After the Fall: The Normativity of Nature in Protestant Ethics', in *The Ethics of Grace: Engaging Gerald McKenny*, ed. Michael Mawson and Paul Martens, 143–60. London: T&T Clark Bloomsbury, 2022.

'Creatures before God: Bonhoeffer, Disability and Theological Anthropology', in *Christ, Church and World: New Studies in Bonhoeffer's Theology and Ethics*, ed. Michael Mawson and Philip G. Ziegler, 119–40. London: T&T Clark Bloomsbury, 2016.

'The Spirit and the Church: Jenson, Hütter, and Bonhoeffer on Pneumatology and Ecclesiology', *International Journal of Systematic Theology*, 14, no. 3 (2013): 453–68.

'The Politics of Jesus and the Ethics of Christ: Why the differences between Yoder and Bonhoeffer Matter', in *The Freedom of a Christian Ethicist: The Future of a Reformation Legacy*, ed. Brian Brock and Michael Mawson, 127–44. London: T&T Clark Bloomsbury, 2016.

ABBREVIATIONS

DBW 1 — *Sanctorum Communio: Eine dogmatische Untersuchung zur Soziologie der Kirche.* Edited by Joachim von Soosten. Munich: Chr. Kaiser Verlag, 1986.

DBW 2 — *Akt und Sein: Transzendentalphilosophie und Ontologie in der systemantischen Theologie.* Chr. Kaiser Verlag, 1988. Edited by Hans-Richard Reuter. Munich: Chr. Kaiser Verlag, 1988.

DBW 3 — *Schöpfung und Fall: Theologische Auslegung zu Genesis 1–3.* Edited by Martin Rüter and Ilse Tödt. Munich: Chr. Kaiser Verlag, 1989.

DBW 4 — *Nachfolge.* Edited by Martin Kuske and Ilse Tödt. Munich: Chr. Kaiser Verlag, 1989; 2nd edn, Gütersloh: Chr. Kaiser/Gütersloher Verlagshaus, 1994.

DBW 5 — *Gemeinsames Leben/ Das Gebetbuch der Bibel.* Edited by Gerhard Ludwig Müller and Albrecht Schönherr. Munich: Chr. Kaiser Verlag, 1987.

DBW 6 — *Ethik.* Edited by Ilse Tödt, Heinz Eduard Tödt, Ernst Feil, and Clifford Green. Munich: Chr. Kaiser Verlag, 1992; 2nd edn, Gütersloh: Chr. Kaiser/Gütersloher Verlagshaus, 1998.

DBW 7 — *Fragmente aus Tegel.* Edited by Renate Bethge and Ilse Tödt. Gütersloh: Chr. Kaiser/Gütersloher Verlagshaus, 1994.

DBW 8 — *Widerstand und Ergebung.* Edited by Christian Gremmels, Eberhard Bethge, and Renate Bethge, with Ilse Tödt. Gütersloh: Chr. Kaiser/ Güters loher Verlagshaus, 1998.

DBW 9 — *Jugend und Studium, 1918–1927.* Edited by Hans Pfeifer, with Clifford Green and Carl-Jürgen Kaltenborn. Munich: Chr. Kaiser Verlag, 1986.

DBW 10 — *Barcelona, Berlin, Amerika, 1928–1931.* Edited by Reinhard Staats and Hans Christoph von Hase, with Holger Roggelin and Matthias Wünsche. Munich: Chr. Kaiser Verlag, 1991.

DBW 11 — *Ökumene, Universität, Pfarramt, 1931–1932.* Edited by Eberhard Amelung and Christoph Strohm. Gütersloh: Chr. Kaiser/Gütersloher Verlagshaus, 1994.

DBW 12 — *Berlin, 1932–1933.* Edited by Carsten Nicolaisen and Ernst-Albert Scharffenorth. Gütersloh: Chr. Kaiser/Gütersloher Verlagshaus, 1997.

DBW 13 — *London, 1933–1935.* Edited by Hans Goedeking, Martin Heimbucher, and Hans-Walter Schleicher. Gütersloh: Chr. Kaiser/Gütersloher Verlagshaus, 1994.

DBW 14 — *Illegale Theologen-Ausbildung Finkenwalde, 1935–1937.* Edited by Otto Dudzus and Jürgen Henkys, with Sabine Bobert-Stützel, Dirk Schulz, and Ilse Tödt. Gütersloh: Chr. Kaiser/Gütersloher Verlagshaus, 1996.

DBW 15	*Illegale Theologenausbildung Sammelvikariate, 1937–1940.* Edited by Dirk Schulz. Gütersloh: Chr. Kaiser/Gütersloher Verlagshaus, 1998.
DBW 16	*Konspiration und Haft, 1940–1945.* Edited by Jørgen Glenthøj, Ulrich Kabitz, and Wolf Krötke. Gütersloh: Chr. Kaiser/Gütersloher Verlagshaus, 1996.
DBW 17	*Register und Ergänzungen.* Edited by Herbert Anzinger and Hans Pfeifer, assisted by Waltraud Anzinger and Ilse Tödt. Gütersloh: Chr. Kaiser/Gütersloher Verlagshaus, 1999.
DBWE 1	*Sanctorum Communio: A Theological Study of the Sociology of the Church.* In *Dietrich Bonhoeffer Works*, English Edition. Edited by Clifford Green. Translated by Reinhard Krauss and Nancy Lukens. Minneapolis, MN: Fortress Press, 1998.
DBWE 2	*Act and Being: Transcendental Philosophy and Ontology in Systematic Theology.* In *Dietrich Bonhoeffer Works*, English Edition. Edited by Wayne Whitson Floyd, Jr. Translated by H. R. Rumscheidt. Minneapolis, MN: Fortress Press, 1996.
DBWE 3	*Creation and Fall: A Theological Exposition of Genesis 1–3.* In *Dietrich Bonhoeffer Works*, English Edition. Edited by John de Gruchy. Translated by Douglas Stephen Bax. Minneapolis, MN: Fortress Press, 2004.
DBWE 4	*Discipleship.* In *Dietrich Bonhoeffer Works*, English Edition. Edited by Geoffrey Kelly and John D. Godsey. Translated by Barbara Green and Reinhard Krauss. Minneapolis, MN: Fortress Press, 2001.
DBWE 5	*Life Together/Prayerbook of the Bible.* In *Dietrich Bonhoeffer Works*, English Edition. Edited by Geoffrey Kelly. Translated by Daniel Bloesch and James Burtness. Minneapolis, MN: Fortress Press, 1996.
DBWE 6	*Ethics.* In *Dietrich Bonhoeffer Works*, English Edition. Edited by Clifford Green. Translated by Reinhard Krauss, Charles West and Douglas W. Stott. Minneapolis, MN: Fortress Press, 2006.
DBWE 7	*Fiction from Tegel Prison.* In *Dietrich Bonhoeffer Works*, English Edition. Edited by Clifford Green. Translated by Nancy Lukens. Minneapolis, MN: Fortress Press, 2000.
DBWE 8	*Letters and Papers from Prison.* In *Dietrich Bonhoeffer Works*, English Edition. Edited by John W. de Gruchy. Translated by Isabel Best, Lisa E. Dahill, Reinhard Krauss, Nancy Lukens, H. Martin Rumscheidt and Douglas W. Stott. Minneapolis, MN: Fortress Press, 2010.
DBWE 9	*The Young Bonhoeffer: 1918–1927.* In *Dietrich Bonhoeffer Works*, English Edition. Edited by Paul Duane Matheny, Clifford Green and Marshall d Johnson. Translated by Mary C. Nebelsick and Douglas W. Stott. Minneapolis, MN: Fortress Press, 2003.
DBWE 10	*Barcelona, Berlin, New York: 1928–1931.* In *Dietrich Bonhoeffer Works*, English Edition. Edited by Clifford Green. Translated by Douglas W. Stott. Minneapolis, MN: Fortress Press, 2007.
DBWE 11	*Ecumenical, Academic, and Pastoral Work: 1931–1932.* In *Dietrich Bonhoeffer Works*, English Edition. Edited by Victoria J. Barnett, Mark S. Brocker and Michael Lukens. Translated by Anne Schmidt-Lange,

	Isabel Best, Nicolas Humphrey, Marion Pauck and Douglas W. Stott. Minneapolis, MN: Fortress Press, 2012.
DBWE 12	*Berlin: 1932–1933.* In *Dietrich Bonhoeffer Works,* English Edition. Edited by Larry Rasmussen. Translated by Isabelle Best and David Higgins. Minneapolis, MN: Fortress Press, 2009.
DBWE 13	*London: 1933–1935.* In *Dietrich Bonhoeffer Works*, English Edition. Edited by Keith Clements. Translated by Isabel Best and Douglas W. Stott. Minneapolis, MN: Fortress, 2007.
DBWE 14	*Theological Education at Finkenwalde: 1935–1937.* In *Dietrich Bonhoeffer Works*, English Edition. Edited by H. Gaylon Barker and Mark S. Brocker. Translated by Douglas W. Stott. Minneapolis, MN: Fortress Press, 2013.
DBWE 15	*Theological Education Underground, 1937–1940.* In *Dietrich Bonhoeffer Works*, English Edition. Edited by Victoria J. Barnett. Translated by Victoria J. Barnett, Claudia D. Bergmann, Peter Frick, and Scott A. Moore. Minneapolis, MN: Fortress Press, 2012.
DBWE 16	*Conspiracy and Imprisonment: 1940–1945.* In *Dietrich Bonhoeffer Works*, English Edition. Edited by Mark S. Brocker. Translated by Lisa E. Dahill and Douglas W. Stott. Minneapolis, MN: Fortress Press, 2006.
DBWE 17	*Index and Supplementary Materials.* Edited by Victoria J. Barnett and Barbara Wojhoski. Minneapolis, MN: Fortress Press, 2014.

INTRODUCTION

Dietrich Bonhoeffer has been a faithful companion of mine for two decades and across multiple contexts. Despite occasional attempts to move on, to focus more on other theologians and issues, I have continually found myself returning to Bonhoeffer, reading him in new ways and discovering new insights.

Throughout most of my twenties, I lived in an intentional Christian community in Aotearoa New Zealand.[1] This rich season of life involved community work, activism, prayer and radical hospitality. In this context, along with others in the community, I remember reading and discussing Bonhoeffer's *Discipleship* and *Life Together*.[2] Bonhoeffer provided language and theological resources for reflecting on the community and its work. As Bonhoeffer wrote,

> Christian community is not an ideal we have to realize, but rather a reality created by God in Christ in which we may participate. The more clearly we learn to recognize that the ground and strength and promise of all our community is in Jesus Christ alone, the more calmly we will learn to think about our community and pray and hope for it.[3]

In the midst of the busyness of our shared life and activity, Bonhoeffer helped us to orientate ourselves prayerfully to Christ and to be wary of our own agendas and idealism.

---

1. My time in the Urban Vision community included running foster homes for young people in Wellington. Towards the end of my time in the community, I lived for two years at the Ngatiawa River Monastery in Waikanae. For a brief account of living in the Urban Vision community from this time, see Michael Mawson and Justin Duckworth, 'Building Prophetic Community in Aotearoa', in *Small Christian Communities Today: Capturing the Movement*, ed. Joseph G. Healy and Jeanne Hinton (Maryknoll: Orbis, 2006), 148–56.

2. Bonhoeffer, *Discipleship*, DBWE 4, and *Life Together*, DBWE 5. I also remember a series of morning devotions at the Ngatiawa River Monastery with Charles Ringma's *Seize the Day with Dietrich Bonhoeffer* (Carol Stream: Nav Press, 2000).

3. DBWE 5: 28.

When I eventually decided to leave the community and pursue doctoral studies, I applied to universities throughout the United Kingdom and United States.[4] The project that I initially proposed focused on political theology and activism; it made absolutely no reference to Bonhoeffer. I accepted an offer of study from the University of Notre Dame in South Bend, Indiana. (Neither my partner nor I had ever travelled to the United States, so on receiving the offer we were surprised to learn that Notre Dame was not on the East Coast.) While the programme was overwhelming at first, Notre Dame provided a rich context for deepening and expanding my intellectual interests.

The programme at Notre Dame had particular strengths in fundamental theology and the Western Christian tradition, what Bonhoeffer had once recommended to his students as 'the company of honest theologians from Paul to Augustine, from Thomas to Luther'.[5] I was able to attend doctoral seminars on the Reformation and Protestant theology with Jerry McKenny and Randall Zachman, to study Aquinas and medieval natural law with Jean Porter and to read key texts in phenomenology and modern philosophy with Kevin Hart and Cyril O'Regan. One summer I was even assigned as a teaching assistant to Gustavo Gutiérrez. We had a lengthy conversation over lunch about Bonhoeffer and liberation theology, and I was delighted to discover his essay on Bonhoeffer.[6] During our six years living in South Bend, we were involved in the local Community of Sant'Egidio,[7] made friends with Catholic Workers and attended Holy Trinity Episcopal Church.

Early in my doctoral studies, I enrolled in a seminar on modern Protestant ethics with Jerry McKenny. One of the assigned texts was a recently translated edition of Bonhoeffer's *Ethics*.[8] I recall finding *Ethics* to be extraordinarily rich and stimulating, even while feeling unsure that I had really grasped what Bonhoeffer was doing. In the seminar, there were a number of long discussions about the details and nuances of this text, as well as about the tensions between different manuscripts and their claims. In 'Natural Life', for example, Bonhoeffer writes that human reason (*Vernunft*) is 'the organ for recognizing the natural' and is 'able to perceive the universal in what is given'.[9] However in 'God's Love and the Disintegration of the World', he is more pessimistic about human reasoning and

---

4. Alongside my involvement in the community, I had competed undergraduate and postgraduate degrees in Religious Studies at Victoria University of Wellington.

5. DBWE 12: 433.

6. Gustavo Gutiérrez, 'The Limitations of Modern Theology: On a Letter of Dietrich Bonhoeffer', in *The Power of the Poor in History: Selected Writings*, ed. Gustavo Gutiérrez, 222–44 (London: SCM, 1983).

7. For an overview of Sant'Egidio's work and history, see Sarah Moses, *Ethics and the Elderly: The Challenge of Long-Term Care* (Maryknoll: Orbis, 2015). See also Austen Ivereigh, 'Sant'Egidio: Prophets of the Poor and of Peace', in *Small Christian Communities: Capturing the Movement*, ed. Joseph G. Healy and Jeanne Hinton, 170–6 (Maryknoll: Orbis, 2006).

8. That is, DBWE 6.

9. DBWE 6: 174–5.

discernment: the goal of Christian ethics is to 'supersede' any attempt to 'know about good and evil' and pursue a 'simplicity of action' in Christ.[10]

In the same semester, a small group of us convinced Cyril O'Regan to provide a directed reading course on the philosophy of G. W. F. Hegel.[11] I became intrigued by some of the resonances and divergences between these two very different German thinkers. This eventually led to an ambitious idea for a new doctoral dissertation: a systematic examination of Bonhoeffer's use and critique of Hegelian idealism.[12] Preparing for this bold undertaking involved learning German, working my way through Bonhoeffer's and Hegel's collected works and familiarizing myself with the relevant secondary literature. Of course, a project of this kind required spending a year living in Berlin to continue improving my German and undertake archival research at the Staatsbibliothek.[13]

When it came time for actually writing my dissertation, it made sense to begin with a chapter on Bonhoeffer's engagements with idealism in *Sanctorum Communio* and *Act and Being*.[14] After a busy year of reading and writing, however, I found that I was still immersed in the details of Bonhoeffer's first dissertation. Following a meeting with my supervisor, the project was hastily reconfigured as an exposition of *Sanctorum Communio* and its theology.[15] This new dissertation would demonstrate that Bonhoeffer's early ecclesiology provided something important

---

10. DBWE 6: 313.

11. This followed from my attempt to work through Cyril O'Regan's *The Heterodox Hegel* (New York: SUNY, 1994). In the reading course, we read 'The Positivity of Christian Religions', in *On Christianity: Early Theological Writings* (Philadelphia: University of Pennsylvania Press, 1971), *Phenomenology of Spirit*, trans. A. V. Miller (Oxford: Oxford University Press, 1977), parts of the *Lectures on the Philosophy of Religion: One Volume Edition, the Lectures of 1827*, ed. Peter Hodgson (Berkeley: University of California Press, 1988), as well as some secondary literature.

12. While my own attempt to relate these two thinkers never eventuated, others have subsequently taken up this challenge. See especially David S. Robinson, *Christ and Revelatory Community in Bonhoeffer's Reception of Hegel* (Tübingen: Mohr Siebeck, 2018). See also my review, Michael Mawson, 'Review of David S. Robinson's *Christ and Revelatory Community*', *Scottish Journal of Theology* 73, no. 2 (2020): 182–3.

13. During our time in Berlin, I was the Eberhard Bethge Fellow in Residence at the Bonhoeffer House in Charlottenburg. This allowed me to work on my dissertation in the same attic study where Bonhoeffer had composed parts of his *Ethics*. For some rich reflections on the Bonhoeffer Haus, see Laura M. Fabrycky, *Keys to Bonhoeffer's Haus: Exploring the World and Wisdom of Dietrich Bonhoeffer* (Minneapolis: Fortress Press, 2020). During the year in Germany, I also had opportunities to discuss Bonhoeffer and philosophy with some leading German Bonhoeffer scholars, including Christiane Tietz, Isle Tödt and Ralf Wüstenberg.

14. That is, Bonhoeffer's first two published works, DBWE 1 and DBWE 2.

15. A substantially reworked version of this dissertation was eventually published as Michael Mawson, *Christ Existing as Community: Bonhoeffer's Ecclesiology* (Oxford: Oxford University Press, 2018).

in the context of early-twentieth-century German theology. Building on both dialectical and liberal theology, Bonhoeffer provided an account of the church as simultaneously 'a reality of revelation' and 'a concrete historical community'.[16] While working on this more modest project, I also had the opportunity to organize a conference on Bonhoeffer at Notre Dame with my friend Adam Clark. We later co-edited the papers as *Ontology and Ethics: Bonhoeffer and Contemporary Scholarship*, published in 2013.[17]

While in the final throes of my dissertation, I was offered and accepted a position at the University of Aberdeen in Scotland. Aberdeen was one of the best places in the world for systematic theology and Christian ethics. The programme had a strong emphasis on the Western tradition and modern Protestant theology. When I arrived in 2012, colleagues with interests in Bonhoeffer included Brian Brock, Tom Greggs, John Swinton, Bernd Wannenwetsch, John Webster and Philip Ziegler.[18] Over the next few years there were ample opportunities for extending and enriching my understanding of Bonhoeffer and theology. Indeed, many of the essays included in this volume began as presentations in seminars or as public lectures in Aberdeen.

In 2014, Philip Ziegler and I received a grant from the Royal Society of Edinburgh to host a series of workshops and public lectures on Bonhoeffer. We collected and edited this material as *Christ, Church and World: New Studies in Bonhoeffer's Theology and Ethics*, published in 2016.[19] This volume sought to capture some of the dynamic and innovative work being done on Bonhoeffer by scholars from around the world. The following year we proposed and began working on *The Oxford Handbook of Dietrich Bonhoeffer*, which consisted of thirty-two chapters and eventually appeared in 2019.[20] This slow, laborious editorial work exposed me to the diverse scholarship of historians, theologians and ethicists working on

---

16. DBWE 1: 127, 209.

17. Adam C. Clark and Michael Mawson, eds, *Ontology and Ethics: Bonhoeffer and Contemporary Scholarship* (Eugene: Pickwick Publications, 2013).

18. Later Mike Laffin joined the department. Conversations with Mike helped to deepen my understanding of Bonhoeffer's relationship to Luther and Lutheran theology. See his important book, Michael Laffin, *The Promise of Martin Luther's Political Theology: Freeing Luther from the Modern Political Narrative* (London: T&T Clark Bloomsbury, 2016).

19. Michael Mawson and Philip Ziegler, eds, *Christ, Church and World: Bonhoeffer's Theology and Ethics* (London: T&T Clark Bloomsbury, 2016).

20. Michael Mawson and Philip Ziegler, eds, *The Oxford Handbook of Dietrich Bonhoeffer* (Oxford: Oxford University Press, 2019). Another highlight from this period was a conference on Protestant ethics, The Freedom of a Christian Ethicist, which I co-organized with Brian Brock. While not on Bonhoeffer directly, contributors like Hans Ulrich and Rachel Muers made reference to Bonhoeffer. The presentations were all collected and published as Brian Brock and Michael Mawson, eds, *The Freedom of a Christian Ethicist: The Future of a Reformation Legacy* (London: T&T Clark Bloomsbury, 2016).

Bonhoeffer in Germany, North America, the United Kingdom, South Africa and Australasia.

While at Aberdeen University, I developed and taught a new course on Bonhoeffer for the undergraduate programme.[21] The cohorts of students who took this course would read and engage Bonhoeffer's theology in light of their own experiences and ethical commitments. In addition, I began supervising and working with a number of brilliant doctoral students, who were either writing on Bonhoeffer directly or drawing on him for other projects (e.g. on ecumenism, ecotheology, race and ageing and vulnerability).[22] Partly due to the new translations and editions of the Dietrich Bonhoeffer Works series, there had been an explosion of scholarly and student interest in Bonhoeffer.[23] Alongside regular supervision meetings, there were frequent reading groups and stimulating discussions at Kilau café or the Bobbin.[24]

My family and I left Scotland and relocated to Australia in 2019. I accepted a position at the United Theological College (UTC) of Charles Sturt University, a college of the Uniting Church of Australia.[25] The decision to leave Aberdeen was partly driven by financial and familial pressures, but I was also ready for a context that would require some different kinds of teaching and engagement. My new role involved teaching a wider range of courses and working with ministry candidates

---

21. The course was called 'Theology against the Nazis: The Writings of Dietrich Bonhoeffer'. For background we read Christiane Tietz's *Theologian of Resistance: The Life and Thought of Dietrich Bonhoeffer* (Minneapolis: Fortress Press, 2016). For the course itself, we read selections from Michael P. DeJonge and Clifford J. Green, eds, *The Bonhoeffer Reader* (Minneapolis: Fortress Press, 2013).

22. Some of the doctoral students I directly supervised or co-supervised included Caireen Likely, Justin Pritchett, Cole Jodon, Kevin O'Farrell, Jin Kim, Claire Hein Blanton and Brandin Francabandera.

23. This was a massive translation and editorial project. The final volume of the Dietrich Bonhoeffer Works project (DBWE 14) appeared in English in 2014.

24. Some examples of the published dissertations on Bonhoeffer that emerged from this time include Chris Dodson, *The God Who Is Given: Bonhoeffer's Sacramentality and Religionless Christianity* (Langham: Lexington, 2021); David Emerton, *God's Church-Community: The Ecclesiology of Dietrich Bonhoeffer* (London: T&T Clark Bloomsbury, 2020); Ross E. Halbach, *Bonhoeffer and the Racialized Church* (Waco: Baylor University Press, 2020); Cole Jodon, *Discipleship and Unity: Bonhoeffer's Ecumenical Theology* (Langham: Lexington, 2022); Hyun Joo Kim, *Bearing Sin as Church Community: Bonhoeffer's Hamartiology* (London: T&T Clark Bloomsbury, 2022) and Joel Looper, *Bonhoeffer's America: A Land without Reformation* (Waco: Baylor University Press, 2021).

25. On the Uniting Church and its theology, see Geoff Thompson, *A Genuinely Theological Church: Ministry, Theology and the Uniting Church* (Sydney: Morning Star Publishing, 2018); *Disturbing Much, Disturbing Many: Theology Provoked by the Basis of Union* (Eugene: Wipf & Stock, 2016); and William Emilsen, ed., *An Informed Faith: The Uniting Church at the Beginning of the 21st Century* (Sydney: Morning Star Publishing, 2014).

and students from diverse cultural backgrounds (e.g. Aboriginal, Tongan, Fijian, Samoan, Chinese, Korean and white).

In this new context, I began discovering and learning from some of the rich, concrete scholarship that was emerging in the region. Reading Bonhoeffer's late theology had already inculcated an openness to diverse and surprising forms of Christ's presence, to expressions of faith that 'speak in a "worldly" way about God' and that break with the 'temporally conditioned presuppositions of [Western] metaphysics, the inner life, and so on'.[26] I soon read work by indigenous scholars Anne Pattel-Gray, Garry Deverell, Hirini Kaa and Naomi Wolfe, who highlighted the devasting effects of missionary Christianity on First Peoples, as well as ongoing problems being caused by imported forms of Western theology and education.[27] Friends like Jione Havea and Brian Kolia introduced me to the dynamic, creative work being done by Pasifika scholars in the areas of hermeneutics and biblical studies.[28] And students at the college pressed me to give greater attention to disruptive and marginal voices and positions (e.g. indigenous, Pasifika, Minjung, Dalit, womanist and queer theologies).[29] Soon after moving to Australia, bushfires, flooding, global pandemics and new activist movements all began to frame and impact my scholarship.[30]

These relationships and pressures have helped me to read and teach Bonhoeffer in ways that are more contextual, fluid and open-ended. While I have continued to draw on Bonhoeffer for deepening discussions about discipleship and formation, I am now more careful to ensure that this is not at the expense of engaging and

---

26. DBWE 8: 778.

27. See Anne Pattel-Gray, *The Great White Flood: Racism in Australia* (Atlanta: Scholar's Press, 1998); Garry Worete Deverell, *Gondwana Theology: A Trawloolway Man Reflects on Christian Faith* (Sydney: Morning Star Publishing, 2018); Hirini Kaa, *Te Hāhi Mihinare: The Māori Anglican Church* (Wellington: Bridget Williams Books, 2020); and Mark G. Brett and Naomi Wolfe, 'Sovereignty: Indigenous Counter-Examples', *International Journal of Public Theology* 14, no. 1 (2020): 24–40.

28. For some examples of work in this area, see Jione Havea, ed., *Theologies from the Pacific* (London: Palgrave, 2021); Nāsili Vaka'uta, *Reading Ezra 9–10 Tu'a-wise Rethinking Biblical Interpretation in Oceania* (Atlanta: SBL Press, 2011); and Brian Kolia, '*Maota Tau Ave*: Towards an Australian-Samoan Diasporic Understanding of Wisdom in Ecclesiastes', PhD Dissertation, University of Divinity, 2021.

29. In 2021, I organized my course on Christian ethics around liberation theologies that have emerged in different contexts, inviting friends to contribute lectures to the course.

30. I reflect on some of these issues in the first chapter of this book, 'Studying Theology in a Time of Crisis: Bonhoefferian Insights for Theological Thinking Today'. In addition, see Michael Mawson, 'Speaking of God: Unruly God-Talk with Julian of Norwich', in *Doing Theology in the New Normal: Global Perspectives*, ed. Jione Havea, 196–208 (London: SCM Press, 2021).

drawing on marginal voices and insights directly.³¹ When I taught a postgraduate seminar on Bonhoeffer in 2019, we also explored how Bonhoeffer's theology has been taken up and creatively reworked in liberation and resistance movements (e.g. in Latin America, South Africa and Hong Kong).³² Some of my more recent essays have begun to reflect on aspects of Bonhoeffer's theology that are in need of supplementation and repair.³³ Finally, I have learnt from my colleagues Di Rayson and Peter Walker how Bonhoeffer's theology can be constructively developed and deployed for responding to issues like climate change or engaging in interreligious dialogue.³⁴

The chapters in this volume reflect these various contexts and the twists and turns of my journey with Bonhoeffer. While I have revised and updated all of the essays, engaging with new scholarship and rewriting sections, I have not sought to erase or diminish the particular situations and events that gave rise to these ideas. In addition, I have not tried to smooth over the tensions that exist between some of these essays and their claims. These tensions can partly be attributed to the ways in which my own theology and understanding of Bonhoeffer has developed and changed. And of course, Bonhoeffer's theology itself is sufficiently complex and rich enough to allow for a variety of readings.

Many of the essays in this volume proceed by comparing or contrasting a particular aspect of Bonhoeffer's theology with that of another theologian or ethicist. My goal with this approach is to draw out some of the complexities and nuances of Bonhoeffer's thinking and to indicate what is at stake with some of his specific claims and insights.

The first chapter, 'Studying Theology in a Time of Crisis', has been reworked from a 2022 essay that I contributed to an edited book, *Letters to a Young Theologian*.³⁵ In this chapter, I use Bonhoeffer to reflect on some of the challenges facing theology students today, as well as on how studying theology can potentially assist with

---

31. On this point, see a rich reflection by Peter Kline, 'Dietrich Bonhoeffer: Faith as Unsovereign Attention', *Anglican Focus*, April 2019, https://anglicanfocus.org.au/2019/04/05/dietrich-bonhoeffer-faith-as-unsovereign-attention/. Accessed 15 March 2023.

32. I organized a number of guest lecturers for the course, including Di Rayson, Carlos Caldas, Ockert Meyer and Jason Lam. We read Bonhoeffer's theology alongside secondary scholarship that explored his reception in various contexts and struggles.

33. An example of this can be found in the final chapter of this book, 'The Stumbling Block and the Lynching Tree'.

34. See Dianne Rayson, *Bonhoeffer and Climate Change: Theology and Ethics for the Anthropocene* (Langham: Lexington, 2021). With Di Rayson, Peter Walker and others, I am organizing the XIV International Bonhoeffer Congress, which will take place in Sydney in January 2024. The title and theme of the Congress, 'Crisis and Hope: Reading Bonhoeffer for Today', is intended to encourage these kinds of constructive reflections.

35. Henco van der Westhuizen, ed., *Letters to a Young Theologian* (Minneapolis: Fortress Press, 2022).

responding to some of the crises that we are facing. The essay is programmatic and has been intentionally placed at the beginning to frame the volume as a whole.

The remaining chapters have been organized into three parts. Part I, 'The Forms of the Word', has a broad focus on hermeneutics. Chapters 2 and 3 explore Bonhoeffer's approach to Scripture. The former does so directly by presenting Bonhoeffer's reflections on biblical interpretation and providing some examples from his work. Chapter 3 compares Bonhoeffer's and the Jewish thinker Franz Rosenzweig's focus on the substance and materiality (*Sachlichkeit*) of biblical texts. I argue that Bonhoeffer and Rosenzweig can make an important contribution to ongoing work in the area of apocalyptic theology and biblical studies.

Chapters 4 and 5 focus on hermeneutics by reflecting on Bonhoeffer's relationship to Luther. While Chapter 4 establishes the Lutheran provenance of Bonhoeffer's thinking – drawing out their shared emphasis on the cross as a grammar for Christian living – Chapter 5 narrows in on the question of *how* we should frame Bonhoeffer's relationship to Luther. This essay was originally written as a response to Michael DeJonge's 2018 book *Bonhoeffer's Reception of Luther*[36] for a book symposium in the journal *Modern Theology*.[37] Despite the specific focus of this essay on DeJonge's work, it has broad implications for how we understand Bonhoeffer's theology as simultaneously Lutheran and modern.

Part II, 'The Vulnerabilities of Bodily Life', consists of three chapters on suffering and vulnerability. Chapter 6 draws on Bonhoeffer's anthropology in his 1933 *Creation and Fall* to supplement and deepen the relational turn in recent disability theology. Chapter 7 brings Bonhoeffer's 'Natural Life' manuscript from *Ethics* into dialogue with Gerald McKenny's work on the normativity of human nature in his 2018 *Biotechnology, Human Nature, and Christian Ethics*.[38] Along similar lines, Chapter 8 reflects on how Karl Barth and Bonhoeffer can assist with responding to challenges presented by technologies aiming to radically extend the human lifespan.

Part III, 'A Community of the Cross', draws together several essays that focus on community, discipleship and the cross. Chapter 9 contrasts Bonhoeffer's and Jürgen Moltmann's language of the suffering God and draws out the implications of their differences for who we are before God and in relation to one another. Chapter 10 compares how Robert Jenson, Reinhard Hütter and Bonhoeffer each construes the relationship between the Holy Spirit and the existing church. I argue that Bonhoeffer sets up this relationship in ways that allow him to more clearly affirm the sinfulness of the church.

Chapter 11 contrasts Bonhoeffer with John Howard Yoder on discipleship, thereby criticizing the work of some of Bonhoeffer's Anabaptist interpreters who

---

36. Michael P. DeJonge, *Bonhoeffer's Reception of Luther* (Oxford: Oxford University Press, 2017).

37. *Modern Theology* 35, no. 2 (2019): 352–81.

38. Gerald McKenny, *Biotechnology, Human Nature, and Christian Ethics* (Cambridge: Cambridge University Press, 2018).

have tended to conflate their approaches. Finally, Chapter 12 supplements and deepens Bonhoeffer's understanding of Christ's humiliation in his 'Lectures on Christology' by drawing on James Cone's Black theology. In particular, I argue that Cone provides a more concrete account of what crucifixion under Roman Empire actually entailed.

Chapter 1

STUDYING THEOLOGY IN A TIME OF CRISIS: BONHOEFFERIAN INSIGHTS FOR THEOLOGICAL THINKING TODAY

In mid-1933, following Adolf Hitler's appointment as chancellor and a series of disappointments in the Church Struggle, Bonhoeffer composed a short essay for his students, 'What Should a Student of Theology Do Today?'[1] Much of this essay straightforwardly reflects upon the nature of theological study and the temptations besetting young students eager to prove themselves through their studies. At various points, however, Bonhoeffer makes reference to the wider crisis engulfing church and academy: 'One must learn to recognise where and when the church of Christ reaches the hour of its decision, when it is time for confession – the *status confessionis*.'[2] In light of the challenges of this new situation, the student of theology must learn to discern when and how to take a stand.

One way of reading Bonhoeffer's essay is as a reflection on how theological study can support and sustain Christian witness during difficult times. How can study help Christians to find a way forward, to remain faithful to Christ's call in the midst of complex situations and crises? In particular, Bonhoeffer proposes going back to the basics: 'One should, in such times of confusion, go back to the very beginning, to our wellsprings, to the true Bible, to the true Luther.'[3] In times of crisis and confusion, the student should return to Scripture and those voices from the tradition that remain close to Scripture: 'the company of honest theologians from Paul to Augustine, from Thomas to Luther.'[4]

As is well known, Bonhoeffer himself sought to follow Christ faithfully during the next decade under National Socialism. His theological education and commitments were central to how he made sense of this evolving context and what it required: assisting with the formation of the Confessing Church, the pursuit of peace through ecumenical activities, running an illegal seminary in Finkenwalde and his conspiratorial involvements in the plot to assassinate Hitler. Bonhoeffer's theological commitments were central to his ability to survive and adapt, to

---

1. Bonhoeffer, 'What Should a Student of Theology Do Today?', DBWE 12: 432–5.
2. DBWE 12: 434.
3. DBWE 12: 435.
4. DBWE 12: 433.

continually reassess and relinquish previously held assumptions and positions and to be open to following Christ in new and unexpected ways.

Almost a century later, we too are in a situation of crisis. In the 2020s, the extent of the challenges that are confronting us are becoming increasingly apparent. In Australia, for example, the decade began with a series of bushfires which destroyed countless homes and livelihoods, devastating many rural communities. In New South Wales, fires consumed 5.22 million hectares of bushland. Estimates indicate that more than a billion animals, birds and reptiles perished, including many from endangered species.[5] In subsequent years, New South Wales and other parts of Australia experienced unprecedented levels of rainfall and flooding.[6] These fires and floods were, of course, just symptoms of wider processes of anthropogenic climate change. Unless these processes are arrested and reversed, the continued existence of human beings is uncertain.[7]

Also in 2020, a global pandemic swept the world. As well as its direct impact through illness and loss of life, the wider effects of Covid-19 have been catastrophic. Attempts to respond through closing national borders, social distancing and lockdowns, and by shutting schools and businesses have interrupted every aspect of life.[8] Statistics suggest that rates of depression and mental illness have skyrocketed during the pandemic.[9] Many countries have documented escalating levels of violence and domestic abuse during and after the pandemic.[10] And incidents of suicide similarly increased.[11] In the wake of the pandemic, large numbers of people have found themselves unemployed or financially insecure. The virus exposed the deep inequities already present in our societies, which disproportionately affect

---

5. 'Have More Than a Billion Animals Perished Nationwide This Bushfire Season? Here Are the Facts', *ABC News*, 31 January 2020, www.abc.net.au/news/2020-01-31/fact-check-have-bushfires-killed-more-than-a-billion-animals/11912538.

6. For a snapshot of the flooding and its impact, see Phil Mercer, 'Australia Seeks International Help as Flood Crisis Worsens', *VOA News*, 15 November 2022, www.voanews.com/a/australia-seeks-international-help-as-flood-crisis-worsens/6834792.html.

7. See Clive Hamilton, *Defiant Earth: The Fate of Humans in the Anthropocene* (Sydney: Allen and Unwin, 2017). See also a recent collection edited by Peter Walker and Jonathan Cole, *Theology on a Defiant Earth* (Lanham: Lexington, 2022).

8. See, for example, Ed Yong, 'How the Virus Defeated America', *The Atlantic*, 4 August 2020.

9. For example, see Rachel Schraer, 'Depression Doubles during Coronavirus Pandemic', BBC, 18 August 2020, https://www.bbc.com/news/health-53820425.

10. For example, see '"Alarming but Not Unexpected": Increase in Domestic Violence in NSW during Covid-19 Crisis', *The Guardian*, 4 June 2020, https://www.theguardian.com/society/2020/jun/04/alarming-but-not-unexpected-increase-in-domestic-violence-in-nsw-during-covid-19-crisis.

11. Leo Sher, 'The Impact of the COVID-19 Pandemic on Suicide Rates', *An International Journal of Medicine* 113, no. 10 (2020): 707–12, https://doi.org/10.1093/qjmed/hcaa202.

people of colour, women,¹² those without access to healthcare and those without the freedom to work remotely and in safety.

On 25 May 2020, the killing of George Floyd in Minneapolis, Minnesota, gave renewed focus to problems of systemic racism in the United States and beyond. Floyd became the latest in a long list of African Americans killed while in police custody. When the graphic footage circulated of an officer kneeling on Floyd's neck – for 8 minutes and 46 seconds while he cried out repeatedly, 'I can't breathe' – protesters began gathering to call for recognition and justice. The issues raised by these largely peaceful protests remain unresolved; Black Lives Matter and related groups continue to work to draw attention to the plight of black and indigenous lives.¹³

We will be grappling with these crises and the realities they represent into the foreseeable future.¹⁴ We are continuing to experience the economic and social fallout from Covid-19 and the way that political leaders and regimes took advantage of these crises to consolidate power and advance their agendas.¹⁵ The world as we know it has changed irrevocably. And Christians must again be prepared to discern when and how to declare a *status confessionis*.¹⁶

Temptations in theological study

This leads to the title and question of Bonhoeffer's short essay: 'What Should a Student of Theology Do Today?'¹⁷ Before even addressing this question, we should consider whether anyone should be devoting time and resources to theological study. This should remain an open question. Those who are beginning theological study do so today without any real prospect of stable employment or advancement.

---

12. On the impact of the virus on women in particular, see 'How Covid-19 Could Set Back Women by a Generation', *The Guardian*, 28 August 2020, www.theguardian.com/australia-news/audio/2020/aug/28/how-covid-19-could-set-back-women-by-a-generation.

13. In Sydney, several protests centred around the case of the twenty-six-year-old Aboriginal man, David Dungay, who died in Long Bay Jail in 2015. Dungay is reported to have called out 'I can't breathe' twelve times while being restrained by guards, none of whom faced any disciplinary action.

14. While I've chosen to highlight these three examples from 2020, there are obviously other crises with which we need to continue to wrestle, including realities highlighted by the #MeToo movement.

15. Timothy McLaughlin, 'Where the Virus Is Cover for Authoritarianism', *The Atlantic*, 25 August 2020. McLaughlin's examples include Hong Kong, Thailand, Algeria, Hungary and Israel.

16. While Bonhoeffer uses '*status confessionis*' to refer to how confessing Christians need to break with the established church, I am using it a little more expansively here.

17. I have in mind not only students in the formal sense, but also all of us who pursue theological study as a central part of our activity.

And this is especially the case for those committing to the slow and painful work of advanced research. For many of us there may be better ways of following Christ and responding to the current situation.[18]

Those of us who do continue should, like Bonhoeffer's students, be wary of several temptations. First of all, theological study can easily become a means of simply avoiding the crises and challenges that surround us. Theology can become a means of retreating into speculation or abstraction, of exchanging the concerns of the present for an idealized vision of the past.[19] As Bonhoeffer sympathetically notes in a lecture contemporaneous with his essay, 'When life begins to be difficult and oppressive, one leaps boldly into the air and soars, relieved and worry free, in the so-called eternal realm.'[20] If one continues with studies and research, this must be in a way that eventually presses back into the world and the present challenges.

To be clear, this is not to suggest that study and research should at every moment be directly orientated to and by a given issue. The work of faithfully understanding and responding to the present situation may at times require long excursions into unfamiliar territory. Unravelling the anthropological assumptions underlying and contributing to climate change, for example, may involve closely reading and grappling with figures such as Karl Barth or Maximus the Confessor.[21] Alternatively, as Willie Jennings has shown, understanding the logics of race and racism, as well as how such logics keep Christians separated from one another, may require attending to fifteenth- and sixteenth-century figures such as Gomes Eanes de Azurara or José de Acosta.[22]

Similarly, if theological study is to assist with faithfully following God and responding to the world, this may require convoluted and indirect ways of speaking and writing. Judith Butler has drawn attention to how familiar, common-sense language too often serves the status quo: 'Why are some of the most trenchant social criticisms often expressed through difficult and demanding

---

18. As Bonhoeffer writes in his letter, 'Far less harm is done if many who might have become good pastors or teachers of religion instead become good lawyers or physicians, than if a single person pursues theology who should not have done so'. DBWE 12: 432.

19. This accusation has often been levelled at the Radical Orthodoxy movement. For example, see Douglas Hedley's review of John Milbank, Catherine Pitstock and Graham Ward, eds, *Radical Orthodoxy: A New Theology* (London: Routledge, 1999) in *The Journal of Theological Studies* 51, no. 1 (2000): 405–8. In a late letter from prison, Bonhoeffer himself is wary of attempts at 'conservative restoration' in response to 'the world come of age'. DBWE 8: 328.

20. Bonhoeffer, 'Thy Kingdom Come: The Prayer of the Church-Community: God's Kingdom on Earth', DBWE 12: 286.

21. I have in mind here Willis Jenkins, *Ecologies of Grace: Environmental Ethics and Christian Theology* (Oxford: Oxford University Press, 2013), especially 154–206.

22. Willie Jennings, *The Christian Imagination: Theology and the Origins of Race* (New Haven: Yale University Press, 2010).

language?'²³ If theological study is to aid in responding to these challenges in all their complexity, and to help us begin to see and act otherwise and differently, this will require pressing beyond the utilitarian language that is prevalent in our churches and societies. Following God into the unknown will require complex and nuanced patterns of thinking and speaking. We should resist the temptation to think that theology can always be done in ways that are straightforward and accessible.²⁴

In addition, those who proceed with studying theology should be alert to certain institutional pressures.²⁵ At this time of economic rationalization, with universities cutting funding and shedding staff, there is a temptation to pursue only projects that make a clear and positive contribution to our churches and societies. Increasingly, theology is being promoted and defended for its ability to build resilience, promote flourishing or contribute to the common good.²⁶ If such justifications are at times expedient and even necessary, they can begin to direct our efforts away from more risky and critical ventures. Put differently, these framings can begin to locate theological study within horizons that have already been set. Can we really know at the outset what resilience, flourishing or the common good even are? Do these framings limit an openness to how theology should more radically disrupt and reconfigure general notions of what resilience or flourishing entails?

Finally, pressure in the form of global rankings and research frameworks can tempt institutions to value 'internationally recognized' research at the expense of local and situated forms of engagement. This is a particular challenge for those of us studying and working in the Antipodes.²⁷ As Mark Brett has suggested, 'we need a deliberate strategy to link international research to local interests and to local

---

23. See Judith Butler, 'A Bad Writer Bites Back', *New York Times*, 20 March 1999. Butler is responding to her being awarded first prize in the Bad Writing Competition, sponsored by the relatively obscure conservative journal *Philosophy and Literature*.

24. While I'm committed to an understanding of theology as in service to the church, this is a service that must at times cause discomfort. This is especially difficult to accomplish in contexts like Australia where theological education is so closely tied to denominational structures and identities.

25. Linn Tonstad provides a rich reflection on the relationship between globalization and theology's operations and status in the university. In particular, she draws attention to the naivety and inadequacy of attempts to simply focus on the virtuous formation of individual theologians. See Linn Marie Tonstad, '(Un)wise Theologians: Systematic Theology in the University', *International Journal of Systematic Theology* 22, no. 4 (2020): 494–511.

26. This is a particular temptation and problem for those of us working in the areas of Christian ethics and public theology. These framings can too quickly come to substitute and displace language that runs closer to Scripture and the complexity and messiness of lived existence.

27. Especially in New Zealand and Australia, far too much time and attention is given to trying to replicate the kind of work being done in elite northern hemisphere institutions.

understandings of shalom/salaam. As part of that strategy, it will be necessary to deconstruct the hierarchy that currently separates elite, internationally recognized scholarship from lower-status efforts that reflect community engagement in a local context.'[28]

Encountering the cross

How can theological study proceed in a way that remains alert to these temptations? In his short essay, Bonhoeffer provides us with some guidance. In particular, he suggests that genuine theological study proceeds from the cross: 'The real study of *theologia sacra* begins when, in the midst of questioning and seeking, human beings encounter the cross; when they recognize the endpoint of all their own passions in the suffering of God at the hands of humankind, and realize that their entire vitality stands under judgment.'[29] That all Christian theology ultimately proceeds from the cross, and attends to Scripture and other voices in their witness to the cross, has implications for how we understand and pursue the work of theology.

First, the cross has significance for the *disposition* of those studying theology. The cross makes clear that theological study is not simply and primarily about our own efforts and abilities, but about allowing our thinking to be interrupted and shaped from without. As students of the cross, we are called to engage Scripture and other voices in ways that keep an encounter with Christ at the centre. Among other things, this means that we should proceed without a view to mastery, without needing to know at the outset where we are being led.[30] Similarly, the cross frees us to hold lightly our cherished commitments and conclusions, recognizing that these stand under God's judgement.[31] And for those of us accustomed to a level of privilege and control, the cross disposes us to begin surrendering power and making room for others.[32]

---

28. Mark G. Brett, 'Past and Future of Biblical Studies in Australia', *Australian Biblical Review* 67 (2019): 96.

29. DBWE 12: 433.

30. Again, Tonstad's rich article is useful on this point. She writes in her conclusion: 'If the wisdom and foolishness of the cross is the logic of choosing things that have no being, then any claim to wisdom or rulership that is grounded in the participation of things in divine being must be set aside.' Tonstad, '(Un)wise Theologians', 511.

31. For many of us, theological study needs to take the form of acknowledging guilt and repentance. For a recent example of this, see Ross Halbach, *Bonhoeffer and the Racialized Church* (Waco: Baylor University Press, 2000). See also Jennifer M. McBride, *The Church for the World: A Theology of Public Witness* (New York: Oxford University Press, 2011).

32. There have, of course, been important critiques of this kind of kenotic divestment by feminist theologians and others, as well as more recent attempts to recover and reframe kenosis. For example, see Sarah Coakley, '*Kenōsis* and Subversion: On the Repression of

Second, the cross has implications for *how we approach and engage Scripture*.[33] Specifically, it frees us from needing to understand Scripture simply as a deposit of divine wisdom or truth, something which we from our side must take possession of, interpret and make our own. In other words, studying theology does not primarily involve deriving dogmatic truths or moral principles *from* Scripture.[34] Rather, as students of the cross we are free for more fluid and open-ended styles of engagement and immersion, ones that remain closer to the irreducibility of the diverse biblical texts and forms, thereby allowing ourselves to be formed by these texts in their witness to Christ.[35]

Third, the cross has implications for what we should be *reading beyond Scripture*. (On this point Bonhoeffer's 'company of honest theologians' is in need of a little expansion.[36]) If the pluriformity of Scripture testifies to the diverse ways God is present and at work in the world, the particularity and scandal of the cross lends priority to disruptive and confronting voices. While as students and theologians we should read widely, in and beyond theology, we should pay particular attention to voices challenging and destabilizing assumptions and norms.[37] In light of our current situation and crises – to update Karl Barth just a little[38] – we should 'read with the Bible in one hand …' and with the prophetic speeches of Greta Thunberg or Kimberley Jones in the other.[39]

"Vulnerability" in Christian Feminist Writing', in *Powers and Submissions: Spirituality, Philosophy and Gender* (Malden: Blackwell, 2002), 3–39.

33. I've explored some of these ways of thinking about Scripture in more detail elsewhere. For example, see Chapter 2 in this volume.

34. Or at least this should not be our primary posture with respect to the text.

35. We can see examples of this kind of fluid, immersive engagement in Bonhoeffer's *Creation and Fall*, DBWE 3, and also in Martin Luther's expositional theology. For a reading of Luther along these lines, see Brian Brock, *Singing the Ethos of God: On the Place of Christian Ethics in Scripture* (Grand Rapids: Eerdmans, 2007), especially chapters 5 and 7. For a very different kind of example of this immersive approach to Scripture, see Jione Havea's recent *Jonah: An Earth Bible Commentary* (London: T&T Clark, 2020).

36. As quoted earlier. 'What Should a Student of Theology', DBWE 12: 433.

37. To be clear, it is not that disruptive or destabilizing voices have priority in and of themselves. Rather, as Christians, as those who see the world through the cross, we are able to attend to such voices as a place that God encounters and challenges us.

38. While Barth is often attributed with saying that 'one should preach with the Bible in one hand and the newspaper in the other', to the best of my knowledge this has not, in fact, been substantiated.

39. I have in mind here Greta Thunberg's 2019 speech to the United Nations, 'WATCH: Greta Thunberg's Full Speech to World Leaders at UN Climate Action Summit', 24 September 2019, www.youtube.com/watch?v=KAJsdgTPJpU. See also Kimberly Jones's speech in Atlanta, '#BLM How Can We Win? Kimberly Jones Powerful Speech Video Full Length Black Lives Matter #BLM 2020', 10 June 2020, https://www.youtube.com/watch?v=llci8MVh8J4.

On this question of reading, I have found Stephen Chin Ming Lim's idea of 'reading from elsewhere' to be salutary. Engaging the Malay (Muslim) poet and writer Alfian Sa'at, Lim has shown how reading Scripture in dialogue with marginal voices can disrupt and displace 'objectivist desires of reading from *nowhere*' and 'nativist inclinations of reading from *here*'.[40] Such an approach, he reflects, 'has at the very least edged me out of my comfort zone to re-read the text [of Daniel 1] as an ambivalent one rather than the superficial triumphalistic message that it most probably is trying to project'.[41] Attending to particular voices from elsewhere can both open up Scripture and press us out into the world in richer and deeper ways.

Fourth, the cross has implications for *theological writing*. As mentioned earlier, following God into the unknown will at times involve complex and indirect forms of writing. As students and theologians, we are of course required at times to adopt and operate within set forms and conventions. Nonetheless, we should still be prepared to write in ways that are riskier, that run closer to the ground. On the one hand, this may involve writing in ways that stay close to the poetical, performative language and forms displayed by various biblical texts. On the other hand, it may involve kinds of writing that expose the hybridity and fluidity at the heart of all language, that attend to how the very ruptures, limits and spaces of language can be places of God's presence.[42]

Finally, all of this means that as students and theologians we need not fear or withdraw from the challenges confronting us. As Amy Laura Hall has reflected,[43] 'Jesus' suffering invites his followers powerfully to refuse a cautious, calculated distance from suffering'. 'Those who follow Jesus', she continues, 'do not run in the other direction or distract ourselves from the misery of domination of people around us'.[44] If all Christian theology is ultimately oriented to and by Jesus' suffering, then in our studies and lives we are free to acknowledge suffering and confront the domination that surrounds us.

And this is because the cross gives us grounds for hope. As students and theologians, we hold in faith that suffering and crisis do not have the final word.

---

40. Stephen Chin Ming Lim, 'The Impe(/a)rative of Dialogue in Asian Hermeneutics within the Modern/Colonial World System: Renegotiating Biblical Pasts for Planetary Futures', *Biblical Interpretation* 25 (2017): 663.

41. Lim, 'The Impe(/a)rative of Dialogue in Asian Hermeneutics', 676. See also Lim, *Contextual Biblical Hermeneutics as Multicentric Dialogue: Towards a Singaporean Reading of Daniel* (Leiden: Brill, 2020).

42. See, for example, Rowan Williams, *The Edge of Words: God and the Habits of Language* (London: Bloomsbury, 2014).

43. Hall's *Laughing at the Devil: Seeing the World with Julian of Norwich* (Durham: Duke University Press, 2018) exemplifies the kind of theological engagement and writing that I have in mind. In this short book, Hall allows Julian of Norwich's complex, vernacular theology to shed light on her own personal experience and contemporary political realities, even while these realities press her into the detail and substance of Julian's text and language.

44. Hall, *Laughing at the Devil*, 87.

James Cone has profoundly articulated the nature of this hope when reflecting on black experience in the United States: 'Christ crucified manifested God's loving and liberating presence *in* the contradictions of black life – that transcendent presence in the lives of black Christians that empowered them to believe that *ultimately*, in God's eschatological future, they would not be defeated by the "trouble of this world".'[45] For Christians, God's presence and work on the cross reminds us that God comes to and encounters us in the midst of contradiction. It reminds us that, ultimately, those who suffer now will one day be redeemed. Accordingly, in light of our current situation and pressing challenges, to quote Bonhoeffer's final words in his essay, 'one should keep on, ever more undaunted and joyfully, becoming a theologian ἀληθεύοντες δὲ ἐν ἀγάπῃ [speaking the truth in love, Eph. 4:15]'.[46]

---

45. James Cone, *The Cross and the Lynching Tree* (Maryknoll: Orbis, 2011), 3.
46. DBWE 12: 435.

PART I

THE FORMS OF THE WORD

Chapter 2

'AS A WHOLE AND IN ITS PARTS': BONHOEFFER'S APPROACH TO SCRIPTURE

In a 2001 essay John Webster observed, 'the significance of Scripture and its interpretation for understanding ... Bonhoeffer has often been passed over rather quickly'.[1] Since Webster's remark there have been a number of important articles and monographs on Bonhoeffer's use of Scripture.[2] But there is still room for more research and reflection on this vital area of Bonhoeffer's theology. This is especially the case given how extensively Bonhoeffer engaged with and reflected upon biblical texts in his sermons, essays, books, commentaries and letters.

The aim of this chapter is to indicate some of the broad contours of Bonhoeffer's theological uses of Scripture. In pursuing this task, I draw on material from across

---

1. John Webster, 'Reading the Bible: The Example of Barth and Bonhoeffer', in *Word and Church: Essays in Christian Dogmatics* (London: T&T Clark, 2001), 89.

2. Examples of some articles on this topic include: Sean Winter, 'Present-ing the Word: The Use and Abuse of Bonhoeffer on the Bible', *The Bonhoeffer Legacy: The Australasian Journal of Bonhoeffer Studies* 2, no. 2 (2014): 17–35; Sean Winter, 'Word and World: Dietrich Bonhoeffer and Biblical Interpretation Today', *Pacifica: Australasian Theological Studies* 25, no. 2 (2012): 161–75; and Jens Zimmermann, 'Reading the Book of the Church: Bonhoeffer's Christological Hermeneutics', *Modern Theology* 28, no. 4 (2012): 763–80. There have also been a number of recent books: Stephen J. Plant, *Taking Stock of Bonhoeffer: Essays in Biblical Interpretation and Scripture* (Farnham: Ashgate, 2014); Nadine Hamilton, *Dietrich Bonhoeffers Hermeneutik Der Responsivitat: Ein Kapital Schriftlehre im Anschluss an 'Schopfung und Fall'* (Göttingen: Vandenhoeck & Ruprecht, 2016); Brad Pribbenow, *Prayerbook of Christ: Dietrich Bonhoeffer's Christological Interpretation of the Psalms* (Lanham: Rowman and Littlefield, 2018); Derek W. Taylor, *Reading Scripture as the Church: Bonhoeffer's Hermeneutic of Discipleship* (Downers Grove: IVP Academic, 2020); Joel Banman, *Reading in the Presence of Christ: A Study of Dietrich Bonhoeffer's Bibliology and Exegesis* (London: T&T Clark Bloomsbury, 2021); and Jameson Ross, *Bonhoeffer as Biblical Interpreter: Reading Scripture in 1930s Germany* (London: T&T Clark Bloomsbury, 2021).

his writings, giving particular attention to places where he explicitly reflects upon the nature and interpretation of Scripture. This includes two important essays, the 1925 'The Historical and Pneumatological Interpretation of Scripture'[3] and the 1935 'Contemporizing New Testament Texts',[4] and a brief 1936 letter from Bonhoeffer to his brother-in-law, Rüdiger Schleicher.[5] In outlining Bonhoeffer's approach, I draw examples from his sermons and expositional texts, especially *Creation and Fall*, *Discipleship* and his writings on the Psalms: namely, parts of *Life Together*,[6] *The Prayerbook of the Bible*,[7] an unfinished meditation on Psalm 119[8] and a lecture at Finkenwalde.[9]

The Bible in Bonhoeffer's life and work

In an oft-quoted letter from 1936, Bonhoeffer reflects upon his earlier academic studies and subsequent 'discovery' of the Bible:

> I threw myself into my work in an extremely un-Christian and not at all humble fashion ... At that time, I was terribly alone and left to myself. It was quite bad. But then something different came, something that has changed and transformed my life to this day. For the first time, I came to the Bible ... The Bible, especially the Sermon on the Mount, freed me from all this.[10]

At the time when he made these remarks, Bonhoeffer was engaged in training seminarians for the Confessing Church in Finkenwalde.[11] This period of his life was marked by intensive scriptural engagement: he taught numerous courses on biblical books for his students, he preached regularly and he wrote some of his best-known works: *Life Together*,[12] *The Prayerbook of the Bible*[13] and *Discipleship*. This activity displays the profound impact of the earlier 'discovery'. It was also at

---

3. Bonhoeffer, 'Paper on the Historical and Pneumatological Interpretation of Scripture', DBWE 9: 285–300.
4. Bonhoeffer, 'Contemporizing New Testament Texts', DBWE 14: 413–33.
5. Bonhoeffer, 'Letter to Rüdiger Schleicher', 8 April 1936, DBWE 14: 166–70.
6. DBWE 5: 48–80.
7. DBWE 5: 155–77.
8. Bonhoeffer, 'Meditation on Psalm 119', DBWE 15: 496–528.
9. Bonhoeffer, 'Lecture on Christ in the Psalms', DBWE 14: 386–93.
10. Bonhoeffer, 'To Elizabeth Zinn', 27 January 1936, DBWE 14: 134.
11. For background on this, see Matthew Hockenos, 'Bonhoeffer and the Church Struggle', in *The Oxford Handbook of Dietrich Bonhoeffer*, ed. Michael Mawson and Philip G. Ziegler (Oxford: Oxford University Press, 2019), 52–64.
12. DBWE 5: 25–118.
13. DBWE 5: 155–77.

this time that Bonhoeffer wrote the provocative and insightful essay on scriptural interpretation, 'Contemporizing New Testament Texts'.[14]

During his later incarceration in Tegel Prison, Bonhoeffer again turned to the Bible with a particular intensity. In a letter dated 18 November 1943, he notes in passing that he had just 'read the Old Testament two and half times through' and 'learnt a great deal'.[15] In another letter, he reflects that his experiences have given him a deeper appreciation of certain biblical texts and themes.[16] And even when he recounts 'going through weeks without reading much of the Bible', he expresses confidence that 'after a time I'll be ravenous again'.[17] As Martin Kuske has shown, many of the provocative insights and concepts that Bonhoeffer developed in his late theology emerged from engagements with Old Testament texts.[18]

Nonetheless, if Bonhoeffer's letter from 1936 testifies to his 'coming to the Bible', and if the impact of this discovery is then apparent in both his Finkenwalde writings and prison theology, many features of his basic approach to Scripture were already in place much earlier. Even if he had been proceeding in an 'un-Christian fashion', his academic dissertations, for example, were permeated with biblical concepts and references, in ways that have not always received sufficient recognition.[19] During his academic studies, Bonhoeffer also wrote a number of short essays and seminar papers engaging closely with biblical texts, including on John and Paul's letters,[20] Job[21] and Amos 9.[22] These early essays already display inchoate insights and claims that Bonhoeffer would take up and develop in his later writings.

While a student in Berlin, Bonhoeffer also wrote another important essay that explicitly reflects on the Bible and its interpretation: the 1925 'The Pneumatological and Historical Understanding of Scripture'.[23] Even if this early essay is somewhat schematic and overdrawn, it still displays a commitment to the Bible as 'God's word' and 'where God speaks',[24] which would remain central to Bonhoeffer's approach. This early essay is further significant in that it displays the two main influences on

---

14. In the year following this essay, Bonhoeffer wrote in a letter to a friend, 'I would really like to try my hand at a book on hermeneutics.' 'To Erwin Sutz', 24 October 1936, DBWE 14: 273.

15. Bonhoeffer, 'To Eberhard Bethge', 18 November 1943, DBWE 8: 181.

16. Bonhoeffer, 'To Karl and Paula Bonhoeffer', 15 May 1943, DBWE 8: 79.

17. Bonhoeffer, 'To Eberhard Bethge', 19 March 1944, DBWE 8: 326.

18. Martin Kuske, *The Old Testament as the Book of Christ: An Appraisal of Bonhoeffer's Interpretation*, trans. S. T. Kimbrough, Jr. (Philadelphia: The Westminster Press, 1976), 132–59.

19. For example, limited attention has been given to the organizing role of 1 Cor. 15 for the last section of *Act and Being*, DBWE 2: 136–61.

20. For example, Bonhoeffer, 'Paper on John and Paul', DBWE 9: 395–404.

21. Bonhoeffer, 'Seminar Paper on Job', DBWE 9: 420–36.

22. Bonhoeffer, 'Old Testament Examination on Amos 9', DBWE 9: 447–9.

23. 'Interpretation of Scripture', DBWE 9: 285–300.

24. DBWE 9: 288.

Bonhoeffer's approach to Scripture (and indeed his wider theology): Karl Barth and Martin Luther.

On the one hand, scholars have pointed to this essay as evidence of Barth's impact upon the young Bonhoeffer.[25] Having only recently encountered Barth, Bonhoeffer enthusiastically promotes an understanding of the Bible as God's freely chosen place of revelation. As Barth had asserted just the previous year (and as Bonhoeffer had read), 'The Bible tells us not how we are supposed to talk with God, but rather what God says to us. It does not say how we are to find our way to him, but how God has sought and found the way to us.'[26] Bonhoeffer's early essay is perhaps best read as an enthusiastic endorsement of and expansion on this key Barthian claim.

On the other hand, while Barth may have provided the proximate impetus for Bonhoeffer's approach to Scripture, this early essay also displays the formative influence of Luther. Even more than Barth, references to Luther abound in Bonhoeffer's scriptural engagements and theology, here and elsewhere.[27] Luther's influence is especially evident in Bonhoeffer's deep insistence on the historicity (*Geschichtlichkeit*) of the Bible and the hiddenness of God's word within these human words and texts.[28]

The Bible as God's word in human history and language

In line with Barth and Luther, a central commitment of Bonhoeffer's approach to the Bible is that it is *here* that God has chosen to reveal Godself. God has chosen Scripture as the place of self-revelation. This means, among other things, that it is pointless to search for God elsewhere and otherwise.[29] In the essay 'Interpretation of Scripture', Bonhoeffer asserts that 'revelation can be found for us only in scripture'.[30] In line with Luther's *sola scriptura*, he holds that there is no sure access to and knowledge of God apart from the biblical texts: 'To the question of why revelation is to be found precisely here the answer must simply be that this is where

---

25. For example, Ferdinand Schlingensiepen, *Dietrich Bonhoeffer: 1906-1945*, trans. Isabel Best (London: T&T Clark, 2010), 30.

26. Karl Barth, *The Word of God and Theology*, trans. Amy Marga (London: T&T Clark, 2011), 25.

27. See Wolf Krötke, 'Dietrich Bonhoeffer and Martin Luther', in *Bonhoeffer's Intellectual Formation*, ed. Peter Frick (Tübingen: Mohr Siebeck, 2008), 57–60.

28. DBWE 9: 293–4.

29. Martin Luther, 'That These Words of Christ, "This Is My Body," Etc. Still Stand Firm against the Fanatics (1527)', in *Luther's Works* 37, ed. and trans. R. H. Fischer (Minneapolis: Fortress Press, 1961), 342. On this issue, see also Philip G. Ziegler, 'God', in *Oxford Handbook of Dietrich Bonhoeffer*, 137–49.

30. DBWE 9: 289.

2. 'As a Whole and in Its Parts'

God speaks and this is where it pleases God to be personally revealed.'[31] God has chosen to reveal Godself through the Bible, meaning that from our side we are to simply accept and attend to these texts as the place of revelation.[32] As Bonhoeffer formulates this claim in a later lecture at Finkenwalde, 'It pleased God to speak to us in the word of the Bible alone.'[33]

What immediately follows from this claim is that the Bible discloses and directs us to God in and as Jesus Christ.[34] This is because, as Bonhoeffer insists in the essay 'Contemporizing New Testament Texts', *'as a whole and in all its parts, it [the Bible] is nothing other than this witness of Christ, Christ's life, death and resurrection'*.[35] The Bible's sole task as God's chosen place and means of revelation is to witness to Christ.[36] And once again, the Bible is the only means by which God has chosen to do this.[37] As he reflects in *Discipleship*, 'For how do we know that Christ is still present with us today in the way that Paul proclaims? How else, but from scripture itself?'[38] By attending to the Bible as God's word and witness, Christ encounters us and we begin to learn who God is.

Nonetheless, Bonhoeffer is clear that affirming the Bible as God's word and witness in no way undermines its status as a set of historical, human texts. Indeed, for Bonhoeffer the Bible is God's word *only* in terms of its historical, temporally bound forms. He lays this out in 'Contemporizing New Testament Texts':

> The word of God and the word of human beings are bound together in the Holy Scriptures, but they are bound such that God himself states where his word is and that he speaks that word *within the word of human beings*. The human word does not cease being temporally bound and transient by becoming God's word; instead, it is precisely as such a historic, temporal word that it is indeed the word of God.[39]

That God 'speaks within the word of human beings' means that the Bible is and remains a set of human texts and words. And this means that God's word is bound up with all the ambiguities and contingencies of history. We encounter God only in the unstable and fragile histories and language of the Bible's human authors.

---

31. DBWE 9: 289. Bonhoeffer also quotes Luther at this point: 'If God gives me wooden apples and tells me to take and eat, I should not ask why.'
32. See DBWE 4: 260; and 'Contemporizing New Testament Texts', DBWE 14: 421.
33. 'Lecture on Homiletics', DBWE 14: 492.
34. On this point see Krötke, 'Dietrich Bonhoeffer and Martin Luther', 56.
35. DBWE 14: 424. Emphasis added.
36. Bonhoeffer had most likely taken this language of 'witness' from Barth. For example, see Barth, *The Göttingen Dogmatics: Instruction in the Christian Religion*, trans. Geoffrey W. Bromiley (Grand Rapids: Eerdmans, 1991), 201–2.
37. See 'The Bethel Confession', DBWE 12: 376.
38. DBWE 4: 206.
39. DBWE 14: 421. Italics original.

This emphasis on God's word in human history and language is especially apparent in Bonhoeffer's meditations on the Psalms. For Bonhoeffer, the Psalter is 'God's word, and at the same time with few exceptions the prayers of human beings'.[40] In his 1940 *Prayerbook of the Bible*, for example, Bonhoeffer notes that many of the Psalms are attributed to David, who 'according to the witness of the Bible … is a prototype of Jesus Christ'.[41] Accordingly, he reflects, 'It is important for us that even David not only prayed out of the personal raptures of his heart, but from Christ dwelling in him. To be sure, the one who prays these Psalms, David, remains himself; but Christ dwells in him and with him.'[42] When reading the Psalms, we are to attend to David's words and prayers as those of Christ and the church, yet simultaneously as David's own. For Bonhoeffer, we are to attend to the Bible as God's word in the specific language and histories of David and the Bible's other all-too-human authors.

Finally, all of this is significant for how Bonhoeffer negotiates historical criticism. In his early studies in Tübingen and Berlin, he had been trained in the dominant methods of early-twentieth-century biblical scholarship.[43] However, following his encounter with Barth, he immediately began raising concerns with the methods and conclusions of historical-critical approaches.[44] In 'Interpretation of Scripture', he programmatically asserts: 'We must say a priori that it is unacceptable for a pneumatological, faith-based interpretation to be dependent on historical methods of reading Scripture with their shifting results.'[45] Bonhoeffer construed his own faith-based mode of interpretation in opposition to the historical-critical pursuit of neutral, scientific (*wissenschaftlich*) objectivity, methods and criteria 'attainable by every reasonable person'.[46]

Nonetheless, Bonhoeffer also recognized that we cannot 'go back' to a time before historical-critical methods and insights[47]: 'As long as we live on earth, we must go ahead and use historical criticism, inadequate though it is.'[48] Indeed, he even suggests that historical criticism renders a valuable service to theology: 'Its value is that the *full historicity* of revelation comes to expression.'[49] By insisting on treating the Bible as simply a set of historical texts, historical-critical scholars testify to the *hiddenness* of God's word and revelation in these texts.[50] In so doing,

---

40. DBWE 5: 53.
41. DBWE 5: 158.
42. DBWE 5: 159.
43. Winter, 'Word and World', 2–6.
44. See Eberhard Bethge, *Dietrich Bonhoeffer: A Biography*, ed. Victoria Barnett (Minneapolis: Fortress Press, 2000), 68, 78.
45. 'Interpretation of Scripture', DBWE 9: 294.
46. DBWE 9: 286.
47. Bonhoeffer, 'Lecture on Christ in the Psalms', DBWE 14: 389
48. Bonhoeffer, 'Thy Kingdom Come', DBWE 12: 288.
49. DBWE 14: 390. Emphasis original.
50. See DBWE 14: 391–2.

historical-critical scholars help theologians resist a temptation to regard the Bible as God's revelation directly or unambiguously (e.g. as verbally inspired).[51] When theologians do this, it 'eternalizes the historical instead of recognizing the historical as coming from God's eternity and God's resurrection'.[52] Historical criticism thus properly affirms that the biblical texts are and remain historical and human all the way down. If these same texts are also God's word and witness to Christ, this can only be a claim of faith.

The whole of the Bible

As a quotation in the preceding section indicated, Bonhoeffer holds that the Bible is God's word and witness to Christ 'as a whole and in all its parts'. To understand Bonhoeffer's way of approaching the Bible in its specific historical and human forms, it is useful to reflect upon each part of this claim. First, what is entailed in insisting that the Bible '*as a whole*' witnesses to Christ? For Bonhoeffer, this means that we are to attend to Christ's presence and call *in the entirety* of the Bible or across the breadth and diversity of the biblical texts. 'To express the full witness of Christ requires more than a single set of terms', as he notes in *Discipleship*.[53] Crucially, the Bible directs us to Christ in the very multiplicity of its texts and their forms, meaning that we are not to unduly privilege or prefer certain passages or texts for understanding who Christ is.[54]

On this basis, Bonhoeffer insists that Scripture as a whole is *unified* in its witness to Christ. He argues, for example, that the gospels and Pauline epistles are unified precisely in their witness, a claim that is at the centre of *Discipleship*.[55] When making the transition between the two main parts of this work (each of which draws predominantly upon synoptic and Pauline material), he explains that, 'the synoptic Christ is neither more nor less distant from us than the Christ of Paul. … The different terminology with which the Synoptic Gospels and Paul communicate this message does not undermine the unity of the scriptural testimony.'[56] Against any who would either prioritize the synoptic material (in order to understand Christ on historical grounds) or begin with the epistles (for doctrinal reasons), Bonhoeffer insists that it is only these two parts of the New Testament *together* that can direct us to living Christ. Any distinction between more historical and more doctrinal material in the New Testament texts is strictly relative and not fundamental: 'Both are equally *witnesses to the unique Christ*.'[57]

51. See DBWE 14: 390.
52. 'Thy Kingdom Come', DBWE 12: 288.
53. DBWE 4: 206.
54. For some examples, see 'The Bethel Confession', DBWE 12: 380; 'Contemporizing New Testament Texts', DBWE 14: 421; DBWE 5: 60.
55. See DBWE 4: 205–7.
56. DBWE 4: 206.
57. 'Contemporizing New Testament Texts', DBWE 14: 424. Italics original.

Moreover, Bonhoeffer is careful to note that it is only in their witness to Christ that these texts can be drawn and held together, not on their own terms or more directly.[58]

These comments also find expression in how Bonhoeffer treats the Old Testament in his theology. That Scripture 'as a whole' witnesses to Christ means that the Old Testament texts, too, are not to be neglected in their witness. This claim is significant. Along with Barth, Wilhelm Vischer and several others, Bonhoeffer insisted upon the importance of the Old Testament for Christians; and he did so over against all those who in his own immediate context had sought to expunge these texts from the canon or construe them as of lesser significance. The former included, for example, scholars associated with the Institute for the Study and Eradication of Jewish Influence on German Religious Life and other German Christians (*Deutsche Christen*);[59] the latter included Bonhoeffer's own teacher and mentor, Adolf von Harnack, whom he explicitly criticized on this basis.[60]

Accordingly, Bonhoeffer insists that 'the full witness to Jesus Christ the Lord can be clearly heard only in its immeasurable inner relationships, in the connection of Old and New Testaments, Promise and Fulfilment'.[61] In their witness to Christ and the promise of Christ, the Old Testament is held to be integral to God's revelation. God's work in and as Christ can only properly be understood as the fulfilment of God's promise in the Old Testament texts.

This means that Bonhoeffer attends to and reads the Old Testament *Christologically*. If this is apparent throughout his engagements with a wide variety of texts, it is especially so in his opening comments in the 1933 *Creation and Fall*,[62] as well as in his meditations on the Psalms.[63] Bonhoeffer frames his readings of these biblical texts with direct reference to Christ and the church. As he states bluntly in a Bible study: 'The Old Testament must be read from the perspective of the incarnation and the cross, i.e., from the perspective of the revelation given to us.'[64] Indeed, Bonhoeffer relates these texts to Christ to such an extent that he was

---

58. The Bethel Confession states that 'the unity of the Holy Scriptures in their entirety and their unity alone is Christ'. DBWE 12: 379. In the essay 'Contemporizing New Testament Texts', Bonhoeffer writes: 'The New Testament is not something *itself* but witnesses to something else; it has no inherent value but value only as a witness to Christ.' DBWE 14: 425.

59. For background and detail on the German Christian movement, see Robert P. Erickson, *Theologians under Hitler* (New Haven: Yale University Press, 1985); and Susannah Herschel, *The Aryan Jesus: Christian Theologians and the Bible in Nazi Germany* (Princeton: Princeton University Press, 2008).

60. DBWE 3: 156–7. See Adolf von Harnack, *Marcion: The Gospel of the Alien God* (1900), trans. John E. Steely and Lyle D. Bierma (Grand Rapids: Baker Books, 1995).

61. DBWE 5: 60.

62. DBWE 3: 21–2.

63. For example, see DBWE 5 158–9; and 'Meditation on Psalm 119', DBWE 15: 496–527.

64. Bonhoeffer, 'Bible Study: King David', DBWE 14: 871.

accused by some of his contemporaries of simply 'plundering' (*Preisgabe*) the Old Testament.[65]

On the topic of the Old Testament, as noted briefly earlier, Bonhoeffer read and engaged with Old Testament texts in an especially focused way during his incarceration in Tegel prison.[66] Many of his best-known concepts and innovations during these final years – for example, 'religionless Christianity', 'world come of age', 'non-religious interpretation of biblical concepts', and so on – can be partly traced to this engagement.[67] Indeed, in his prison letters Bonhoeffer appears to privilege the Old Testament for understanding Christ and what it means to be Christian: 'Only when one knows the name of God may not be uttered may one sometimes speak the name of Jesus Christ. … Only when one accepts the law of God as binding for oneself may one perhaps sometimes speak of grace.'[68] In other words, the Old Testament is integral to the all-important question of 'who is Christ actually for us today?'[69]

The Bible in all its parts

For Bonhoeffer, the Bible 'as a whole' not only witnesses to Christ, but also 'in all its parts'.[70] What is entailed in the second part of this claim? Without this additional clarification, we might be tempted to read and interpret a given text or passage of the Bible *simply* and *primarily* with reference to the whole. We might be tempted, for example, to understand a given text or passage with reference to certain themes it shares with other, clearer parts of Scripture, or in light of some overarching biblical narrative or even in terms of the Bible simply as canon.[71] Such perspectives, of course, all have their place, and are prevalent in many more recent theological engagements with Scripture.[72] But Bonhoeffer wants to make it clear that it is ultimately only in their witness to Christ that these diverse texts can be understood and held together.

---

65. See Bethge, *Dietrich Bonhoeffer*, 526–9. Stephen Haynes has also criticized Bonhoeffer along these lines. See Stephen R. Haynes, *The Bonhoeffer Legacy: Post-Holocaust Perspectives* (Minneapolis: Fortress Press, 2006), 97–8.

66. For example, see Bonhoeffer, 'To Eberhard Bethge', 18 November 1943, DBWE 8: 181. See also 'To Eberhard Bethge, December 5 1943', DBWE 8: 213.

67. For example, see Bonhoeffer, 'To Eberhard Bethge', 30 April 1944, DBWE 8: 367–76; and 'To Eberhard Bethge', 28 July 1944, DBWE 8: 491. See also Kuske, *The Old Testament as the Book of Christ*, 132–59.

68. 'To Eberhard Bethge', 5 December 1943, DBWE 8: 213.

69. 'To Eberhard Bethge', 30 April 1944, DBWE 8: 362.

70. 'To Eberhard Bethge', 8 June 1944, DBWE 14: 424. As quoted earlier.

71. On this issue see, 'Interpretation of Scripture', DBWE 9: 297 n8.

72. For a Bonhoefferian critique of some of these approaches, see Brock, *Singing the Ethos of God*, 3–70.

Indeed, it is because Christ alone provides the substantive basis for approaching and unifying the biblical texts that we are freed to listen to Scripture *in its parts*. In Christ, we become free to attend to each specific text or word of the Bible in the particularity of its own witness. Put differently, Christians are freed to listen and attend a given text, passage or word of the Bible *in terms of its* own witness to Christ, without subordinating it to something else.

In 'Contemporizing New Testament Texts', Bonhoeffer further clarifies this way of approaching the Bible as an 'orientation to substance [*Sachlichkeit*]'.[73] It is the very substance or materiality of the texts that witnesses to Christ. An orientation to substance, therefore, entails carefully and continually attending to each text or word in its own grammatical, linguistic and material specificity. As Bonhoeffer made this same point earlier in 'Interpretation of Scripture', 'each of these written words … is an incarnate image of the person of Jesus Christ himself'.[74] That every single word of the Bible images or witnesses to Christ means that we are to listen to each of these words in order to learn who Christ is. Because Christ's speaking 'takes place not outside or alongside but only and exclusively *through the word* of Scripture itself, one puts one's confidence in the *substance itself*.[75] Bonhoeffer's orientation to substance in this way resonates with Hans Ulrich's more recent suggestion that 'every word of scripture demands its own hermeneutic'.[76]

Bonhoeffer's orientation to substance is central for how he relates Scripture to the present, the core preoccupation of 'Contemporizing New Testament Texts': 'The only *method* of contemporization', he writes, is 'the substantive textual exposition [of the holy Scriptures] as the witness of Christ, and as such exegesis has the promise of Christ's presence'.[77] On the one hand, this deepens and reinforces his claim that Christ is present and to be found in the detail and substance of the texts. On the other hand, if Scripture in its very substance witnesses to Christ, this means that the primary work of theology should be exegetical or expositional in nature.[78] Rather than trying to understand and interpret a given part of the Bible, and to *then* proceed to show how it relates to our present situation, through this 'substantive textual exposition' we instead allow the substance of the texts themselves to disclose and determine the present for us. Put differently, by attending to and expositing Scripture in its substance, we begin to discover what

---

73. 'Contemporizing New Testament Texts', DBWE 14: 417. See also Bonhoeffer's earlier remarks in DBWE 3: 22.
74. 'Interpretation of Scripture', DBWE 9: 294.
75. 'Contemporizing New Testament Texts', DBWE 14: 417. Italics original.
76. Quoted in Brian Brock and Bernd Wannenwetsch, *The Malady of the Christian Body: A Theological Exposition of Paul's First Letter to the Corinthians*, vol. 1 (Eugene: Cascade, 2016), xv.
77. DBWE 14: 422.
78. See 'Interpretation of Scripture', DBWE 9: 294; and 'Contemporizing New Testament Texts', DBWE 14: 418.

the present itself is. Following Bonhoeffer, it is through engaging and expositing the Bible that we begin to discover who and what we are in our real situation or standing with others and before God in the world: 'Not where the present registers its own claims before Christ but rather where that present itself stands before the claims of Christ.'[79]

If this basic orientation and expositional approach is apparent throughout Bonhoeffer's theology, especially following his academic dissertations and his 'coming to the Bible', a striking example can be seen in the 1933 lectures published as *Creation and Fall*. In these lectures, he continually allows the substance and language of the opening chapters of Genesis to guide his reflections, rather than attempting to set out a more systematic treatise or ordered reflection on creation. He moves carefully through these chapters verse by verse, word by word, meditating at length on the language and imagery of each given word or phrase.[80] Indeed, Bonhoeffer often reflects at length on a single sentence or word; he spends the first four pages of *Creation and Fall* reflecting on 'In the beginning' (*Am Anfang*).[81] In the later 'Guide to Scriptural Meditation', he observes: 'Sometimes we may linger for days over a single word.'[82]

Finally, it is noteworthy that Bonhoeffer's orientation to substance and expositional approach to the Bible allow for attending to and affirming conflicts and contradictions in and among biblical texts. In *Creation and Fall*, he draws out the differences between the first and second creation narratives (Gen. 1–2.3 and 2.4-25) and the divergent ways that these narratives portray both God and creation.[83] By holding that Scripture witnesses to Christ *in its parts*, and that these specific parts can be unified only in their witness to Christ, Bonhoeffer is freed from having to try to reconcile or overcome these differences directly. When reflecting on Genesis 2.7, he simply notes that 'we are directed to the earth in a distinct and exclusive way that is quite different from before'.[84] An orientation to substance frees him from undue anxiety about whether or how a given passage or text might fit with some other part of God's witness. If the Bible witnesses to Christ 'as a whole and in all its parts', then we in our place are freed simply to listen to and remain with these words and texts.

---

79. DBWE 14: 17.
80. DBWE 3: 75-6. Another example of Bonhoeffer allowing the text itself to guide his thinking is his unfinished 'Meditation on Psalm 119', DBWE 15: 496–528. On this meditation, see a rich article by Brian Brock, 'Bonhoeffer and the Bible in Christian Ethics: Psalm 119, the Mandates and Ethics as a Way', *Studies in Christian Ethics* 18, no. 3 (2005): 7–29.
81. DBWE 3: 25–9.
82. Bonhoeffer, 'Guide to Scriptural Meditation', DBWE 14: 933.
83. DBWE 3: 72.
84. DBWE 3: 74.

The Bible in its witness to the cross

If Bonhoeffer approaches the Bible in its witness to Christ, 'as a whole and in its parts', he also insists that the Bible witnesses to Christ as *the crucified one*.[85] As he writes in 'Contemporizing New Testament Texts', the 'turn back to Scripture corresponds exactly to the turn undertaken by Christian faith and Christian hope, namely, back to the cross of Christ. In both cases, it is the historicity of God's revelation that comes to expression.'[86] Attending to God in the suffering and human Christ orientates us to God's presence in the fragile, flawed human texts of the Bible. Attending to the Bible in its historicity and substance directs us to a God who suffers a human death on the cross.

Bonhoeffer reflects explicitly on this correspondence between the Bible and cross in a 1936 letter to his brother-in-law, Rüdiger Schleicher. He affirms the cross as 'the very place where God chose to encounter us.'[87] And he again identifies the cross as the meaning and message of the entire Bible. 'Precisely this', he writes, 'is the message of the Bible, not only the New but also in the Old Testament (Isa.53!) In any event both Jesus and Paul intended it thus: the cross of Jesus fulfils Scripture.'[88] The texts of the Bible are continually directing us to God's presence and work in and as the crucified Christ.[89]

In this short letter, Bonhoeffer gives particular emphasis to how the cross offends and stands against us: 'It is not at all a place that we find pleasant or that might be clear a priori, but a place alien to us in every way, a place utterly repugnant to us.'[90] That God is present in Christ's human suffering challenges our assumptions about who God is and how God works. And this, of course, is the whole point: 'If it is God who says where he is to be found, then it will probably be a place that is not at all commensurate with my own nature and that does not please me at all.'[91] The offence of the cross helps us to relinquish our own assumptions and ideas, and instead turn to and wait upon the God who comes to us on the cross. This *theologia crucis* is therefore deepening and expanding upon Bonhoeffer's claim, as outlined earlier, that all true knowledge of God proceeds from God alone. In particular, this emphasis on the alien and scandalous nature of Scripture fits with Bonhoeffer's Lutheran (and Barthian) commitment to *scriptura sacra est sui ipsius interpretes*.[92]

---

85. See Gaylon H. Barker, *The Cross of Reality: Luther's Theologia Crucis and Bonhoeffer's Christology* (Minneapolis: Fortress Press, 2015).
86. 'Contemporizing New Testament Texts', DBWE 14: 419.
87. DBWE 14: 168.
88. 'To Rüdiger Schleicher', DBWE 14: 168.
89. See Bonhoeffer, 'To Eberhard Bethge', 16 July 1944, DBWE 8: 479.
90. DBWE 14: 168.
91. DBWE 14: 168.
92. On this point see 'Interpretation of Scripture', DBWE 9: 290; and 'Lecture on Homiletics', DBWE 14: 497.

That the Bible 'interprets itself' means that our primary posture should be one of openness to how God comes to us through the texts.

The correspondence between the Bible and the cross has implications for how we are to approach the biblical texts. In his writings, Bonhoeffer attempts to engage the Bible in ways that remain continually alert to the offence of God's word: 'Can you somehow understand', he asks Schleicher, 'that I do not wish to surrender the Bible as this alien word of God in any point and instead will ask with all my powers what God is trying to say to us here?'[93] Bonhoeffer had made this same point at a conference in Geneva a few years earlier: 'We prefer our own thoughts to those of the Bible. We no longer read the Bible seriously. We read it no longer against ourselves but only for ourselves.'[94] What might it mean to read the Bible 'against ourselves'?

In his 1939 classic *Life Together*, Bonhoeffer suggests a number of practices and strategies for reading the Bible in precisely this manner,[95] for allowing the biblical texts and words themselves to govern and interrupt our reading. To take one example, he recommends that the Christian community commits to reading and listening to 'at least a chapter of the Old Testament and at least half a chapter of the New Testament every morning and evening'.[96] While acknowledging that this amount is simply too much for many people, he suggests that this in itself can be a reminder of how Scripture always exceeds our understanding: 'It can only be a good thing when we are daily reminded of this fact, which again refers us to Jesus Christ himself "in whom are *hidden* all the treasures of wisdom and knowledge" (Col. 2:3).'[97]

To take a second example, Bonhoeffer insists that the Christian community should not neglect parts of the Bible that seem wholly irrelevant to its needs, those parts that seem 'obsolete and antiquated'.[98] Accordingly, when reflecting on Psalms of innocence, vengeance and suffering, he asserts:

> The psalms that will not cross our lips as prayers, those that make us falter and offend us, make us suspect that here someone else is praying, not we – that the one who is here affirming his innocence, who is calling for God's judgment, who has come to such infinite depths of suffering, is none other than Jesus Christ himself.[99]

By confounding and offending us, these Psalms direct us away from ourselves and towards Christ. Reading the biblical texts against ourselves, in their offence and

---

93. DBWE 14: 169.
94. Bonhoeffer, 'Address at the International Youth Conference in Gland', DBWE 11: 377.
95. See especially DBWE 5: 51–68.
96. DBWE 5: 60.
97. DBWE 5: 61.
98. DBWE 5: 53.
99. DBWE 5: 54.

cruciform witness, therefore, means allowing them to challenge and unravel our assumptions and ideas. As Bonhoeffer makes this point in 'Contemporizing New Testament Texts', 'an orientation toward substance will consist in allowing that external element ... to come to expression as the present – the alien gospel, not the familiar gospel. ... Point of contact with the scandalum!'[100]

Finally, this relates to Bonhoeffer's aversion to metaphysical and moral readings of Scripture. Throughout his writings he frequently criticizes attempts to approach or understand the Bible as disclosing truths or norms that have validity of a general kind:[101] 'It is not a book *containing* eternal truths, teaching, norms, or myths, but the sole *witness* of the God-human Jesus Christ.'[102] As he writes elsewhere, the 'New Testament contains no ethical prescription that we are supposed to adopt literally or even that we could so adopt.'[103] If God's word and witness is the very substance of these texts, then this prevents us from locating or extracting truths or moral prescriptions *from* these texts. Because of their witness to the cross, these texts and words are just as likely to confound and offend as they are to illuminate. The problem with metaphysical and moral readings, therefore, is that they understand the Bible as containing truths or norms translatable into a non-scriptural theological or philosophical idiom. In contrast, Bonhoeffer insists on attending to and remaining with the texts as they stand. As Webster summarizes, 'Scripture is irreducible for Bonhoeffer; it is not a means of attaining moral concreteness, but, quite simply, the concrete point at which Christian thought and action begin and end.'[104]

Conclusion: Preaching and pondering the word of God

In his brief 1936 'Guide to Scriptural Meditation', Bonhoeffer states that 'as a Christian ... it is only through hearing preaching and prayerful meditation that

---

100. DBWE 14: 418.

101. For example, see Bonhoeffer, 'Sermon on John 8: 32', DBWE 11: 446–67; and DBWE 4: 82.

102. 'Contemporizing New Testament Texts', DBWE 14: 424. Emphasis added.

103. Bonhoeffer, 'Basic Questions of a Christian Ethic', DBWE 10: 368.

104. Webster, 'Reading the Bible: The Example of Barth and Bonhoeffer', 96. Bonhoeffer's aversion to metaphysical and moral readings of the Bible is of course central for his reflections during in Tegel Prison. In a letter to Bethge, he famously proposes 'a non-religious interpretation of biblical concepts'. 'To Eberhard Bethge', 16 July 1944, DBWE 8: 475. In an earlier letter, he had defined 'religion' here as the 'temporally conditioned presuppositions of metaphysics, the inner life'. Bonhoeffer, 'Letter to Karl and Paula Bonhoeffer', 26 April 1944, DBWE 8: 364. So, in significant respects, Bonhoeffer's prison theology reflects and extends his wider approach to the Bible. And as suggested earlier, his late reflections also emerged from engagements with the Bible, in particular the Old Testament.

I come to know Holy Scripture'.[105] This remark is useful for guiding some summary reflections on Bonhoeffer's approach to the Bible and its significance.

As we have seen, Bonhoeffer displays a deep and consistent commitment to the Bible as God's word and witness to Christ in the historicity and substance of its texts. As a whole and in its parts, the Bible is continually witnessing and directing us to Christ as the crucified one. And Bonhoeffer positions this approach over against other approaches that begin with or rely upon our own assumptions and ideas (e.g. historical criticism, moral and metaphysical readings, etc.).

On the one hand, Bonhoeffer's claim that we come to know the Bible as God's word in *preaching* reflects and extends all of these insights.[106] Indeed, Bonhoeffer's entire approach to the Bible, as outlined earlier, is directed towards preaching and the life of the community.[107] In particular, preaching as the word of a concrete human other reminds us that God's word always comes to and confronts us from without. Even while God's word is present in and as the Bible, preaching makes clear that this is *God's* word for us. At the same time, preaching facilitates a recognition that God's word in and as the Bible is also *for us*. It is through preaching that God's word in Scripture becomes concrete in the life of the church: 'The particular goal of any individual sermon', Bonhoeffer writes in another lecture from Finkenwalde, 'is that *the text itself* comes to expression'.[108] Quite simply, preaching itself contemporizes biblical texts.

On the other hand, Bonhoeffer's emphasis on *prayerfully mediating* on the Bible similarly expands on and deepens his wider approach. In the 1936 reflection, he gives particular attention to how prayerful meditation allows the biblical texts to discipline us as preachers and servants of God's word. By meditating on the Bible, we allow the substance and words of the Bible to begin to form and shape us: 'Reading by itself is never enough. We must give God's word the time to "enter us deeply", dwell in us like the Holiest of Holies in the sanctuary.'[109] Even more than preaching, prayerful meditation acknowledges and attends to God's presence in the very historicity and substance of the texts. Prayerful meditation attends to God's word in these fragile and unstable human forms. Accordingly, to give Bonhoeffer himself the final word:

---

105. 'Guide to Scriptural Meditation', DBWE 14: 933. In a lecture from this same period, Bonhoeffer writes: 'All study of scripture should serve humility and an improved ability to pray and to preach.' 'Lecture on Homiletics', DBWE 14: 517.

106. As Bonhoeffer had once quoted Barth in *Sanctorum Communio*, 'The preaching of the word of God is the word of God.' DBWE 1: 233.

107. I have discussed Bonhoeffer's understanding of the role of preaching in relation to the church elsewhere. See Michael Mawson, *Christ Existing as Community: Bonhoeffer's Ecclesiology* (Oxford: Oxford University Press, 2018), 161–6. See also David Lose, 'Bonhoeffer the Preacher', in *Oxford Handbook of Dietrich Bonhoeffer*, 108–20.

108. 'Lecture on Homiletics', DBWE 14: 497.

109. 'Meditation on Psalm 119', DBWE 15: 514.

Just as the words of someone dear to you can follow you around the entire day, so also should the word of Scripture resonate in your ears incessantly and work on you. Just as you do not analyse the words of someone dear to you and simply accept them as they are spoken to you, so also accept the word of Scripture, pondering it in your heart just as Mary did. And that is all. That is meditation ... Then ponder these words for a long time in your own heart until they completely enter into you and take possession of you.[110]

---

110. 'Guide to Scriptural Meditation', DBWE 14: 933.

Chapter 3

LIVING IN THE FORMS OF THE WORD: BONHOEFFER AND FRANZ ROSENZWEIG ON THE APOCALYPTIC MATERIALITY OF SCRIPTURE

In his Habilitationshrift, *Act and Being*, Bonhoeffer famously insisted that 'God *is* present, that is, not in eternal nonobjectivity but – to put it quite provisionally for now – "haveable", graspable in the Word within the church'.[1] Along similar lines, the Jewish philosopher Franz Rosenzweig once reflected that 'the faraway God is none other than the near God, the unknown God none other than the revealed one, the Creator none other than the Redeemer'.[2]

This chapter explores possibilities for an apocalyptic theological ethics by reflecting upon resonances between how Bonhoeffer and Rosenzweig (1886–1929) approached the Bible. In particular, I attend to ways in which both thinkers strove to recognize and respond to God's alterity or disruptive presence within the materiality or phenomenality of biblical texts. Rather than just interpreting and deriving meaning *from* the Bible, they sought strategies for attending to God's revelation and presence *in* the very substance and forms of the texts themselves.

The first section of this chapter sets out some of the basic emphases that have emerged in recent apocalyptic biblical studies and theology, giving attention to the role of Karl Barth. The second and third sections examine how Rosenzweig and Bonhoeffer each approach Scripture. In these sections, I explore how each approaches the text by expanding and placing pressure on the understanding of revelation found in apocalyptic theology. Building upon this, the final section makes some comparisons between Bonhoeffer and Rosenzweig, before drawing out the ethic of responsibility that is inherent in how they attend to and live in the forms of God's word.

---

1. DBWE 2: 91.
2. Quoted in Samuel Moyn, *The Origins of the Other: Emmanuel Levinas between Revelation and Ethics* (Ithaca: Cornell University Press, 2005), 159.

Apocalyptic biblical studies and theology

A growing body of work in biblical studies and systematic theology is giving renewed attention to the disruptive and invasive character of God's revelation (ἀποκάλυψις) in Christ. This development can in part be traced to J. Louis Martyn's ground-breaking 1997 commentary on Galatians.[3] In this massive work, Martyn consistently characterizes Paul's theology as a 'cosmological apocalyptic eschatology'.[4] For Martyn, as one reviewer has summarized, Paul's God 'inaugurates a war of liberation against hostile powers that hold human beings captive'.[5] Following Martyn's commentary, other biblical scholars have similarly drawn out this militant, disruptive character of Paul's evangelical witness,[6] as well as its implications for epistemology and human agency.

What is entailed in this Pauline apocalyptic? Central to this reading of Paul is an emphasis on the disjunctive and disruptive character of God's revelation in Christ, that is, the ways in which this revelation radically overturns all claims to knowledge by its human recipients. Furthermore, this revelation not only has epistemological significance, but also is ontological and cosmological in its scope; it does not simply provide new information but brings about a whole new reality. As Paul himself proclaims, 'there is a new creation: everything old has become new!' (2 Cor. 5.16).[7]

It is worth noting that this reading indicates a departure from 'salvation-historical' approaches to Paul, as exemplified by the late E. P. Sanders and N. T. Wright.[8] Indeed, Wright has forcefully and directly challenged this apocalyptic turn: 'The "apocalyptic" reading of Paul offered by Martyn in particular must … be questioned as a complete or adequate account.'[9] Among other things, he worries

---

3. J. Louis Martyn, *Galatians: A New Translation with Introduction and Commentary* (New Haven: Yale University Press, 1997).

4. Here Martyn is drawing on his student Martin de Boer's distinction between 'forensic' and 'cosmological' apocalpytic. See Martin de Boer, *The Defeat of Death: Apocalpytic Eschatology in 1 Corinthians 15 and Romans 5* (London: T&T Clark, 1988).

5. Richard B. Hays, 'Review of J. Louis Martyn's *Galatians: A New Translation*', *Journal of Biblical Literature* 119, no. 2 (2000): 375.

6. Some examples include Douglas Campbell, *The Deliverance of God: An Apocalyptic Rereading of Justification in Paul* (Grand Rapids: Eerdmans, 2009); Susan Eastman, *Recovering Paul's Mother Tongue: Language and Theology in Galatians* (Grand Rapids: Eerdmans, 2007) and Beverly Gaventa, *When in Romans: An Invitation to Linger with the Gospel according to Paul* (Grand Rapids: Baker, 2016).

7. As Philip Ziegler has summarized, 'God's redemptive invasion of the fallen order of things' is 'such that reality itself is decisively re-made in the event.' Philip G. Ziegler, *Militant Grace: The Apocalyptic Turn and the Future of Christian Theology* (Grand Rapids: Baker Academic, 2018), 170.

8. See E. P. Sanders, *Paul and Palestinian Judaism* (Minneapolis: Fortress Press, 1977); N. T. Wright, *Paul and the Faithfulness of God* (Minneapolis: Fortress Press, 2013).

9. N. T. Wright, *Paul and His Recent Interpreters* (London: SPCK, 2015), 18.

that this apocalyptic reading narrowly focuses on the singularity of the Christ event at the expense of Christ being the fulfilment of God's covenant and history with Israel.[10]

Alongside biblical scholars, systematic theologians have contributed to the recent 'apocalyptic turn'.[11] Most notably, Philip Ziegler has connected this Pauline scholarship to broader insights and themes in Protestant theology.[12] In his 2018 book, *Militant Grace: The Apocalyptic Turn and the Future of Christian Theology*, Ziegler draws out the full implications of Paul's apocalypticism for Christian doctrine. Indeed, Ziegler programmatically pursues 'a Christian theology funded by a fresh hearing of New Testament apocalyptic', which stresses 'the unexpected, new, and disjunctive character of the divine work of salvation that comes on the world of sin in and through Christ'.[13]

Ziegler and others have linked this apocalyptic turn to the earlier work of Karl Barth.[14] Especially in his second *Romans* commentary, Barth had likewise emphasized the 'absolute qualitative distinction' or 'eschatological contrast' between God's revelation and all human reality.[15] In ways that resonate with Martyn, Barth structured his reading of Romans around a series of juxtapositions: God and humanity, transcendence and finitude, eternity and time, divine freedom and human sin, revelation and religion.[16] As Ziegler observes, Barth thereby provides an important precedent for more recent apocalyptic theology: 'We have good reason to see contemporary efforts to win through to a form of Christian theology

---

10. Wright, *Paul and His Recent Interperters*, 217–18. See also Michael Bird, *An Anomalous Jew: Paul among Jews, Greeks and Romans* (Grand Rapids: Eerdmans, 2016), 108–69.

11. See for example Walter Lowe, *Theology and Difference* (Bloomington: Indiana University Press, 1993); Douglas Harink, *Paul among the Postliberals: Pauline Theology beyond Christendom and Modernity* (Eugene: Wipf & Stock, 2003). See also the rich collection of essays edited by Joshua B. Davis and Douglas Harink, eds, *Apocalyptic and the Future of Theology: With and beyond J. Louis Martyn* (Eugene: Cascade, 2012).

12. Ziegler writes of a need to 'fill out the wider theological context' of the 'apocalpytic turn' in contemporary theology and biblical studies. Ziegler, *Militant Grace*, 19.

13. This is the third of six 'doctrinal theses' that Ziegler sets out at the end of the first section of his book. Ziegler, *Militant Grace*, 30.

14. Ziegler provides a useful overview of some of those who have connected Barth to the more recent apocalyptic turn. Ziegler, *Militant Grace*, 20–5. For a rich reading of Barth's mature theology in relation to Pauline apocalyptic, see Shannon Nicole Smythe, *Forensic Apocalpytic Theology: Karl Barth and the Doctrine of Divine Justification* (Minneapolis: Fortress Press, 2016).

15. Karl Barth, *The Epistle to the Romans*, 2nd edn, trans. Edwyn C. Hoskyns (London: Oxford University Press, 1968), xiii.

16. On these oppositions in Barth's early theology, see especially Bruce McCormack, *Karl Barth's Critically Realistic Dialectical Theology: Its Genesis and Development 1909-1936* (New York: Oxford University Press, 1995).

that is particularly alert to and shaped by Paul's apocalyptic gospel as … a ripening fruit of that particular sowing.'[17]

For our purposes, Dietrich Bonhoeffer and Franz Rosenzweig were already responding to the provocation of Barth's eschatology in their own contexts.[18] The theology of Barth's *Romans* commentary sits in the background of their respective understandings of and approaches to Scripture. In line with Barth, they give consistent emphasis to the alterity of God's revelation. At the same time, they develop their approaches in ways that move beyond or resituate the sharp antinomies of both Barth and recent apocalyptic scholarship.[19]

Bonhoeffer on approaching the Bible Christologically

Barth's direct and profound influence on Bonhoeffer's theology has been widely recognized and well documented.[20] It is significant that Barth's impact on Bonhoeffer first becomes apparent through a student essay on scriptural interpretation: 'The Pneumatological and Historical Understanding of Scripture'. In this early essay, Bonhoeffer maintains that a properly theological or 'spiritual' (*pneumatische*) approach to Scripture involves recognizing that 'the Bible is not only a word about God but God's word itself'.[21] Inspired by Barth, Bonhoeffer insists that the Bible is the sole place where God has chosen to encounter the human being.

From this essay until his late prison letters, Bonhoeffer consistently understands the Bible as God's word and witness to Christ; he reads the New and

---

17. Ziegler, *Militant Grace*, 25.

18. There have been a number of recent studies positioning Bonhoeffer's theology in relation to the apocalyptic turn. See in particular Philip Ziegler, 'Dietrich Bonhoeffer', 579–94; David Congdon, 'Bonhoeffer and Barth: Toward an Apocalyptic Rapprochement', *International Journal of Systematic Theology* 15, no. 2 (2013): 172–95; and Koert Verhagen, *Being and Action* Coram Deo: *Bonhoeffer and the Retrieval of Justification's Social Import* (London: T&T Clark Bloomsbury, 2021), 77–91.

19. Alternatively, Bonhoeffer and Rosenzweig might instead be seen as emphasizing one aspect of recent apocalyptic theology. For instance, Ziegler has written that 'as a theology of revelation, apocalyptic theology is committed to knowing and speaking of the God of the gospel where the Lord gives himself to be known'. Philip G. Ziegler, 'A Response', *International Journal of Systematic Theology* 22, no. 3 (2020): 331. This resonates closely with the two quotes at the start of this chapter.

20. Some of the most thoroughgoing treatments of this relationship include Andreas Pangritz, *Karl Barth in the Theology of Dietrich Bonhoeffer* (Grand Rapids: Eerdmans, 2000); Edward Van't Slot, *Negativism of Revelation? Bonhoeffer and Barth on Faith and Actualism* (Tübingen: Mohr Siebeck, 2015) and Michael P. DeJonge, *Bonhoeffer's Theological Formation: Berlin, Barth, and Protestant Theology* (Oxford: Oxford University Press, 2012).

21. Bonhoeffer, 'Paper on the Historical and Pneumatological Interpretation of Scripture', DBWE 9: 287.

Old Testaments in light of their Christological witness. Furthermore, Bonhoeffer emphasizes God's own agency and freedom with respect to this witness. God has freely chosen Scripture as the place and means of God's revelation, meaning that from our side we are to attend to these texts as the place where God claims us and directs us towards Christ.

On the one hand, this suggests that attending to the Bible as God's word requires affirming the *alterity* of the biblical texts. In these texts, God comes to us and encounters us from without. For Bonhoeffer, there is always a sense in which the texts themselves stand over against us. As *God's* word and witness, they continually exceed and disrupt our best attempts to interpret and make sense of them. Indeed, Bonhoeffer expressed this point at a conference in Geneva in mid-1932: 'We prefer our own thoughts to those of the Bible. We no longer read the Bible seriously. We read it no longer against ourselves but only for ourselves.'[22] In other words, to 'read the Bible seriously' involves allowing the biblical texts themselves to interrupt and reorientate our reading. In this respect, his approach resonates with the disruptive emphases of recent apocalyptic theology.

On the other hand, Bonhoeffer is clear that reading the Bible as God's word and witness – in its alterity – in no way undermines its status as a set of fully human and historical texts. In his 1935 essay 'Contemporizing New Testament Texts', he rejects the view that 'in the Bible we can distinguish the word of God from the word of human beings and extract it.'[23] God's word remains bound to human history and language. As Bonhoeffer continues, 'the human word does not cease being temporally bound and transient by becoming God's word.'[24] The Bible, as God's word and witness to Christ, is bound to all the ambiguities and contingencies of history. We encounter God only in the unstable and fragile histories and language of the Bible's authors, not otherwise or more directly: 'Through the Bible in its fragility, God comes to meet us.'[25]

As outlined in the previous chapter, attending to the Bible as God's word and witness involves an 'orientation to substance (*Sachlichkeit*)'. For Bonhoeffer, because this witness 'takes place not outside or alongside but only and exclusively *through the word* of Scripture itself, one puts one's confidence in the *substance itself*.'[26] Approaching the Bible in its otherness involves pressing into its substance and detail; it requires attending to every given text, passage or word in its historical and linguistic specificity. The goal of theology and biblical exposition is to allow the substance and materiality of the texts to come to expression.

What this indicates, therefore, is that Bonhoeffer's Christological approach to the Bible continually orientates him into the concrete forms of biblical texts. As Joel Banman has observed, 'Bonhoeffer's Christological exegetical lens has an

---

22. Bonhoeffer, 'Address at the International Youth Conference in Gland', DBWE 11: 377.
23. Bonhoeffer, 'Contemporizing New Testament Texts', DBWE 14: 420–1.
24. DBWE 14: 421.
25. Bonhoeffer, 'Thy Kingdom Come', DBWE 12: 288.
26. DBWE 14: 417. Italics original.

expansive rather than a reductive effect. Christology is not something he pulls out of the text, but rather that pulls him more deeply into it.[27] Paradoxically, Bonhoeffer's claim that the biblical texts witness to Christ frees him to attend to and remain with them as they stand. This is illustrated in a late letter to Eberhard Bethge, in which he makes a surprising claim that reading the Song of Solomon as 'a song of earthly love' is the 'best "Christological interpretation"'.[28] Approaching a given text or word as its own specific word about Christ means attending to what it actually is.

In his theology, Bonhoeffer thus consistently sought to attend closely to the substance of biblical texts. This is evident, for example, in an incomplete exposition of Psalm 119, which he worked on in 1939–40. In this exposition, Bonhoeffer moves through the text slowly, meditating at length on each verse: 'I need time for God's word and often have to ponder the words for a long time in order to understand the precepts of God correctly.'[29] What gradually emerges from his exposition is an account of 'ethics as a way'. As Brian Brock has summarized, 'Bonhoeffer was replacing the [abstract] philosophical concept of ethics with the biblical concept of torah.'[30] The substance of the Psalm provides material forms for Christian freedom and obedience.

Finally, this leads us to Bonhoeffer's emphasis in his theology on the *preaching* of Scripture: 'The preaching of the word of God is the word of God.'[31] It is through preaching that the substance of Scripture comes to expression and encounters a community. As David Lose summarizes, for Bonhoeffer preaching is the 'attempt to speak Scripture into the present on its own terms in order to see what questions and answers, problems and responses Scripture itself elicits'.[32] Through preaching, Scripture itself sheds light on our situation and teaches us who we are.[33] For Bonhoeffer, the very act of preaching – as a free translating of Scripture into the present – reflects and serves the alterity of the text. The fluidity of the spoken word safeguards God's word from being fixed or domesticated by our own interpretations and agendas.

To summarize, for Bonhoeffer we encounter (or are encountered by) Christ only by attending to and immersing ourselves within the substance and diverse forms of the biblical texts. It is through this substance that the Bible as God's word and witness to Christ forms us from without. Practices of meditation and

---

27. Banman, *Reading in the Presence of Christ*, 100.
28. Bonhoeffer, 'To Eberhard Bethge', 2 June 1944, DBWE 8: 410.
29. Bonhoeffer, 'Meditation on Psalm 119', DBWE 15: 517.
30. Brock, 'Bonhoeffer and the Bible in Christian Ethics': 8.
31. DBWE 1: 233, quoting Barth.
32. David J. Lose, 'Bonhoeffer the Preacher', in *The Oxford Handbook of Dietrich Bonhoeffer*, ed. Michael Mawson and Philip Ziegler (Oxford: Oxford University Press, 2019), 113.
33. As Bonhoeffer reflects, 'my true concrete situation as revealed and resolved for me by the sermon'. 'Contemporizing New Testament Texts', DBWE 14: 423.

preaching orientate us to the substance of Scripture as the place of God's alterity and presence.

Franz Rosenzweig on the work of translation

A number of important studies have drawn attention to Barth's and Rosenzweig's shared commitment to revelation,[34] even while noting that the latter often expressed concerns about the 'sheer negativism' of Barth's early theology.[35] Against the early Barth, Rosenzweig too sought ways of attending to God's otherness in the midst of worldly reality. As he put it in a conversation with his friend Eugen Rosenstock, 'God created the world and [is] not just the God of revelation.'[36] This attentiveness to God's revelation in the midst of creaturely living frames Rosenzweig's understanding of and approach to Scripture.

In a series of important essays from the mid-1920s, Rosenzweig reflects on his work with Martin Buber translating the Torah into German.[37] In their translation,[38] they sought to reinvigorate the relationship between the biblical texts and a new community of readers. In particular, they had sought ways of freeing the Bible's texts and language from how it had become reified and overly familiar through existing translations. As Leora Batnitzky has observed, 'the task of the translator for Rosenzweig is to produce shocked attention in the reader. Only by encountering the alien, he argued, could the Jewish people be led back to what was already its own.'[39]

In these essays, Rosenzweig therefore proposes that the work of translation involves producing and preserving a certain distance between a text and its modern readers. This distance is necessary for a new community to be able to receive and engage the Bible as God's word. Specifically, the biblical texts must be

---

34. Important studies on this relationship include Randi Rashover, *Revelation and Theopolitics: Barth, Rosenzweig and the Politics of Praise* (London: T&T Clark, 2005); and Jennifer M. Rosner, *Healing the Schism: Barth, Rosenzweig, and the New Jewish-Christian Encounter* (Minneapolis: Fortress Press, 2005).

35. On this critique see especially Daniel Herskowitz, 'Franz Rosenzweig and Karl Barth: A Chapter in the Jewish Reception of Dialectical Theology', *Journal of Religion* 97, no. 1 (2017): 79–100.

36. Quoted in Herskowitz, 'Franz Rosenzweig and Karl Barth', 84.

37. Martin Buber and Franz Rosenzweig, *Scripture and Translation*, trans. Lawrence Rosenwald with Everett Fox (Bloomington: Indiana University Press, 1993).

38. For their translation itself, see Martin Buber and Franz Rosenzweig, *Die Schrift* (Stuttgart: Deutsche Bibelgesellschaft, 1993).

39. Leora Batnitzky, *Idolatry and Representation: The Philosophy of Franz Rosenzweig Reconsidered* (Princeton: Princeton University Press, 2000), 105. As Batnitzky clarifies, 'the text itself must be made uncanny so that modern people would have the capacity to respond to it'. *Idolatry and Representation*, 106.

able to exert claims upon this community, to both challenge the members of this community and cause them to question themselves from a different place.

This becomes clear in an important essay from July 1926, 'Scripture and Luther'.[40] Here Rosenzweig suggests that translating involves two principles: moving a text towards the reader and moving the reader closer the text. He notes that the former is the primary strategy for the vast majority of translators, including Martin Luther himself. The goal is to make a given text as accessible and comprehensible as possible in the host language. As Luther had put it, the task is 'to produce clear language, comprehensible to everyone, with an undistorted sense of meaning'.[41]

Yet Rosenzweig also notes that Luther found it necessary to occasionally 'give the Hebrew some room', namely, at those points 'where it does better than the German'.[42] Luther had at times sought to translate in ways that stayed much closer to the Hebrew, even when this stretched and disrupted the linguistic patterns and possibilities of German. As Rosenzweig quotes Luther: 'We have also sometimes translated word for word, though we could have done it otherwise and more clearly … Psalm 68:18, for example: "Thou has gone up on high and hast led captivity captive." An idiomatic translation would be, "hast freed the prisoners." But that is too weak and does not yield the rich, subtle sense of the Hebrew.'[43]

In his own translating, Rosenzweig thus aimed to take up this second principle and make it axiomatic. With Buber, he sought to translate in ways that 'give the Hebrew some room', even and perhaps especially when this creates difficulties for the German language. How can the very otherness or subtle sense of the Hebrew be conveyed through a new kind of translating? How can this facilitate deeper and richer engagement with the Bible by a new community?

Indeed, in Rosenzweig's view, translating in this new way had become necessary in part due to the very success of Luther's translation. If the Luther Bible had been revolutionary in its own time,[44] it had quickly come to attain the status of *Shriftsprache* (literature). In another essay he lays out this movement as a continual and 'fateful scripturalization of the word'.[45] The dynamism of language is continually in the process of becoming fixed and contained, that is, as either literature or as

---

40. Franz Rosenzweig, 'Scripture and Luther', in Buber and Rosenzweig, *Scripture and Translation*, 47–69.

41. Rosenzweig here quotes Luther's 1924 preface to the book of Job. Franz Rosenzweig, 'Scripture and Luther', in *Scripture and Translation*, ed. Martin Buber and Franz Rosenzweig, 48 (Bloomington: Indiana University Press, 1994).

42. Here Rosenzweig is quoting Luther's late preface to the Psalter. Rosenzweig, 'Scripture and Luther', 49.

43. Rosenzweig, 'Scripture and Luther', 48.

44. 'The Luther Bible was, then, a trumpet-call in the ear of those who had fallen asleep happy in their possession of the "received and certified text." But it did not remain that; it became itself a possession, a national possession.' Rosenzweig, 'Scripture and Luther', 57.

45. Rosenzweig, 'Scripture and Word', in *Scripture and Translation*, ed. Martin Buber and Franz Rosenzweig, 41 (Bloomington: Indiana University Press, 1994).

Holy Scripture. In the case of Luther, Rosenzweig notes that his translation soon 'broke free of its maker's religious life, and became the fundamental book not only of a particular church but of the national language itself'.[46] Even its Hebraisms and idiosyncrasies had become static and entirely familiar, hence no longer requiring any movement and struggle on the part of its community.

Given this, Rosenzweig suggested that what had saved Protestantism was the place it assigned to the sermon. Protestant preaching supplied and facilitated the requisite distance and disruption now lacking within the text itself. On the one hand, this was because Protestant preachers were steeped in Hebrew and Greek, and thus always 'prepared the sermon in consultation with the original text'.[47] Protestant preaching was never simply reducible to or derived from Luther's Bible as a familiar and domesticated text. On the other hand, the very orality of the sermon supplied a kind of dynamism and unpredictability that again facilitated distance and difference, thereby still requiring movement and engagement from the Protestant community.[48] Accordingly, Rosenzweig concludes, preaching 'offers through the very fact of its orality the deliverance of humankind'.[49]

In their own translation, Buber and Rosenzweig sought a different strategy for maintaining this distance and difference for their modern, secular Jewish community. Specifically, they sought to incorporate the otherness and orality of the Hebrew *into* their translation. Two main examples of this can be seen in their translation techniques of *Leitworte* (leading words) and *Kolometrie* (colometry).

First, Buber and Rosenzweig famously pursued a *Leitworte* (leading words) technique in their translation, whereby they used the same German word to translate a given Hebrew word and its cognates.[50] The impact of this was that the translated text retains more of the internal, material connections and resonances found in the Hebrew. Indeed, Buber and Rosenzweig sought to retain these connections even at the expense of clear, readable German.[51] As Mara Benjamin has noted, 'Champions and critics of the Buber-Rosenzweig Bible alike agreed that

---

46. Rosenzweig, 'Scripture and Luther', 51.

47. Rosenzweig, 'Scripture and Luther', 55.

48. For a reflection on the role of orality in translation, see James A. Maxey and Ernst Wendland, *Translating Scripture for Sound and Performance: Biblical Performance Criticism* (Eugene: Wipf & Stock, 2012).

49. He continues: 'However merciful a mouth may be, it is still flesh and blood and not paper; it becomes weary … it must eat, and at least then it will find a moment to chat. But the book is indefatigable, cares nothing for day and night, has no sense of the human need for relaxation and change.' Rosenzweig, 'Scripture and Word', 41.

50. On the *Leitwort* style, see especially Buber's essay, '*Leitwort* Style in Pentateuch Narrative', in *Scripture and Translation*, 114–28.

51. As Nahum Glatzer has observed, 'Some critics [of the translation] pointed to the fact that translation was more Hebraic than German and that, indeed, the rules and style were not followed.' Glatzer, 'Editor's Postscript', in Martin Buber, *On the Bible: Eighteen Studies* (Syracuse: Syracuse University Press, 2000), 235.

the translation's abundant neologisms and verbal contortions were its signature quality.'[52]

Second, Buber and Rosenzweig attempted to convey the otherness and orality of the Hebrew through a technique called colometry (*Kolometrie*). Colometry involves dividing and reorganizing the biblical prose into units the length of a human breath.[53] Rosenzweig reflects, for example, on the effects of this technique in their translation of Genesis 14.2: 'Cain's appalling answer – "I do not know. Am I my brother's keeper?" – are by the rendering of the vital, breathing course of speech brought together in a single movement, and thus given their full horror, previously covered-over by the logical punctuation.'[54] Drawing Cain's answer into one unit restores the sense of this and other such passages as a vital, living word, in ways that punctuation and logical form by themselves tend to diminish.

In short, through these and other such techniques, Rosenzweig (and Buber) tried to capture and convey some of the deep internal rhythms and forms of the Hebrew texts. In so doing, he sought to facilitate these texts being spoken or read aloud as God's word in and for a new community. In this way, Rosenzweig too locates God's disruptive presence in the midst of the substance and forms of the biblical texts.

The forms of the word: Bonhoeffer, Rosenzweig and ethics

As a theology of revelation, apocalyptic theology is committed to knowing and speaking of the God of the gospel where the Lord gives himself to be known. Without denying the differences between Bonhoeffer and Rosenzweig, there are some notable overlaps between their approaches to Scripture. First, they both sought ways of attending to the Bible *in its otherness*. In order for the biblical texts to confront us and call out a new community, they needed to provide something new and unfamiliar. As Batnitzky notes in relation to Rosenzweig, 'questioning comes from the tension of the awareness of difference, and not from

---

52. Mara Benjamin, *Rosenzweig's Bible: Reinventing Scripture for Jewish Modernity* (Cambridge: Cambridge University Press, 2009), 146. On the critical reception of the translation also see Lawrence Rosenwald, 'On the Reception of Buber and Rosenzweig's Bible', *Prooftexts: A Journal of Jewish Literary History* 14, no. 2 (1994): 141–65.

53. On this use of colometry see Benjamin, *Rosenzweig's Bible*, 154–60. See also Hans-Christoph Askani, *Das Problem der Übersetzung dargestellt an Franz Rosenzweig* (Tübingen: Mohr Siebeck, 1997), 230–47.

54. Rosenzweig, 'Scripture and Word', *Scripture and Translation*, 43. As Rosenzweig continues, 'commas retain their logical function as subordinate distinctions; but through the added modulation of breathing they acquire a quiet resonance … which would otherwise get lost'.

the mediation of sameness. Only because the Bible looks so different can we have an opportunity to relate it to our lives today'.[55] For Bonhoeffer, as we have seen, taking the 'Bible seriously' as God's word involves finding ways of reading it 'against ourselves'.[56]

At the same time, Bonhoeffer and Rosenzweig insist on locating this otherness *within*, not above or apart from, the very substance of the biblical texts. Put differently, the Bible is God's revelation only in the concrete details of its human language and forms, meaning that we must continually immerse ourselves in these details.[57] As Marius Mjaaland has written in another context, 'the otherness thus situated within the text makes it necessary to read it all the more carefully, as long as we suspect that it still has secrets in reserve'.[58]

Furthermore, Bonhoeffer and Rosenzweig recognize the centrality of the body in approaching Scripture in this way. For both of them, attending to the Bible as God's word involves bodily practices and activity. They are not simply interested in intellectual comprehension, in meaning in the abstract, but in the physical and direct ways that we encounter and relate to texts. For Bonhoeffer, this is apparent in his focus on preaching and also meditative reading.[59] Rosenzweig, as we have seen, sought to produce a translation that would be read aloud within a community. The verbal resonances and effects of his (and Buber's) translation are inaccessible to the isolated individual. Techniques such as colometry, as Mara Benjamin observes, 'puts the authority for establishing the rhythm of the text squarely in the body – the mouth, the lungs, and the spirit – of the reader'.[60]

These overlaps are significant for drawing attention to an ethic that is inherent in Bonhoeffer's and Rosenzweig's approaches. To quote Batnitzky again, 'the text as other is always in service of recognising the other in another human being'.[61] The community that gathers around God's word is and becomes open to what lies beyond it. The text as other elicits an openness and response to the world and to other human beings.

Therefore, Bonhoeffer's and Rosenzweig's approaches in this way facilitate an awareness that we exist in deep relationship with others. Their work engenders a recognition of how we are bound up with others in ways we can neither fully comprehend nor control. Responsibility to others, as Bonhoeffer writes, 'is not fixed in advance once and for all by a principle, but develops together with the

---

55. Batnitzky, *Idolatry and Representation*, 111.

56. 'Address in Gland', DBWE 11: 378.

57. As Rosenzweig writes, 'The word of God cannot dispense with the word of man – the true, spoken, sounding word of man.' Rosenzweig, 'Scripture and Word', 42.

58. Marius Mjaaland, *The Hidden God: Luther, Philosophy, and Political Theology* (Bloomington: Indiana University Press, 2015), 60.

59. On meditative reading, see the final section of the previous chapter.

60. Benjamin, *Rosenzweig's Bible*, 156.

61. Batnitzky, *Idolatry and Representation*, 127.

given situation'.⁶² Scripture in its alterity presses us to recognize and remain alert to the other human being.⁶³

Because Bonhoeffer and Rosenzweig locate the otherness of Scripture in the *substance* of biblical texts, this recognition of the human other becomes similarly concrete. Their work engenders close attention to the *particular* situation and needs of the other human being: 'The attention of responsible people is directed to concrete neighbours in their concrete reality.'⁶⁴ Following Bonhoeffer and Rosenzweig, attending to the other means attending to *this* human being in their *specific* situation.

Finally, Bonhoeffer's and Rosenzweig's shared attention to the body encourages a recognition of bodily rhythms and movements of this relationship. By drawing attention to bodily practices in relation to Scripture, they help us to recognize the centrality of the body for our relationships to one another. Following Bonhoeffer and Rosenzweig, responding to the other involves a bodily presence and attention.⁶⁵ This stands in contrast to a certain neglect of the body in more mainstream ethical approaches.

In all these ways, Bonhoeffer's and Rosenzweig's approaches to Scripture have something to offer for the ongoing work of developing an apocalyptic theological ethic. Their work helps to facilitate close attention to God's presence and militant grace in the midst of concrete relationships. Likewise, their attempts at living in the forms of God's word can provide rich insight for attending and responding to others.

---

62. DBWE 6: 261.

63. Or, as Emmanuel Levinas puts it, 'the other *as* other'. Levinas acknoweldges the extent of Rosenzweig's influence on his ethics of alterity. Levinas, *Totality and Infinity: An Essay on Exteriority* (Pittsburgh: Dusquene Univeristy Press, 1969), 28.

64. DBWE 6: 261.

65. I engage with Bonhoeffer's account of responsibility in more detail in Chapter 6.

Chapter 4

THE WEAKNESS OF THE WORD AND THE REALITY OF GOD: BONHOEFFER'S GRAMMAR OF WORLDLY LIVING

In a rich essay on Bonhoeffer's poem, 'Stations on the Way to Freedom', the German ethicist Hans Ulrich reflects upon the ways in which Bonhoeffer's writings – and this prison poem in particular – provide us with a 'grammar of theological work' and Christian discipleship.[1] 'What Bonhoeffer articulates in his writings', Ulrich insists, 'is the life of a human being in patient and attentive expectation of God's action, ready to surrender to God's will and plan – which makes him a disciple.'[2] In his essay, Ulrich gives particular attention to the significance of divine and human suffering for what it means to become a disciple. He draws out some important and neglected Lutheran themes of Bonhoeffer's late theology.

In his earlier 1937 *Discipleship*, one of Bonhoeffer's surprising (and again neglected) claims is that 'the Word of God is so weak that it suffers to be despised and rejected by people'. For the word, Bonhoeffer continues, 'there are such things as hardened hearts and locked doors'.[3] Bonhoeffer's point here is that God comes to and dwells within the world in the weakness and suffering of the word, not through divine authority or strength more directly. Furthermore, he insists that this weakness is at the heart of what it means to become a disciple: 'This weakness liberates them [the disciples] from the sick restlessness of a fanatic; they suffer with the Word.'[4] The word's very weakness is what frees Christ's followers to attend to and suffer in the world, that is, without needing to interpret

---

1. Hans Ulrich's essay, 'Stations on the Way to Freedom: The Presence of God – The Freedom of the Disciples' appears in Bernd Wannenwetsch, ed., *Who Am I? Bonhoeffer's Theology through His Poetry* (London: T&T Clark, 2009). In particular, this essay helped me to recognize how we might attend to God's suffering (in Christ) as at the very heart of Christian theology and discipleship, while avoiding speculation *about* the nature of God, that is, in ways that are characteristic of most modern theological attempts to speak of divine suffering. For further reflection along these lines, see Chapter 6 in this volume.

2. Ulrich, 'Stations on the Way to Freedom', 150.

3. Bonhoeffer, *Discipleship*, DBWE 4: 172.

4. DBWE 4: 172.

or make sense of this suffering in reference to some external principle or higher ideal. Indeed, this weakness is what allows for a kind of witness and mission that is *genuinely* Christian. The word's weakness discloses a new Christian and theological grammar, a framework for speaking of and attending to God's own presence and work.

Drawing inspiration from Ulrich's essay, this chapter explores and reflects upon Luther's and Bonhoeffer's theology of weakness and its implications for Christian mission. In the first section, I outline Luther's *theologia crucis*, as presented in the Heidelberg Disputation. I suggest that Luther's disputation provides a basic framework for a theology of discipleship and suffering. In the second section, I consider the theme of the word's weakness in Bonhoeffer's *Discipleship*. I briefly draw out and develop these themes with reference to the apostle Paul's language of hope, faith and love in the third section. To conclude, I offer some broad reflections on the significance of these Lutheran and Bonhoefferian themes for Christian mission and evangelism.

Martin Luther's Theologia Crucis

In his 1518 Heidelberg Disputation, Martin Luther provided the classic formulation of his own early theological programme and that of the emerging reform movement. At the heart of the Disputation is thesis 23: 'A theologian of glory calls evil good and good evil. A theologian of the cross calls a thing what it actually is' (*theologia crucis quod res est*).[5] Luther draws a sharp distinction here between two different dispositions or grammars: two ways of naming things, of positioning ourselves (or of being positioned) with respect to God, one another and the world.

First, Luther's 'theologian of glory' names what human beings are on their own terms apart from how God comes to and encounters us in Christ. Luther uses this designation to diagnose the kind of grammar that proceeds from our own natural knowledge of and assumptions about God and reality. Fundamentally, this disposition is marked by a self-confidence or even hubris; it is marked by a belief that we ourselves can recognize and speak of God, that we are able to understand who God is and how God is present to and active in the world.

The one who operates from within this grammar, therefore, understands and speaks of God in terms of various *positive* attributes and qualities: goodness, holiness, wisdom, justice and so on. Accordingly, this theologian of glory assumes a basic adequacy and stability of such concepts and language, and hence a level of continuity or analogy between all that we think is good, holy and true, and God's

---

5. Martin Luther, 'Heidelberg Disputation', in *Luther's Works, Volume 31: Career of the Reformer I*, trans. Helmut T. Lehmann, ed. Harold J. Grimm (Philadelphia: Fortress Press, 1957), 53.

own being and action.⁶ Following Luther, this theologian assumes that God is to be found in and behind those things and values that we collectively endorse. God's ultimate judgement and grace is anticipated by, or at least reflected by, our own penultimate understanding and pursuit of such values.⁷

Furthermore, this means that this grammar is marked by a certain confidence with respect to reality. The theologian of glory assumes that we can recognize those things that are good and evil in the world. Put differently, there is a confidence that the meaning of reality itself is straightforwardly available to us. As Gerhard Forde has summarized, 'theologians of glory operate on the assumption that creation and history are transparent to human intellect'.⁸ At the heart of this disposition or grammar, therefore, is a conviction that we can know what is what.⁹ This kind of theologian or human being assumes that she has the capacity to recognize and speak of what things are and what they mean. In Aquinas' language, there is a confidence that the 'good is to be done and pursued, and evil is to be avoided'.¹⁰

Luther's point, of course, is that this theologian of glory is mistaken. Theologically speaking, this person is mistaken in that her thinking and speech, at least on some level, is proceeding from her own assumptions and resources, rather than from God's revelation in and as Christ. In thesis 19 of the Disputation, he writes: 'That person does not deserve to be called a theologian who looks upon the invisible things of God as though they were clearly perceptible in those things that have actually happened.'¹¹ The mistake of this would-be theologian is that she does not recognize that it is God who discloses who God is and what things mean:¹² 'Reality is God's reality, and we are involved in that reality as he is.'¹³ Accordingly, any genuine knowledge that we have of God and of the meaning of things proceeds from and is tied to God's word. Following Luther, this is because we ourselves have

---

6. Luther anticipated and was influential for Ludwig Feuerbach's critique of Christianity in his 1841 *The Essence of Christianity*, trans. George Eliot (New York: Dover, 2008). After this work, Feuerbach also wrote *The Essence of Faith according to Martin Luther*, trans. Melvin Cherno (London: Harper and Row, 1967).

7. Against this assumption, thesis 28 in the Disputation states: 'The love of God does not find, but creates, that which is pleasing to it.' Luther, 'Heidelberg Disputation', 57.

8. Gerhard Forde, *On Being a Theologian of the Cross* (Grand Rapids: Eerdmans, 1997), 72.

9. As Ulrich writes, understanding of reality 'is not generated by interpreting history – as theologians often have – pretending to know God's will'. Ulrich, 'Stations on the Way to Freedom', 169.

10. Thomas Aquinas, *Summa Theologiae* II.1, translated by Fathers of the English Dominican Province, paragraph 94.2, Westminster: Christian Classics, 1981.

11. Luther, 'Heidelberg Disputation', 52.

12. As Bonhoeffer makes this point in his *Ethics*, 'we cannot speak rightly of either God or the world without speaking of Jesus Christ. All concepts of reality that ignore Jesus Christ are abstractions.' DBWE 6: 54.

13. Ulrich, 'Stations on the Way to Freedom', 158.

no stable or independent vantage point from which to approach God or the world. There is no human being as such, only the one who stands before God *simul justus et peccator*.

In the Disputation, Luther is not only concerned with diagnosing this *theologia gloriae*, a sinful human disposition with all its assumptions about God and the world, but also with setting forth a more *genuinely* theological disposition or grammar. For Luther, the cross is the way in which God interrupts and overturns our natural assumptions and dispositions, re-orientating us and setting us within a different story.[14] Luther's *theologia crucis* is thus an attempt to set forth a living grammar tied to God's disruptive revelation as the crucified one. The theologian of the cross is therefore the one who properly attends to the cross and its significance for who we are before God and in the world: 'He deserves to be called a theologian, however, who comprehends the visible and manifest things of God seen through suffering and the cross.'[15]

On the one hand, this makes clear that for Luther we are to know and speak of God from the standpoint of the cross: 'God can only be found in suffering and the cross.'[16] As Luther elsewhere insists, 'Christ alone, and no other God.'[17] We have no knowledge of who or what God is prior to and apart from Christ.[18] And this always means Christ as the one who was humiliated, who suffered and who was crucified: 'True theology and the recognition of God are in the crucified Christ.'[19] If, as Christians, we can properly speak of God only with reference to the cross, any attempt to understand or speak of God otherwise is futile. As Paul famously makes this point in 1 Corinthians, 'I decided to know nothing among you except Jesus Christ, and him crucified' (1 Cor. 2.2). Luther's Pauline insistence on the cross is intended to shut down speculative attempts to understand God in terms of the attributes or qualities of a perfect being (i.e. goodness, pure being, wisdom,

---

14. It is important to clarify that the *theologia gloriae* and *theologia crucis* are not available to us as two possibilities or alternatives that stand alongside one another. Strictly speaking, we do not *choose* which story or grammar we live by. Following Luther, as I have sought to demonstrate, *theologia gloriae* is describing the grammar or story that we all natively assume as sinful human beings, whereas the *theologia crucis* is describing God's own story that we are drawn into in Christ and through the church.

15. Luther, 'Heidelberg Disputation', 52.

16. Luther, 'Heidelberg Disputation', 53.

17. Martin Luther, 'On the Councils of the Church', in *Luther's Works, Volume 41: Church and Ministry III*, trans. Helmut T. Lehman, ed. Eric W. Gritsch (Philadelphia: Fortress Press, 1966), 286. In the Heidelberg Disputation, he writes: 'None of us can talk adequately or profitably about God's glory and majesty unless we see God also in the lowliness and humiliation of the cross.' Luther, 'Heidelberg Disputation', 52.

18. Hans Ulrich writes, 'Jesus is not the last triumphant representative of our God – he is the one in whom God himself suffers, stepping into our human powerlessness and loneliness.' Ulrich, 'Stations on the Way to Freedom', 163.

19. Luther, 'Heidelberg Disputation', 53.

power and so forth). As Bonhoeffer will later make this point in his Christology lectures: 'If we are to describe Jesus as God, we would not speak of his being all-powerful or all-knowing; we would speak of his birth in a manger and of his cross.'[20]

On the other hand, the cross is not only decisive for how we speak of God, but again includes a grammar for attending to reality as such, reality as it is before God. In thesis 21 of the Disputation, Luther writes: 'He who does not know Christ does not know God hidden in suffering. Therefore he prefers glory to the cross, strength to weakness, wisdom to folly, and, in general, good to evil.'[21] Apart from the cross, we are disposed to look for meaning in the things that appear good. We look for God's presence, or try to discern God's hand, in and through those things that we most value. Luther's point, then, is that it is the cross that allows us to perceive reality differently, that is, to perceive reality as it truly is. As Marius Mjaaland writes: 'Suffering and cross thus function as the *prism* through which the world is perceived, or, rather, the grammar which structures thought and perception in light of scripture.'[22] The cross allows us to see that God is, in fact, present and at work precisely where we least expect it, even and especially in the depths of suffering and apparent failure. Hence such things mean something different from what we assume.

What is clear, therefore, is that in both instances there is a rupture or break between what we think we know about God and reality, and what God discloses and teaches us in Christ.[23] Thus, there is a discontinuity between what we assume and what God reveals is the case. This means that God's revelation as Christ invariably subverts our own assumptions. Luther is of course taking up a familiar Pauline theme here: 'I will destroy the wisdom of the wise, and the discernment of the discerning I will thwart' (1 Cor. 1.18-19). The theologian of the cross is the one who attends and remains open to the disruptive force of God's death on the cross and its impact on human wisdom. To be Christian, a theologian, involves allowing our assumptions and self-confidence to be overturned (and continually overturned) by God in Christ. On the cross, God confronts and disrupts our basic self-confidence and redirects us to the human suffering of Christ as the truth of God.[24]

Finally, for Luther the grammar or disposition of the *theologia crucis* entails a further re-evaluation of our own suffering. When we view God and reality

---

20. Bonhoeffer, 'Lectures on Christology', DBWE 12: 354. In Chapter 13, 'The Cross and the Lynching Tree', I draw on James Cone to raise questions about whether Bonhoeffer's *theologia crucis* in the Christology lectures is sufficiently concrete.

21. Luther, 'Heidelberg Disputation', 53.

22. Mjaaland, *The Hidden God*, 42.

23. For a rich reflection on this rupture that draws out its significance for systematic theology, see Ziegler, *Militant Grace*.

24. It is important to note here that Luther is not endorsing suffering per se. His claim is not that suffering on its own terms provides some vantage point from which to interpret and understand the world. For Luther, as for Bonhoeffer, suffering has significance only as and when God uses it to redirect human beings to Godself.

through the prism of the cross, we can begin to recognize God as present and at work in our own suffering and failure: 'He who has been emptied through suffering no longer does works but knows that God works and does all things in him.'[25] Through our own suffering and weakness, God helps us to relinquish our reliance on ourselves and makes us available for Christ. That is why 'I am content with weaknesses, insults, hardships, persecutions, and calamities for the sake of Christ', Pauls tells us, 'for whenever I am weak, then I am strong' (2 Cor. 2.10). Such weakness and hardships help us to surrender our own agendas and prepare us for God's own work.[26] Ulrich echoes this point: 'To suffer means to give oneself over to God and his story, which through Jesus has already been revealed to be precisely that suffering.'[27] Through the cross, Christ's followers are freed from their native grammar and disposition of glory and are drawn into a different kind of grammar or story.

Bonhoeffer and the weakness of the word

Luther's central distinction between the *theologia gloriae* and *theologia crucis* provides the context for understanding the theme of the weakness of God's word in Bonhoeffer's theology. Indeed, Luther's distinction between the two dispositions discloses what Ulrich describes as 'the Lutheran grammar of Bonhoeffer's theology'.[28] Bonhoeffer's rich mediations and comments on this theme develop and expand upon Luther's earlier insights.[29]

Bonhoeffer makes a similar distinction between two dispositions or grammars at the heart of his 1937 *Discipleship*. On the one hand, he again diagnoses the

---

25. That is, thesis 24.

26. Feminist theologians have rightly pointed out how appeals to embracing suffering and self-emptying have been problematic (and even abusive) with respect to women and other marginalized persons. Interestingly, there have been some feminist scholars who have more recently suggested how a broadly Lutheran *theologia crucis* could, in fact, have resources for advancing feminist concerns. See Anna Mercedes, *Power For: Feminism and Christ's Self-Giving* (London: T&T Clark Bloomsbury, 2011); and Arnfríður Guðmundsdóttir, *Meeting God on the Cross: Christ, The Cross and the Feminist Critique* (Oxford: Oxford University Press, 2011).

27. Hans Ulrich, 'Stations on the Way to Freedom', 163–4. Ulrich continues: 'One's suffering must be part of that story if it is not the making of our own story.' Ulrich, 'Stations on the Way to Freedom', 164.

28. Ulrich, 'Stations on the Way to Freedom', 161.

29. Recently, there has been a resurgence of interest in the theological connections between Luther and Bonhoeffer. See especially Barker, *The Cross of Reality*; Michael DeJonge, *Bonhoeffer's Reception of Luther* (Oxford: Oxford University Press, 2017); and Brandin Francabandera, 'Reading beneath the Cross: Dietrich Bonhoeffer's Doctrine of Scripture as *Theologia Crucis*', PhD Dissertation, University of Aberdeen, 2022.

attempt to engage God and reality through our own active efforts or strivings: 'All our urging, running after people, proselytizing, every attempt to accomplish something in another person by our own power is vain and dangerous.'[30] This activity is dangerous in that it depends on and proceeds from our own assumptions and wisdom about God and the world. Bonhoeffer's concern is that through these activities we are trying to impose our own ideas *about* Christ on to others.

Developing Luther's insights in a new context, Bonhoeffer characterizes this *theologia gloriae* as a kind of idealism. Those who operate from within this disposition are governed by adherence to an ideal rather than by the concrete reality of the word: 'The driving restlessness of the group of disciples, who do not want to accept any limitation on their effectiveness, and their zeal, which does not respect resistance, confuses the word of the gospel with a conquering idea.'[31] These would-be disciples speak and act on the basis of an idealized version of what the gospel is and means. In so doing, they fail to recognize God's word itself, to attend to how God actually comes to us and claims us.

In particular, Bonhoeffer suggests that these would-be disciples neglect the weakness of God's word. They neglect the concrete, specific nature of God's own revelation or address, that is, how God has actually spoken and speaks to us in Christ and through Scripture: 'The idea is strong. But the word of God is so weak that it suffers to be despised and rejected by people.'[32] In preferring the strength of the idea, Christ's would-be followers give priority to their own assumptions and wisdom. They remain committed to the certainty and stability of their own knowledge *about* God, rather than attending to God's own surprising and unexpected address in Christ's weakness.

Bonhoeffer claims that this commitment to human wisdom and stability pre-empts and prevents attending to the God who comes to us in Scripture. Attending to the cross presses us back into Scripture in its concrete materiality and vice versa. In an important essay from the Finkenwalde period, 'Contemporizing New Testament Texts',[33] he writes that the 'turn back to Scripture corresponds exactly to the turn undertaken by Christian faith and Christian hope, namely, back to the cross of Christ. In both cases, it is the historicity of God's revelation that comes to expression.'[34] Attending to God in the suffering and human Christ, therefore, helps us to recognize that God is present and speaking to us through these fragile human texts.[35] At the same time, attending to Scripture in its historicity directs us

---

30. DBWE 4: 172.
31. DBWE 4: 173.
32. DBWE 4: 173.
33. It is worth noting that Bonhoeffer approaches Old Testament texts in this same manner. For example, see the notes for his lecture on 'Christ in the Psalms', DBWE 14: 387. See also Chapter 2, 'As a Whole and in Its Parts'.
34. DBWE 14: 419.
35. This close correspondence between Scripture and the cross in Bonhoeffer and Luther has deep significance for how we approach the biblical texts. Rather than deriving principles

back to a God who suffers a human death on a cross. As Bonhoeffer puts this in a later letter from Tegel prison, 'The Bible directs people towards the powerlessness and suffering of God.'[36]

Following Bonhoeffer, this means that we are to attend to these texts as the place of God's revelation and witness in their entirety and simply as they stand: 'It is precisely as such a historic, temporary word that it is indeed the word of God.'[37] This means that Scripture as God's word and address to us, the place where God calls and claims us in Christ, is and remains a thoroughly human word. God is present in this human word, making it God's own. But Scripture is God's word, Bonhoeffer insists, in such a way that 'the human word does not cease being temporary bound and transient'.[38]

As with Luther, this means that God's presence in revelation – in Christ and through Scripture – remains a hidden presence. In both cases, God's revelation remains concealed under the form of fragility and weakness.[39] In his 1933 Christology lectures, Bonhoeffer asserts that Christ 'comes among us humans not in Godly form, but rather incognito, as a beggar among beggars, an outcast among outcasts; he comes among sinners as the one without sin, but also as a sinner among sinners'.[40] In Christ and through Scripture, God embraces and enters the sinful condition of humanity. This means that God's word is ineluctably tied to human suffering and weakness. As Ulrich makes this same point, 'Jesus therefore is not the last triumphant representative of God – he is the one in whom God himself suffers, stepping into our human powerlessness and loneliness.'[41]

Faith, hope and love

What are the implications of Luther's and Bonhoeffer's theology of the crucified Christ? What does the weakness of God's word, in Christ and through Scripture, mean for the shape of Christian witness? The implications of this theology can be further explicated using Paul's language of hope, faith and love (1 Cor. 13.13).

First, for both Luther and Bonhoeffer, it is because God in Christ takes on and enters into a suffering and sinful world that we have grounds for *hope*. For both

---

or models from the text, Christ encounters us through the texts more directly. As Bonhoeffer notes in *Discipleship*, 'Scripture does not present us with a collection of Christian types to be imitated according to our own choice.' DBWE 4: 204. See also Chapter 2, 'As a Whole and in Its Parts'.

36. Bonhoeffer continues: 'Only the suffering God can help.' See 'To Eberhard Bethge', 15 July 1944, DBWE 8: 479. See also Chapter 9, 'Only the Suffering God Can Help.'

37. Bonhoeffer, 'Contemporizing New Testament Texts', DBWE 12: 421.

38. DBWE 12: 421.

39. See 'Lectures on Christology', DBWE 12: 358–9.

40. DBWE 12: 356.

41. Ulrich, 'Stations on the Way to Freedom', 169.

theologians, it is only *this* kind of God who is able to save us. In his 1535 lectures on Galatians, for instance, Luther reflects: 'Whenever you ... wonder how or where or in what condition to find a God who justifies and accepts sinners, then you must know that there is no other God than this Man Jesus Christ. Take hold of Him, cling to him with all your heart, and spurn all speculation about Divine Majesty.'[42] In preparation for a sermon for Trinity Sunday in April 1936, Bonhoeffer put this same point more bluntly: 'What good does a God do us who is in eternity, stronger than the majesty of the world, stronger than sin and death? This God does not concern us? How can such a god help us?'[43] It is only the God who is present in the suffering of Christ that provides hope in the midst of our own suffering and sin.[44] For Luther and Bonhoeffer, God's presence in Christ means that we are no longer alone in our own suffering. This means that we no longer have to take flight into our own ideas or ideals, but can have hope where we are. As Ulrich reminds us, 'Christian hope is not about expecting another world, but rather an encounter with God himself in this world.'[45]

Second, God's presence in suffering and weakness, in Christ and through Scripture, provides the basis for *faith*. God's presence in suffering and on the cross frees us from having to depend on our own knowledge and instead turns (and continually returns) us to faith in Christ. Following Paul, the very foolishness of the cross (1 Cor. 1.18-20) – the incomprehensibility of God being present and at work in *this* place – helps to disrupt our confidence in our own knowledge and assumptions. In his Christology lectures, Bonhoeffer expresses this Lutheran insight: 'Faith exists when I yield myself to God ... even and especially there where it goes against all visible appearances. Only when I give up having visible confirmation do I believe in God.'[46] The point, then, is that God's suffering on the cross challenges our own knowledge and assumptions about God, helping us to instead trust in and embrace God's own story: 'Faith is trust in God's plan.'[47] By confounding our attempts to speak of God on our own terms, the cross liberates us to attend to how God comes to and is present with us.

Third, God's presence on the cross facilitates Christian *love*. Attending to God's presence as the crucified one frees us to live in the world and for the neighbour. In

---

42. Martin Luther, 'Lectures on Galatians 1535', in *Luther's Works, Volume 26: Lectures on Galatians Chapters 1–4*, ed. Jaroslav Pelikan and Walter A. Hansen (Saint Louis: Concordia Publishing House, 1963), 29.

43. Bonhoeffer, 'Outline on Exodus 20:2-3 as a Sermon for Trinity Sunday', DBWE 14: 636.

44. In a sermon outline on Hebrews 4, Bonhoeffer extends this insight: 'God suffers for your sake, to be with you, like a mother with her child. Hence God's suffering is the throne of his grace, where you can find compassion in the hour of your own temptation.' Bonhoeffer, 'On Hebrews 4:15-16', July 1953, DBWE 14: 367.

45. Ulrich, 'Stations on the Way to Freedom', 167.

46. 'Lectures on Christology', DBWE 12: 358.

47. Ulrich, 'Stations on the Way to Freedom', 160.

Christ, God has embraced humanity in its suffering and fragility. And this, in turn, frees us to similarly embrace others simply as we find them. Put differently, the cross frees us to see and respond to others as they actually are, not with reference to some higher ideal or purpose. This, of course, is the central movement of Luther's 1520 treatise, 'On the Freedom of a Christian': 'From faith … flow forth love and joy in the Lord, and from love a joyful, willing, and free mind that serves one's neighbour willingly and takes no account of gratitude or ingratitute, of praise or blame of gain or loss.'[48] As Bonhoeffer develops this theme in his *Ethics*, 'The cross of reconciliation sets us free to live before God in the midst of the godless world, sets us free to live in genuine worldliness.'[49] God's work on the cross frees us to love the world and attend to those in it as they actually are.

Reframing Christian discipleship and mission

In this final section, by way of conclusion, I will simply draw out a few implications of this *theologia crucis* for Christian mission and evangelism. Given the weakness of God's word, how are we as disciples to witness to and engage with the world today?

First and foremost, the Lutheran theme of God's presence in weakness provides a counterpoint to a continual Christian temptation to pursue missional and evangelistic activities that are triumphalist or even imperialistic. Attending to God's presence on the cross can help to pre-empt a kind of witness and activity that tries to engage the world from a position of strength. In other words, the grammar of the cross frees us from needing to rely on or make use of our own strength in relation to others. More subtly, this grammar frees us from a benevolence that construes the other as a project or object of charity. In either case, the cross reminds us that we do not possess any special knowledge, insight or truth vis-à-vis the other: 'In dealing with other people, the disciples do not possess any special power or right of their own.'[50]

This in turn frees Christians from needing a fixed programme or governing ideal when engaging in mission. As already suggested, by attending to and participating in the suffering of the cross, we are freed from having to depend upon our own wisdom and knowledge about God, other people and the world. The unexpected nature of God's presence in this place frees us from needing to be the ones in control. As Bonhoeffer puts this in *Life Together*, 'this means I must release others from all my attempts to control, coerce, and dominate them with love'.[51] The cross frees us to begin attending to the surprising ways in which God

---

48. Martin Luther, 'The Freedom of a Christian', in *Career of the Reformer I*, 367.
49. DBWE 6: 400
50. DBWE 4: 174.
51. DBWE 5: 44.

continues to be present and at work in the world today, which will often conflict with our own assumptions about who God is and how God works.

If this is the case, then we are never finally in a position to judge the effectiveness of our own witness. God's presence on the cross discloses that God's ways are not our ways (Isa 55:9). This suggests that God may well be present when our attempts at witness and service appear to us to be failing. In a sermon from 1518, Luther suggests that it is through our failure that we begin to rely on God's grace: 'Here is where all who undertake to do something of themselves are compelled to submit and be conquered. ... We must despair of everything that we can do. But those who say, Ah, but I have done as much as I possibly can; I have done enough, and I hope that God will give me grace – they set up an iron wall between themselves and the grace of God.'[52] Our very failure and despair makes room for God working in and through us.

On the other hand, this suggests we should be similarly cautious when our attempts at mission and evangelism seem to succeed. Commenting on success in *Ethics*, Bonhoeffer writes: 'The figure of the judged and crucified one remains alien, and at best pitiable, to a world where success is the measure and justification of all things.'[53] While not suggesting that we should attempt to avoid success – or set out with the intention of failing – Luther and Bonhoeffer hold that success brings with it a temptation to make success into its own justification. When our endeavours do appear to succeed, we can be tempted to claim this success as our own. Put differently, we can be tempted to attribute apparent success to our own strength and wisdom. We know from the gospels, of course, that such apparent success is often fleeting. While large crowds do at times gather to listen attentively to Jesus' teachings, they just as quickly disperse and turn against him.

God's presence on the cross, therefore, directs our attention away from our own activity, endeavours and works, and from any success or failure found therein. The cross reminds us that it is God's own presence in an all-too-human suffering, and not our own knowledge or strivings, that ultimately brings about change and redemption. In light of this, the task given to Christians is to recognize the limits of what we ourselves can know and achieve.[54] Instead, the cross locates us within a new grammar and story; it leads us to be prayerfully attentive to God's own work in Christ and in and through us. To conclude with Bonhoeffer's words:

---

52. Martin Luther, 'Sermon on the Man Born Blind, John 9:1-38, 17 March 1518', in *Luther's Works, Volume 51: Sermons I*, ed. John W. Doberstein (Philadelphia: Fortress Press, 1959), 43.

53. DBWE 6: 88.

54. Bonhoeffer writes: 'The great task of recognising the limits of their mission is given to the disciples.' DBWE 4: 173.

In their own lives, only the saints see strife, hardship, weakness, and sin. And the more maturity they gain in the state of sanctification, the more they recognize themselves as being overcome, as those who are dying according to the flesh. … But because of this very fact, their whole life must now be an act of faith in the Son of God who has begun his own life in them.[55]

---

55. DBWE 4: 267.

Chapter 5

LUTHERAN OR LUTHERISH? ENGAGING MICHAEL DEJONGE ON BONHOEFFER'S RECEPTION OF LUTHER

How do we understand and position Bonhoeffer's theology in relation to some of his preceding influences, particularly Martin Luther and Lutheran theology? Furthermore, what do we gain and lose by locating Bonhoeffer as an example of a wider Lutheran theological tradition?

In his 2017 book *Bonhoeffer's Reception of Luther*, Michael DeJonge provides a rich and compelling reading of Bonhoeffer's theology. His central claim is that 'Bonhoeffer's thinking was Lutheran and should be interpreted as such.'[1] DeJonge develops this claim through a series of careful and nuanced engagements with Bonhoeffer's texts. At times he demonstrates how Bonhoeffer was directly drawing upon Luther and other Lutheran thinkers for his theology. Elsewhere, he indicates how Bonhoeffer's theological positions align with broadly Lutheran ones. In *Bonhoeffer's Reception*, DeJonge focuses especially upon the Lutheran character of Bonhoeffer's Christology (in chapters 1–2) and on how Lutheran two-kingdoms theology fames and informs much of Bonhoeffer's political thinking and action (in chapters 4–7).

Throughout his book, DeJonge also establishes the Lutheran provenance of Bonhoeffer's thinking through a series of polemical engagements with other scholars who have written on Bonhoeffer, including Stanley Hauerwas, Mark Nation, John de Gruchy, Larry Rasmussen and Clifford Green. DeJonge argues that a neglect of Bonhoeffer's Lutheranism by these scholars has led to distortions in their approaches to Bonhoeffer: 'Interpretations that forget about Luther's importance for Bonhoeffer tend toward misinterpretation.'[2] Through these critical engagements, DeJonge thus makes an important intervention into ongoing scholarly work and debates.

---

1. DeJonge, *Bonhoeffer's Reception*, 6.
2. DeJonge, *Bonhoeffer's Reception*, 11.

What is meant by 'Lutheran'?

In his introduction, DeJonge outlines and clarifies how he is using the concept or category 'Lutheran' for his reading of Bonhoeffer. First, he indicates that he is using 'Lutheran' as a hermeneutical concept: 'I argue that generating good interpretations of Bonhoeffer's texts in their context requires approaching them with a proper interpretative framework, one element of which is the recognition of Bonhoeffer's positive relationship to Luther and Lutheranism.'[3] In other words, reading Bonhoeffer as Lutheran provides a means of approaching and organizing the details and complexities of his theology.

DeJonge further clarifies how he is using 'Lutheran' by making a distinction between a first order claim and second order claim in his book. At the first level, DeJonge indicates that he plans to show that Bonhoeffer understood his own thinking to be Lutheran; at the second level, he intends to argue that Bonhoeffer was 'justified in thinking so'.[4] These two claims together, along with their corresponding senses of 'Lutheran', form the very centre of DeJonge's hermeneutical approach.

In clarifying his first order claim, DeJonge sets up 'Lutheran' largely as a confessional and oppositional category.[5] Bonhoeffer understood his thinking to be Lutheran precisely *as opposed to* being 'Catholic', 'Reformed', 'Anabaptist' and so forth. As DeJonge explains, 'the claim that Bonhoeffer understood his theology as Lutheran here means that he understood it to participate in the Lutheran confessional-theological tradition and not another one'.[6] On the one hand, this means that DeJonge frequently argues that Bonhoeffer was *consciously* and *actively* drawing upon Lutheran ideas and resources for this thinking. To take one example, he argues in his final chapter that Bonhoeffer's opposition to National Socialism finds an important Lutheran precedent in Matthias Flacius, namely, in Flacius' opposition to Melanchthon's compromises on matters of adiaphora in the late 1540s. DeJonge contends that Bonhoeffer was both familiar with Flacius' opposition and consciously drawing upon it in conceiving of his own.[7]

On the other hand, DeJonge deploys this confessional and oppositional sense of Lutheran to draw contrasts between Bonhoeffer and various non-Lutheran thinkers and positions. In chapter 2, for example, he draws out subtle yet important differences between Bonhoeffer's and Karl Barth's respective Christologies and

---

3. DeJonge, *Bonhoeffer's Reception*, 6.

4. DeJonge, *Bonhoeffer's Reception*, 7.

5. DeJonge has responded to this point, suggesting that I overplay the extent to which Lutheran operates as an oppositional category in his work and drawing attention to the ways in which his positioning of Bonhoeffer as Lutheran still allows for attending to significant overlaps with other Christian traditions. See Michael P. DeJonge, 'Non-Lutheran Influences, Scholarly Impasses, and Spiritual Influences: A Response to Mawson, Harvey and Plant', *Modern Theology* 35, no. 2 (2019): 374–6.

6. DeJonge, *Bonhoeffer's Reception*, 8.

7. DeJonge, *Bonhoeffer's Reception*, 203–6.

frames these differences using the traditional Reformed-Lutheran *in/capax* debate. In chapter 5, DeJonge traces important differences between Bonhoeffer's account of discipleship and peace and an Anabaptist account, contending that Bonhoeffer 'inherits Luther's broad, polemical and derogatory … way of thinking about Anabaptists'.[8] DeJonge thus demonstrates how Bonhoeffer clarifies and develops his own positions through polemics against *Schwärmer*. Making these kinds of confessional contrasts, therefore, allows him to draw out and sharpen many of the nuances of Bonhoeffer's own commitments and positions.

In clarifying his second order claim, DeJonge's attention shifts to whether we should still understand Bonhoeffer as Lutheran today, that is, irrespective of his own self-understanding and the ways he positions and develops his own thinking. At this second level, DeJonge presents 'Lutheran' as a much broader and internally variegated category, one encompassing a range of more specific and even conflicting Lutheran positions: 'It is an understanding of the Lutheran tradition that does not attempt to adjudicate between competing claims to authentic or true Lutheranism.'[9] What is the value of this broader, 'outsider' sense of 'Lutheran'? Crucially, it allows DeJonge to acknowledge and attend to Bonhoeffer's well-known criticisms of some other Lutheran thinkers (e.g. Melanchthon, Karl Holl, etc.) and other Lutheran theological positions (e.g. orders of creation), while still arguing that Bonhoeffer was making these criticisms from *within* Lutheranism. Put differently, this broader sense of Lutheran allows DeJonge to contest ways in which other readers of Bonhoeffer have often appealed to such criticisms in order to understand him as breaking with or moving beyond Lutheranism.

What is meant by 'tradition'?

One way that DeJonge holds together these differing senses of Lutheran is by appealing to 'the Lutheran tradition'. DeJonge makes numerous references to 'the Lutheran tradition' throughout *Bonhoeffer's Reception*. Indeed, he asserts in his introduction that 'this book attempts to show that Bonhoeffer can profitably be read in light of his positive relationship to the Lutheran theological tradition'.[10] While DeJonge does not directly reflect upon what he means by 'tradition', he deploys this term in ways that broadly resonate with Alasdair MacIntyre's influential and well-known work. It is thus helpful to turn to MacIntyre in order to reflect on DeJonge's use of this language.

There are at least four aspects of MacIntyre's understanding of tradition that are relevant in this context.[11] First, it is significant that in MacIntyre's understanding traditions tend to operate as *stable* and *coherent* streams of intellectual and

---

8. DeJonge, *Bonhoeffer's Reception*, 159.
9. DeJonge, *Bonhoeffer's Reception*, 11.
10. DeJonge, *Bonhoeffer's Reception*, 11.
11. Alasdair MacIntyre's understanding and use of this concept is complex and develops over his major works. For a more detailed analysis of MacIntyre's notion of tradition, see

moral inquiry. As MacIntyre in one place explains, a tradition is 'an historically extended, socially embodied argument, and an argument precisely about those goods which constitute that tradition'.[12] On the one hand, this means that a given tradition unfolds largely on the basis of its own internal logic. As Willis Jenkins helpfully summarizes, MacIntyre 'thinks that traditions differ so much that their conceptual resources must be understood exclusively within the terms of the internal arguments of a tradition'.[13] On the other hand, MacIntyre is clear that as an 'argument extended through time' a tradition is able to contain within itself a range of differing and conflicting viewpoints: 'Traditions, when vital, embody continuities of conflict'.[14]

In addition, this indicates MacIntyre's understanding of different traditions as largely *distinct* and *separate* from one another. He tends to frame and present traditions as '*rival* versions of moral inquiry'.[15] To be clear, he insists that traditions are continually interacting with and clarifying themselves in these interactions with one another. Indeed, for MacIntyre, it is partly these interactions that lead traditions to develop and change over time. But even in and through these interactions, it is noteworthy that traditions themselves usually remain separate from one another and retain their own integrity.[16]

Third, MacIntyre tends to understand traditions as something *available* to us. At least in retrospect, we are able to recognize traditions and actively embrace them. This is broadly apparent, for example, in MacIntyre's emphasis on the inherent 'rationality' of traditions and traditioned forms of inquiry.[17] More specifically, it is apparent in his claim that we can each give our 'allegiance' to a particular tradition. In the final sections of *Whose Justice? Which Rationality*, he suggests that 'each of us' faces a 'question' of whether our own particular tradition provides sufficient resources with which to confront and negotiate the problems and challenges facing us.[18] Following MacIntyre, we are to consciously inhabit and embrace traditions and actively draw upon the conceptual and moral resources that they have to offer.

Jean Porter, 'Tradition in the Recent Work of Alasdair MacIntyre', in *Alasdair MacIntyre*, ed. Mark C. Murphy (Cambridge: Cambridge University Press, 2003), 38–69.

12. Alasdair MacIntyre, *After Virtue: A Study in Moral Theory* (Notre Dame: University of Notre Dame Press, 1981), 222.

13. Willis Jenkins, *The Future of Ethics: Sustainability, Social Justice, and Religious Creativity* (Washington: Georgetown University Press, 2013), 86.

14. MacIntyre, *After Virtue*, 222.

15. This of course refers to Alasdair MacIntyre's *Three Rival Versions of Moral Inquiry: Encyclopaedia, Genealogy and Tradition* (Notre Dame: University of Notre Dame Press, 1990).

16. A notable exception here is MacIntyre's account of Thomism as a synthesis of the preceding Augustinian and Aristotelian intellectual traditions. See Alasdair MacIntyre, *Whose Justice? Which Rationality?* (Notre Dame: Notre Dame University Press, 1988), 164–82.

17. MacIntyre, *Whose Justice? Which Rationality?*

18. MacIntyre, *Whose Justice? Which Rationality?*, 402.

Finally, this leads to how, for MacIntyre, traditions provide resources with which to both respond to present challenges and direct oneself to the future. MacIntyre presents and understands traditions as *teleological*: 'Living traditions, just because they continue a not-yet-completed narrative, confront a future whose determinate and determinable character, so far as it possesses any, derives from the past.'[19] For MacIntyre, the inherent rationality and social practices of a given tradition are always oriented towards a vision of the good. Broadly speaking, this means that for MacIntyre traditions are themselves also partly oriented towards shaping and bringing about an intended future.

Tradition versus habitus

If DeJonge's appeals to 'the Lutheran tradition' in *Bonhoeffer's Reception* seem to align with MacIntyre's work and hermeneutical approach, at least broadly, then an alternative can be identified in Pierre Bourdieu's notion of *habitus*.[20] With this notion, Bourdieu is similarly interested in how past social practices and intellectual arguments can shape and influence present and future ones. However, Bourdieu gives greater emphasis to the messy, more implicit and less contained ways in which such practices and ideas are transmitted into the present. As Bourdieu himself explains in a dense passage, 'a *habitus* consists of systems of durable, transposable dispositions, structured structures predisposed to function as structuring structures, that is, as principles which generate and organize practices and representations that can be objectively adapted to their outcomes without presupposing a conscious aiming at ends or an express mastery of the operations necessary in order to attain them.'[21]

There are several features of Bourdieu's reflections on *habitus* that are useful for reflecting upon DeJonge's (and MacIntyre's) appeals to tradition.

First, Bourdieu here presents a *habitus* as a 'system of dispositions' rather than as a more fully articulated and determined set of positions. As compared with the concept of tradition, *habitus* gives greater emphasis to the fluid and implicit ways in which past practices and ideas can shape and inform present ones. This further means that *habitus*, at least as compared with tradition, is less inherently and internally rational and stable.

In addition, this means that Bourdieu's notion of *habitus* is less dependent on a subject or agent who actively and consciously draws upon the past in order to engage present problems, that is, on a 'conscious aiming at ends or an express

19. MacIntyre, *After Virtue*, 223.
20. In a number of places Ted Smith has contrasted Bourdieu with MacIntyre along these lines. See especially Ted Smith, 'Theories of Practice', in *The Wiley-Blackwell Companion to Practical Theology*, ed. Bonnie J. Miller-McLemore (Oxford: Wiley Blackwell, 2013), 246–50.
21. Pierre Bourdieu, *The Logic of Practice*, trans. Richard Nice (Oxford: Polity Press, 1990), 53.

mastery of operations'.[22] Fundamentally, this is because, for Bourdeiu, a *habitus* informs and shapes how we think and act at the level of the body. As Willis Jenkins summarizes, 'A *habitus* shapes an embodied, practical sense of the world.'[23] While there may still be conscious decision-making and calculation accompanying a given *habitus*, this is not always or necessarily the case.[24]

This means that Bourdieu is less inclined to draw clear boundaries either around a given *habitus* or between different *habitus*. Precisely as a set of 'structuring dispositions' operating at a more intuitive level, *habitus* can overlap, mutate and migrate across different social spheres. The advantage of this, as Ted Smith has suggested, is that 'When *habitus* defines a practice ... extensive traffic across cultures can become visible as something other than slips from idealist purity.'[25] Even while ideas and practices from a past *habitus* continually influence and impact present thinking and action, this need not be in a way that prevents or excludes other *habitus* from simultaneously exerting influence.

Finally, Bourdieu's notion of *habitus* implies a different way of imagining the relationship between past, present and future. Even while the concepts of *habitus* and tradition are both somewhat open ended and creative, orienting thinking and action to present exigencies and future possibilities, Bourdeiu's *habitus* is less teleologically driven than MacIntyre's tradition. Put differently, a *habitus* is less oriented to and directed by intended and manageable outcomes and instead directed to the present and future in ways that are more experimental and more radically open ended.

Framing Bonhoeffer's reception of Luther

What is at stake with these differences between DeJonge's (and MacIntyre's) concept of tradition and Bourdieu's notion of *habitus*? While DeJonge's approach facilitates a rich and compelling reading of Bonhoeffer, as already noted, do his assumptions about 'the Lutheran tradition' lead him to advance claims and draw conclusions that sometimes go beyond Bonhoeffer's own theology? Additionally, does it lead him to emphasize and attend to certain of Bonhoeffer's influences and relationships at the expense of others? In what follows, I expand on these questions and suggest how Bourdieu's notion of *habitus* could facilitate a different framing of Bonhoeffer's reception of Luther.

First, in *Bonhoeffer's Reception*, DeJonge consciously deploys 'Lutheran' and 'the Lutheran tradition' hermeneutically to organize the detail of Bonhoeffer's writings: 'What might otherwise appear as disparate, even contradictory moments

22. Bourdieu, *The Logic of Practice*, 53.
23. Jenkins, *The Future of Ethics*, 90.
24. Bourdieu, *The Logic of Practice*, 53.
25. Ted Smith, *The New Measures: A Theological History of Democratic Practice* (Cambridge: Cambridge University Press, 2007), 28.

or themes can often be read in terms of a consistent commitment to a basic Lutheran theological framework.'[26] For all that this approach allows, are there ways in which this kind of interpretation can begin to *over*-organize or stabilize influences and positions that are more fluid and inchoate in Bonhoeffer's texts themselves? In chapter 2, for example, DeJonge interprets Bonhoeffer as firmly in line with Lutheran *capax* thinking, which requires rejecting Bonhoeffer's own stated reservations about such language.[27] By reading Bonhoeffer as part of 'the Lutheran tradition', is DeJonge here giving sufficient recognition to Bonhoeffer's consistent criticisms of Lutheran orthodoxy and of much Lutheran thinking after Luther? Bourdieu's less stable and more fluid notion of *habitus* might allow for recognizing Bonhoeffer's dependence upon Luther, but without requiring that this becomes fixed and stabilized by a 'Lutheran theological framework' or as part of 'the Lutheran tradition'.[28]

Second, we have seen that DeJonge understands and presents Bonhoeffer as a '*conscious* participant' in the Lutheran tradition, this being part of DeJonge's 'first order' claim. He reads Bonhoeffer as intentionally and actively drawing upon Lutheran thinkers and positions for his own thinking and action. This raises the question of whether Bonhoeffer viewed himself as 'Lutheran' in quite such a determinate manner. What is the significance, for example, of the fact that Bonhoeffer was a member of the Evangelical Church of the Old Prussian Union (until 1933) and then of the Confessing Church, rather than one of the *intact* Lutheran churches? What is the significance of the fact that he tended to position and describe himself as 'Evangelical' or 'Protestant' (*Evangelisch*) broadly, rather than as 'Lutheran' (*Lutheranisch*) specifically? To continue this line of questioning, does DeJonge's way of locating Bonhoeffer as broadly 'Lutheran' conflate or obfuscate important differences between Bonhoeffer and other contemporary Lutheran theologians (e.g. Paul Althaus or Werner Elert)? Can this way of locating Bonhoeffer explain his enthusiastic and consistent support of the Barmen Declaration (with its more Reformed theology), for example, when so many other 'Lutherans' during the 1930s were much more critical of it?

In addition, DeJonge's emphasis on Bonhoeffer as consciously 'Lutheran' leads him to search for and emphasize *explicit* and *direct* connections between

---

26. DeJonge, *Bonhoeffer's Reception*, 259.

27. As DeJonge admits, 'Bonhoeffer's interpretation of Lutheran orthodoxy's relationship to Luther himself differs, then, from the interpretation I have offered'. DeJonge, *Bonhoeffer's Reception*, 74. DeJonge's way of understanding 'the Lutheran tradition' would seem to require this kind of correcting of Bonhoeffer.

28. In a telling passage, DeJonge criticizes Stanley Hauerwas' reading of Bonhoeffer's *Discipleship*: 'Bonhoeffer is not criticizing "Luther's understanding of grace", as Hauerwas puts it, but "the Lutheran doctrine of grace"'. *Bonhoeffer's Reception*, 237. However DeJonge himself then seems to conflate this distinction of Bonhoeffer's (between 'Luther' and 'Lutheran') when he concludes that 'a full account of the *Lutheran* character of *Discipleship* ... remains to be written'. DeJonge, *Bonhoeffer's Reception*, 239. Emphasis added.

Bonhoeffer and the preceding Lutheran thinkers and positions. In discussing a Lutheran precedent for Bonhoeffer's resistance activities, for example, DeJonge speculates that 'one likely course of Bonhoeffer's knowledge of the anti-Interim tradition is his theological conversation partner and first cousin Hans-Christoph von Hase'.[29] Whether or not this was the case, an advantage of Bourdieu's notion of *habitus* is that it does not require transmission in so direct a manner. It leaves more room for the indirect and more intuitive ways that past ideas can exert influence on and re-emerge in new situations.

Third, DeJonge's confessional and oppositional sense of 'the Lutheran tradition' involves positioning Bonhoeffer over against other 'non-Lutheran' influences and positions. As mentioned earlier, this use of 'Lutheran' often allows DeJonge to attend to and draw out nuanced differences between Bonhoeffer and some other thinkers (e.g. Barth, Yoder, etc.). Nonetheless, does positioning Bonhoeffer as 'Lutheran' in this way exclude or at least downplay some important influences on and aspects of Bonhoeffer's thinking? Is it significant, for example, that DeJonge gives relatively limited attention in *Bonhoeffer's Reception* to the role of modern thinkers (e.g. Hegel,[30] Nietzsche,[31] etc.) in Bonhoeffer's ethical thinking, or to ways in which his engagements with social theory (in *Sanctorum Communio*[32]) and phenomenology (in *Act and Being*) are crucial for understanding and attending to his early theology? In other words, does DeJonge locate Bonhoeffer as 'Lutheran' at the expense of him also being a thoroughly modern thinker?[33] Bourdieu's notion of *habitus* would allow for attending to Bonhoeffer's frequent uses of and appeals to Luther, but without downplaying the presence of other, even contradictory influences and ideas. Put differently, it would allow for a reading of Bonhoeffer's thinking as 'Lutheran', without excluding the possibility that he was also thoroughly 'Barthian'. This in turn could facilitate closer attention to the complexities and changes in the relationship between Bonhoeffer's and Barth's theology, that is, in ways that DeJonge's more straightforward framing of 'Lutheran' versus 'Reformed' does not quite capture.[34]

---

29. DeJonge, *Bonhoeffer's Reception*, 206.

30. See David Robinson, *Christ and Revelatory Community in Bonhoeffer's Reception of Hegel* (Tübingen: Mohr Siebeck, 2018).

31. See Peter Frick, *Understanding Bonhoeffer* (Tübingen: Mohr Siebeck, 2017), 78–126.

32. I have argued elsewhere that attending to Bonhoeffer's complex engagement with social theory in *Sanctorum Communio* is essential for understanding his ecclesiology. See Mawson, *Christ Existing as Community*, 121–75.

33. DeJonge, of course, is too subtle and careful a thinker to do this in any direct way. And in response to this question has rightly noted that one book cannot hope to address all of Bonhoeffer's influences and engagements. DeJonge, 'Non-Lutheran Influences, Scholarly Impasses, and Spiritual Influences', 375.

34. For a rich treatment of some these complexities and changes, see Edward van' Slot's recent book: *Negativism of Revelation? Barth and Bonhoeffer on Faith and Actualism* (Tübingen: Mohr Siebeck, 2015).

Furthermore, in *Bonhoeffer's Reception* DeJonge often criticizes scholars who have drawn upon and appealed to Bonhoeffer without taking his 'Lutheranism seriously'.[35] He rightly shows that many such scholars have neglected and misread important features of Bonhoeffer's theology. Even if this is the case, however, does the very existence of such diverse readings (and misreadings) itself complicate attempts to organize and stabilize Bonhoeffer theology as straightforwardly *inside of* 'the Lutheran tradition'? Bourdieu's more fluid and open-ended notion of *habitus* might place fewer limits on how Bonhoeffer could be legitimately drawn upon and appropriated for all kinds of thinking and action.

Finally, this suggests a more complex relationship between past, present and future in Bonhoeffer's reception of Luther. In line with MacIntyre, DeJonge is clear that Bonhoeffer 'does not inherit some pre-existing Lutheran framework whole cloth but develops it through creative collaboration in the tradition. Nor does he rigidly adhere to the framework once he has constructed it, but rather constantly recalibrates it.'[36] In other words, DeJonge understands and presents Bonhoeffer as a 'creative, dynamic participant in the Lutheran theological tradition'.[37] Following Bourdieu, the question is whether this still subtly mitigates some of the more experimental and exploratory aspects of Bonhoeffer's thinking. Does presenting Bonhoeffer as creative *within* the Lutheran tradition make his creativity internal and secondary to a broader Lutheranism?[38] Does this on any level supress or direct attention away from the more radically innovative aspects of his theology, that is, as found in the prison letters or sections of the *Ethics*?[39]

Conclusion

Bonhoeffer's Reception is an impressive and important book by any measure. DeJonge has provided one of the very best scholarly treatments of Bonhoeffer's theology to date. He provides a compelling case for the 'ubiquity' and importance of Luther in Bonhoeffer's thinking and action. Furthermore, he has drawn attention to a number of specific ways in which Luther is present in areas of

---

35. DeJonge, *Bonhoeffer's Reception*, 7.
36. DeJonge, *Bonhoeffer's Reception*, 261.
37. DeJonge, *Bonhoeffer's Reception*, 261.
38. In his introduction, DeJonge indicates his decision to prioritize the claim '*that* Bonhoeffer's thinking was Lutheran' over the question of 'what *kind* of Lutheran thinking Bonhoeffer was'. At least on some level, does this initial decision subtly locate Bonhoeffer's distinctiveness as secondary and internal to a prior category of Lutheranism? See DeJonge, *Bonhoeffer's Reception*, 12. Emphasis added.
39. In *Bonhoeffer's Reception*, DeJonge pays close attention to Bonhoeffer's fairly occasional engagements with Lutheran creeds and confessional documents, but gives relatively limited attention to the more experimental and innovative (perhaps less traditionally Lutheran) claims and insights of texts like *Letters and Papers from Prison*.

Bonhoeffer's theology, especially in his Christology and political theology. The question, however, is whether there are other, less determinate and more fluid ways of attending to this presence, of framing Bonhoeffer's complex reception of Luther.

PART II

THE VULNERABILITIES OF BODILY LIFE

Chapter 6

CREATURES *CORAM DEO*: BONHOEFFER, DISABILITY AND THEOLOGICAL ANTHROPOLOGY

A striking feature of recent work in disability theology has been the turn to the idea of relational personhood to develop a more expansive and inclusive theological anthropology. Theologians working within this field such as Hans Reinders, John Swinton, Amos Yong and Michael Hryniuk have all sought to develop an anthropology along these lines. In addition, these thinkers have sought to show how such an anthropology can provide a basis for an ethic, that is, for actively striving to care for and respond to persons with profound disabilities. In this chapter, I review and endorse this basic development, while also suggesting how the theology of Dietrich Bonhoeffer can assist with overcoming some of the limitations with the turn to relational personhood in disability theology as it stands.

In the first section, I briefly outline one standard way that personhood has often been defined and understood: as involving or requiring the possession of certain capacities or attributes. Second, I outline the alternative that has emerged in disability theology: an understanding of human beings as relational persons gifted to one another by God. On this basis, I indicate how several theologians have sought to ground relational personhood by appealing to the divine persons and relations of the Trinity. For all that this move offers, I suggest how this can obfuscate or downplay the concrete and embodied nature of being human. Finally, I outline Bonhoeffer's account of the human being as a 'being in relation' with a concrete other.[1] I make the case that Bonhoeffer's creaturely anthropology provides a better theological basis for a relational anthropology.

Philosophical and cultural assumptions about personhood

In recent decades, questions such as 'Who is a person?', 'How do persons emerge?' or 'What does personhood entail?' have increasingly come to frame and organize how we negotiate basic issues of rights and responsibilities, as well as how we

---

1. Bonhoeffer, *Creation and Fall*, DBWE 3: 63.

understand our individual and collective identities. How we answer such questions can have profound implications at the level of public policy and practice.

One place where this is apparent is in philosophical approaches to biomedical ethics. For example, in his influential *Practical Ethics*, the utilitarian philosopher Peter Singer has defined personhood in terms of 'self-awareness, self-control, a sense of the future, a sense of the past, the capacity to relate to others, concern for others, communication and others'.[2] Using such criteria, Singer has proposed including some non-animals as persons and – more controversially – excluding human beings with profound intellectual disabilities as well as foetuses, newborn infants, people with advanced dementia and various other groups with limited capacity due to ageing or terminal illness. For Singer, these groups are all essentially made up of non-persons; as such, they have no recognizable human rights and we have strictly limited obligations to and responsibilities for them.[3]

In *Abortion and Infanticide*, Michael Tooley has proposed a definition of personhood with similar ramifications: 'There are a number of necessary conditions that something must satisfy if it is to be a person, including the possession, either now or at some time in the past, of a sense of time, of a concept of a continuing subject of mental states, and of a capacity for thought episodes.'[4] According to Tooley, we are persons by virtue of a capacity to reflect on and be aware of ourselves through time. Moreover, he insists that 'an entity cannot be a person unless it possesses, or has previously possessed, the capacity for thought'.[5] He draws out the implications of this with respect to newborns: It is 'unlikely that humans, in the first few weeks after birth, possess this capacity'.[6] This means, of course, that infanticide should not be considered murder, and that we should reorder our ethical and legal systems accordingly.

If Singer and Tooley both closely identify personhood with the possession of certain attributes or capacities, such a position resonates with many wider cultural assumptions about what it means to be human. Hans Reinders, for instance, suggests that our 'culture is replete with images of self-determining bodies and minds, reflecting the deeply rooted cultural belief that the point of our lives is what we are capable of doing'.[7] Likewise, John Swinton notes that 'within a culture that is marked by ... hypercognition ... and hypermemory ... the temptation to define the nature of personhood and humanness according to such criteria is alluring and perhaps inevitable'.[8] We implicitly understand what it means to be human on the

2. Peter Singer, *Practical Ethics*, 2nd edn (Cambridge: Cambridge University Press, 1993), 74.
3. Singer, *Practical Ethics*, 192.
4. Michael Tooley, *Abortion and Infanticide* (Oxford: Clarendon, 1983), 419–20.
5. Tooley, *Abortion and Infanticide*, 421.
6. Tooley, *Abortion and Infanticide*, 421.
7. Hans Reinders, *Receiving the Gift of Friendship: Profound Disability, Theological Anthropology and Ethics* (Grand Rapids: Eerdmans, 2008), 8.
8. John Swinton, *Dementia: Living in the Memories of God* (Grand Rapids: Eerdmans, 2012), 110.

basis of such cultural values and priorities. To be fully human involves being able to actively pursue and achieve the kind of existence or being that we collectively esteem.[9] It is these kinds of philosophical and cultural conceptions of personhood, then, that recent theologians working in the area of disability theology have sought to contest and overcome.

A theological approach to personhood

What insights does the Christian theological tradition have to offer for how we understand personhood? How can theology contribute to an alternative understanding of human life and its meaning? Traditionally, many Christians have approached and negotiated questions surrounding anthropology with reference to Genesis 1: 'Then God said, "Let us make humankind in our image, according to our likeness ..." So God created humankind, in his image, in the image of God he created them; male and female he created them' (Gen. 1.26-27). Genesis informs us that to be human fundamentally means to be created in the image of God.

On its own terms, however, the text provides few clues as to what this *imago Dei* specifically entails. This has led to diverging interpretations of the *imago Dei* throughout the Christian tradition.[10] In an important book, James Mumford has characterized a dominant strand of interpretation: the 'capacities-based or "immanentist" reading of the *imago* according to which human beings are thought to resemble God in so far as they possess specific attributes or properties'.[11] In line with recent philosophical conceptions of personhood, God created human beings in the *imago Dei* by endowing them with certain attributes. Drawing on Greek philosophy, the candidates for these attributes have typically included reason, language, will and intellect. Thomas Aquinas, for example, observed that 'since it is because of his intellectual nature that man is said to be made to the image of God, it follows that he is made to God's image to the highest degree to the extent that his intellectual nature is able to imitate God to the highest degree'.[12]

Yet if these kinds of interpretations of the *imago Dei* have a long and established pedigree, they have more recently fallen from grace. In recent decades, developments and insights from biology and phenomenology have undermined such immanentist or substantive interpretations. Wentzel Van Huysteen

---

9. Reflecting on this issue, Gilbert Meilaender notes that 'it has become common to define personhood in terms of certain capacities. To be a person one must be conscious, self-aware, productive'. Gilbert Meilaender, *Bioethics: A Primer for Christians* (Grand Rapids: Eerdmans, 2005), 6.

10. On different ways that the *imago Dei* has been interpreted, see Lucy Peppiatt, *Imago Dei* (Eugene: Cascade, 2022).

11. James Mumford, *Ethics at the Beginning of Life* (Oxford: Oxford University Press, 2013), 186.

12. Aquinas, *Summa Theologica,* I. 93.4.

summarizes these developments: 'Substantive interpretations of the *imago Dei* have been replaced ... precisely because substantive views were seen as too static, and too strongly expressive of mind/body dualism.'[13] As scientists and some philosophers have begun attending to the bodily and embodied nature of human identity and cognition, conceptions of human identity primarily in terms of a capacity for reason, language and intellect have become harder to sustain.[14]

The impact of this shift is evident in recent trends in disability theology. Over the last two decades, theologians such as Hans Reinders,[15] Brian Brock,[16] Thomas Reynolds,[17] John Swinton[18] and Amos Yong[19] have all sought to develop insights into theological anthropology by attending to the concrete realities and experiences of persons with physical and intellectual differences. Their interest has especially been in how the lives and experiences of those with profound physical and intellectual differences can help us to clarify the nature of personhood. Assuming that this group of human beings are persons in the full sense, what do their realities and experiences disclose about the nature of personhood as such?

On the one hand, these thinkers have drawn attention to the problems that immanentist or capacity-based interpretations of the *imago Dei* pose for many of those with disabilities. In *Theology and Down Syndrome*, Amos Yong writes, 'This view perpetuates a bias against persons with disabilities who are oftentimes less physically and intellectually capable than others.'[20] In *Receiving the Gift of Friendship*, Hans Reinders similarly insists that 'the history of this doctrine shows' that 'the case for theological inclusiveness grounded in *imago Dei* is at best ambiguous', precisely because 'theological reflection has always been tempted to explain the divine image in terms of human capabilities'.[21] If to be created in the

---

13. J. Wentzel van Huyssteen, *Alone in the World: Human Uniqueness in Science and Theology* (Grand Rapids: Eerdmans, 2006), 134.

14. See Maurice Merleau-Ponty, *Phenomenology of Perception*, trans. Colin Smith (New York: Routledge, 2002), 202–34.

15. Reinders, *Receiving the Gift of Friendship*. See also Hans Reinders, *The Future of the Disabled in Liberal Societies* (Notre Dame: University of Notre Dame Press, 2000); and Hans Reinders, *Disability, Providence and Ethics* (Waco: Baylor University Press, 2014).

16. Brian Brock, *Wondrously Wounded: Theology, Disability and the Body of Christ* (Waco: Baylor University Press, 2019).

17. Thomas Reynolds, *Vulnerable Communion: A Theology of Disability and Hospitality* (Grand Rapids: Brazos Press, 2008).

18. Swinton has published a significant amount in this area. As an example, see Swinton, 'Who Is the God We Worship? Theologies of Disability; Challenges and New Possibilities', *International Journal of Practical Theology* 14, no. 2 (2011): 273–307.

19. Amos Yong, *Theology and Down Syndrome: Reimagining Disability in Late Modernity* (Waco: Baylor University Press, 2007).

20. Yong, *Theology and Down Syndrome*, 173.

21. Reinders, *Receiving the Gift of Friendship*, 229.

imago Dei means to be rational, self-determining or verbal, then the status of those who lack or less clearly display such attributes is ambiguous at best.[22]

On the other hand, these theologians have also sought to recover and develop alternative ways of understanding the human being as *imago Dei*. They have interpreted the *imago Dei* not in terms of a capacity for reason or intellect, but in relational terms. Genesis 1.26-27 can be read in light of Genesis 2.18: 'It is not good that the human being should be alone.' As Martin Buber famously makes this connection: 'In the beginning was the relation.'[23] At the most basic level, what it means to be human or a person is to exist in relation to another.

Reflecting upon this point, Thomas Reynolds writes that 'interdependence is originary. It is the fulcrum from which we emerge as persons.'[24] We emerge as persons in and through our interactions with others. Yong draws out the significance of this insight for persons with disabilities: 'An anthropology of interrelationality is able to account for the interpersonal encounters and intersubjectivity most palpably experienced in and between relationships involving people with disabilities.'[25] If immanentist or capacity-based interpretations of the human being place in question the full humanity or personhood of those with profound disabilities, a more thoroughly relational interpretation of *imago Dei* affirms that we are persons simply by being in relation.

In addition, some of these theologians have insisted that this relational being or personhood must be extrinsically grounded in and gifted by God.[26] They insist that an emphasis on relationality or relational personhood per se is insufficient. There could be a kind of relational personhood, for example, in which a human being must *actively* realize or achieve personhood in and through their interactions with another. This kind of relational personhood, however, would still remain centred on and directed by an active subject or agent, doing little to secure the full humanity of those who less clearly display such agency.[27] Accordingly, such thinkers argue that relational personhood is not primarily something we can achieve or activate; it is, more fundamentally, a gift from God. As Reinders makes this point,

22. See Yong, *Theology and Down Syndrome*, 169–74.
23. Martin Buber, *I and Thou*, trans. Walter Kaufmann (Edinburgh: T&T Clark, 1970), 69.
24. Reynolds, *Vulnerable Communion*, 117.
25. Yong, *Theology and Down Syndrome*, 184.
26. Molly Haslam is an interesting exception here. She directly argues for grounding relationality primarily in inter-human reciprocity and mutuality. Molly Haslam, *A Constructive Theology of Intellectual Disability: Human Being as Mutuality and Response* (New York: Fordham University Press, 2012).
27. This approach could, however, conceivably still secure the significance of recognizing and caring for those with disabilities, insofar as this activity contributes to the cultivation of one's own subjectivity or rationality. This is essentially Alasdair MacIntyre's position in *Dependent Rational Animals: Why Human Beings Need the Virtues* (Chicago: Open Court, 1999), 99–118.

relationality 'is not constituted by our subjectivity but by God's self-giving gift to humankind'.[28] God's free and gratuitous action grounds our relationality *ab extra*. In contrast to Singer and Tooley, such an extrinsic and transcendent grounding makes personhood unconditional and extends it to all human beings. We are related to one another prior to and apart from any capacity to recognize or realize this relationality ourselves.

This relational interpretation of the *imago Dei* not only allows for a more inclusive conception of personhood, but also provides a basis for an ethic, that is, for more actively striving to secure better lives for others, especially those with profound disabilities. Reinders aptly describes this as 'the other side the unconditional gift' of our relational personhood: 'how we respond to it'.[29] As he succinctly puts it, 'the gift entails a mission'.[30] Reinders's basic point, therefore, is that even while relational personhood is itself unconditionally gifted by God, this gift brings with it an opportunity to embrace and serve all those who have been similarly gifted. Attending to the writing of Jean Vanier and the reflections of L'Arche communities,[31] Reinders develops an account of this mission through the language of friendship and hospitality. We have been given an opportunity to embrace and serve our friends precisely because God has given them to us: 'God's gift is the gift that precedes Christian friendship and makes it possible.'[32] Crucially, Reinders's point is that God gives us our friends and that they are 'not chosen' by us.[33] This radically expands our social networks to include all those who are different from us.[34] Christian friendship involves embracing all those who have been gifted to us, in particular those friends who we did not choose or anticipate.

To be clear, however, any such active embrace or service to the other remains secondary and derivative. Neither our relational personhood nor these friendships per se require or depend upon a capacity to actively serve. Fundamentally, we have been given one another as friends; secondarily, this means we have an opportunity to actively serve one another insofar as we are able.

To summarize, the theologians discussed earlier insist on a theological understanding of personhood as relational. Against Singer and Tooley, as well as

---

28. Reinders, *Receiving the Gift of Friendship*, 252.
29. Reinders, *Receiving the Gift of Friendship*, 287.
30. Reinders, *Receiving the Gift of Friendship*, 314.
31. This, of course, was before the revelations about Vanier's sexual abusing became public in February 2020. For an overview and response to the release of these revelations, see Misha Ketchell, 'I Once Thought Catholic Humanist Jean Vanier a Hero. Now I'm Wrestling with His Coercive Legacy', *The Conversation*, 1 May 2020, https://theconversation.com/i-once-thought-catholic-humanist-jean-vanier-a-hero-now-im-wrestling-with-his-coercive-legacy-135794.
32. Reinders, *Receiving the Gift of Friendship*, 15.
33. Reinders, *Receiving the Gift of Friendship*, 355.
34. Reinders contrasts this Christian vision of friendship with an Aristotelian one, in which friendships are governed by rationality and require a certain level of reciprocity. *Receiving the Gift of Friendship*, 358–63.

wider 'immanentist' and 'substantivist' readings of the *imago Dei*, such thinkers recognize that we have all been created as persons in relation to one another. On this basis they affirm the personhood of all human beings, including those with profound intellectual and physical differences. And as Reinders has shown, this relational anthropology includes an ethic. The recognition that we have been gifted to one another provides an opportunity to work to improve the lives of our friends.

Personhood and Trinity

For all that this account of relational personhood (and its related ethic) has to offer, I have concerns with one way in which it is often grounded: with reference to the divine persons and relations of the Trinity. Reinders in particular has sought to understand human relational personhood in terms of divine persons and relations. The Triune God thus provides a model and foundation for relational personhood at the human level.

This basic move has been promoted by a number of prominent modern systematic theologians with diverse commitments, including Jürgen Moltmann,[35] Colin Gunton,[36] John Zizioulas[37] and Miroslav Volf.[38] It appears in the work of feminist theologians such as Catherine LaCugna[39] and Patricia Wilson-Kastner,[40] philosophical theologians, political and liberation theologians such as Leonardo Boff[41] and in the work of pastoral theologians like Peter Holmes and Stanley Grenz.[42] Indeed, Karen Kilby has aptly summarized this trend of modern theology: social trinitarianism 'has been gaining momentum especially since the publication of Jürgen Moltmann's *The Trinity and the Kingdom of God*, and by now has achieved in many quarters dominance – it has become the new orthodoxy'.[43]

---

35. Jürgen Moltmann, *The Trinity and the Kingdom: The Doctrine of God*, trans. Margret Kohl (San Francisco: Harper and Row, 1991).

36. Colin Gunton, *The One, The Three and the Many* (Cambridge: Cambridge University Press, 1993).

37. John Zizioulas, *Being as Communion: Studies in Personhood and the Church* (London: Darton, Longman, and Todd, 1985).

38. Miroslav Volf, *Exclusion and Embrace: Theological Exploration of Identity, Otherness and Reconciliation* (Nashville: Abingdon Press, 1994).

39. Catherine LaCugna, *God for Us: The Trinity and Christian Life* (Chicago: HarperOne, 2000).

40. Patricia Wilson-Kastner, *Faith, Feminism and the Christ* (Philadelphia: Fortress Press, 1983).

41. Leonardo Boff, *Trinity and Society* (Maryknoll: Orbis, 1988).

42. Stanley Grenz, *The Social God and Relational Self: A Trinitarian Theology of the Imago Dei* (Louisville: Westminster John Knox, 2002).

43. Karen Kilby, 'Perichoresis and Projection: Problems with Social Doctrines of the Trinity', *New Blackfriars* 81 (2000): 432-3.

This grounding of relational personhood in the Trinity is also central for several disability theologians. John Swinton claims that 'properly understood, the relational nature of the Trinity is an important key to the relational nature of human beings. Something analogous to this divine dynamic is apparent within human personhood.'[44] Elsewhere Michael Hryniuk has suggested that 'just as God is a communion of persons who would not exist at all if not in relation toward one another and creation, so human beings are likewise persons, that is, existing only in and through relation to another, others, and God'.[45] For Hryniuk, the significance of a turn to the Trinity is that it disrupts our tendency and temptation to understand personhood in individualistic terms and, furthermore, makes possible a 'recognition that personhood is not grounded essentially in one's powers to think, reason or produce'.[46]

As mentioned, Reinders provides a careful and sustained account of how the Trinity can ground a relational anthropology. In the core theological section of *Receiving the Gift of Friendship*, he turns to and draws upon the work of the Orthodox theologian John Zizioulas.[47] First, Reinders repeats and endorses Zizioulas's reading of the Greek Fathers, who, according to Zizioulas, held that '*the being of God himself* was identified with the three persons of the Trinity'.[48] For Zizioulas, Greek patristic theology revolutionized and overturned earlier Classical Greek conceptions of ontology and metaphysics, which had maintained a sharp opposition between *ousia*, as general or universal being, and *hypostasis*, as the particular or concrete person. In Zizioulas's reading, the Greek Fathers disrupted this opposition by making being subordinate to the free relations of the divine persons. The effect of this move, as he summarizes, is that 'to be and to be in relation becomes identical'.[49] For the Greek Fathers, it was no longer possible to think of God prior to the persons and relations of the Trinity.

In addition, Reinders takes over another move in Zizioulas's theology: the claim that human beings are relational by being ecstatically drawn towards and into God's intra-trinitarian relations. 'We are truly human', he summarizes, 'because we are drawn into communion with God the Father, the Son and the Holy Spirit'.[50] Zizioulas himself describes this as opening ourselves up to the perichoretic

---

44. Swinton, *Dementia*, 159 n10. Swinton also writes that 'the inherently relational nature of human beings emerges from the nature and relational shape of the God in whose image they are created'. Swinton, *Dementia*, 158.

45. Michael Hryniuk, *Theology, Disability and Spiritual Transformation: Learning from the Community of L'Arche* (Amherst: Cambria Press, 2010), 247.

46. Hryniuk, *Theology, Disability and Spiritual Transformation*, 249.

47. Reinders writes, 'my being as *imago Dei* is not to be taken ontologically as subsistent being, but as a relationship that is ecstatically grounded in God's loving kindness towards me'. See Reinders, *Receiving the Gift of Friendship*, 273.

48. Reinders, *Receiving the Gift of Friendship*, 258.

49. Zizioulas, *Being as Communion*, 88.

50. Reinders, *Receiving the Gift of Friendship*, 274.

fullness of the divine life: 'The life to which we open ourselves is expansive and unfathomable in its fullness, because it is the divine life: the life of the Trinity.'[51] And Zizioulas maintains that this ecstatic openness to God as Trinity is what grounds our relational personhood in the here and now. He understands the relational personhood of human beings on the basis of their *telos* or final end as union with God.[52]

My concern with this approach is that grounding relational personhood in a social conception of the Trinity can start to obfuscate or downplay the more distinctively human or creaturely nature of human personhood. To put this differently, my concern is that modelling a relational anthropology on trinitarian relations and persons – human beings as relational through being drawn into the intra-trinitarian relations – militates against a more fundamental distinction between God as creator and human beings as creatures. In an important essay critiquing social trinitarianism, Katheryn Tanner has expressed this concern: 'No matter how close the similarities between human and divine persons, differences always remain – God is not us – and this sets up the major problem for theologies that want to base conclusions about human relations on the Trinity.'[53] Tanner locates this key difference in 'the essential finitude of human beings'.[54] Following Tanner, then, social trinitarianism tends to conflate the difference between divine and human persons, thereby marginalizing and downplaying finitude or creaturely limitation in human personhood.[55]

One place where this is apparent in *Being as Communion* is in Zizioulas's central opposition between 'ecclesial being' and 'biological' or 'natural being'.[56] On the one hand, he describes 'ecclesial being' as the new existence that is given in baptism, the free existence or personhood that is constituted in and by God as Trinity. On the other side, he further clarifies this ecclesial being by positioning it over against a prior 'biological' or 'natural existence'. And he construes the latter in largely negative terms: 'Man [*sic*] as a biological hypostasis is intrinsically a tragic figure.'[57] As Zizioulas reiteratates this opposition in a later essay, 'Man is called to preserve the image of God in him as much as possible, striving to free himself from the necessity of nature, to experience "sacramentally" the "new being" as a member of the community of those "born again".'[58] For Zizioulas, we should strive

---

51. Zizioulas, *Being as Communion*, 122.
52. Reinders, *Receiving the Gift of Friendship*, 267.
53. Kathryn Tanner, 'Trinity, Christology, and Community', in *Christology and Ethics*, ed. F. LeRon Shults and Brent Waters (Grand Rapids: Eerdmans, 2010), 65.
54. Tanner, 'Trinity, Christology, and Community', 66.
55. Tanner, 'Trinity, Christology, and Community', 65–9.
56. Zizioulas, *Being as Communion*, 49–65.
57. Zizioulas, *Being as Communion*, 52.
58. John Zizioulas, 'On Being a Person: Towards an Ontology of Personhood', in *Persons, Divine and Human*, ed. Christoph Schwöbel and Colin E. Gunton (Edinburgh: T&T Clark, 1992), 44.

to embrace the freedom of our ecclesial being, moving beyond the necessities and vicissitudes of human nature or natural necessity.

Both Reinders and Hryniuk take up this opposition between ecclesial and biological being in their theological reflections on disability. For example, Reinders insists that being drawn into God 'means that we no longer fear the limitations of our biological and historical being because we have been accepted as who and what we are'.[59] Similarly, Hryniuk (citing Catherine LaCugna) insists that when 'the Spirit deifies human beings', this 'makes them holy, sets them free from sin, free from the conditions of their biological hypostasis'.[60] In other words, Reinders and Hryniuk posit an opposition between the ground of our relational personhood (God) and our natural, embodied limitations. Accordingly, when human beings are drawn into or constituted by the relations of the Trinity, they are simultaneously drawn out of or away from their natural situations and limits. Summarizing this aspect of Zizioulas's theology, Douglas Farrow observes that the human person on its own terms is 'bound by finitude, by his biological nature, by the necessities of his body, and by the self-centredness which all of this inevitably entails'. 'If he is to be free at all', Farrow continues, 'he must overcome his natural or biological hypostasis, and all that it stands for'.[61] For Zizioulas, and consequently for Reinders and Hryniuk, the limits of our biological embodied being are progressively overcome or displaced in our ecstatic transformation.

The problem, therefore, is that this implies that our biological and creaturely limits – including the physical and intellectual limits of persons with disabilities – are overcome in and through this transformation. Bodily limits and experiences play no role in our new ecclesial being or identity. This, in turn, suggests that disability and its realities are not finally constitutive of being human insofar as they do not fundamentally inform our identities as human beings and our standing in relation God and one another.[62]

To be clear, neither Reinders nor Hryniuk *explicitly* advocate dispensing with concrete embodiment or limits. Indeed, Reinders insists that the new 'ecclesial being *does not* abandon the concreteness of the body, nor does it ignore concrete differences between bodies. Both aspects, concreteness and difference, are included in the transformation through the Eucharist.'[63] The issue, however, is that he does not provide an account of *how* this is the case. Reinders's more basic emphasis on

---

59. Reinders, *Receiving the Gift of Friendship*, 368.

60. Hryniuk, *Theology, Disability and Spiritual Transformation*, 265.

61. Douglas Farrow, 'Person and Nature: The Necessity–Freedom Dialectic in John Zizioulas', in *The Theology of John Zizioulas: Personhood and the Church*, ed. Douglas Knight (Burlington: Ashgate, 2007), 111.

62. One of the main claims of disability studies during recent decades is precisely that disability is constitutive of identity. See, for example, Simi Linton, *Claiming Disability: Knowledge and Identity* (New York: New York University Press, 1998).

63. Reinders, *Receiving the Gift of Friendship*, 263.

theosis and deification undermines, or at least sits in tension with, his affirmations of concrete bodily life.[64]

This leads to a second problem. If our ecstatic transformation draws us away from our concrete and embodied limits, then this has implications for the kind of ethics that proceeds from this anthropology. It has implications for how we understand our friendships with and responsibilities to others, including those with profound disabilities. If we are in relation to such persons primarily because we are together being drawn into communion with God, then the mission or ethics that proceeds from this will be similarly directed to and by this ecstatic transformation. We recognize and attend to others not in terms of their natural and biological limits per se, but by looking beyond or behind these limits to who they truly are. My worry, then, is that this means that Christian friendship is not directly determined by embodiment and concrete limitation. If Christian relationality and friendship are directed (at least ultimately) to the inner communion of the divine persons, it is unclear that this is a necessarily embodied and creaturely relationality or friendship.

Finally, this raises the question of whether a trinitarian grounding of relational personhood leaves too much room for an idealization or romanticization of disability and being friends with those with disabilities. If it is not inherently necessary to attend to embodiment and limitation as part of our friendships, would it not be easier to neglect or downplay the ways in which we continually encounter and experience concrete limitation through them? Does a trinitarian approach allow us to neglect the necessarily limited and limiting nature of all human relationships? To put this bluntly, could this lead us to neglect or downplay how such friendships limit us in ways that are often costly and painful?

To reiterate, my concern in this section is that theologically basing a relational anthropology on Triune persons and relations – and our ecstatic transformation towards the communion of the Trinity – threatens to undermine or obfuscate the necessarily bodily and concrete nature of all human relationality. And if such an anthropology provides a basis for an ethics of friendship, then it is similarly left unclear how this is an ethic that *necessarily* attends to what is concretely entailed by our friendships. Rather than viewing the other human being in terms of their transformation away from concrete limits, we need an anthropology and ethic that more clearly places embodiment and concrete limitation at its centre.

Bonhoeffer and creaturely personhood

In this final section, I suggest that Bonhoeffer's theology – in particular in *Creation and Fall* and *Ethics* – provides just such an anthropology. In his 1933 'Theological

---

64. It is significant that this language is largely absent from one of Reinders's subsequent books. Here Reinders draws more heavily on Calvin, which leads to a clearer distinction between creator and creature and avoids the kinds of problems that can result from a trinitarian metaphysics. Reinders, *Disability, Providence and Ethics*, 145–56.

Exposition of Genesis 1–3',[65] Bonhoeffer presents a rich and detailed account of human beings as created by God in relation to one another. Moreover, Bonhoeffer avoids grounding this human relationality in Triune persons and relations, instead insisting on the limited and necessarily creaturely nature of human relationality. In this section, I shall further indicate how Bonhoffer develops and expands on this creaturely anthropology in his *Ethics*, especially in his concepts of 'vicarious representative action' and 'responsibility'.

At the outset, it is important to note the overlaps and resonances between Bonhoeffer's anthropology and the work on personhood in recent disability theology. In *Creation and Fall*, Bonhoeffer similarly provides an account of human beings as fundamentally relational, and he insists that this relationality is grounded in God *ab extra*. Bonhoeffer maintains that God has created human beings in the *imago Dei* by setting them in relation to one another: 'God created them man and woman.' This means, he reflects, that 'the human being is not alone. Human beings exist in duality, and it is in this *dependence on the other that their creatureliness consists*.'[66] Bonhoeffer is clear that human beings have their existence and being only as those who God has set in relation.

Bonhoeffer develops his account of this relational existence with the language of freedom. That God has created human beings as *imago Dei* means we are free for God and one another. Moreover, Bonhoeffer connects this freedom to our relationality directly. For human beings, he writes, 'being free means "being-free-for-the-other", because I am bound to the other. Only by being in relation with the other am I free.'[67] Human beings are truly free only in relation and in service to one another.

Bonhoeffer is clear that this relational freedom is not to be understood as a human possession or capacity. When God sets us in relation to one another, he writes, this 'is not a human potential or possibility or a structure of human existence; instead it is a given relation, a relation in which human beings are set, a *justitia passiva*!'[68] Like Reinders, Bonhoeffer holds that to be created as *imago Dei* does not mean to be given a capacity for relationship. God sets us in relation prior to and more directly than any ability or capacity to understand or actualise this relation.

Nonetheless, while Bonhoeffer is in these ways like Reinders and other recent advocates of relational personhood, it is significant that he avoids grounding this relationality and freedom in a doctrine of the Trinity. Instead, he maintains that we are created as relational and free in a distinctively human way. When discussing human freedom, he insists that this is a distinctively '*created* freedom'.[69] That we

---

65. That is, the subtitle of *Creation and Fall*.
66. DBWE 3: 64. Italics original.
67. DBWE 3: 63.
68. DBWE 3: 65.
69. DBWE 3: 64. Bonhoeffer frames this as a question: 'In what way does the freedom of the Creator differ from the freedom of that which is created?'

are free in relation to the concrete other does not mean that we are free in the same sense that God is free.

Bonhoeffer develops this difference between divine and creaturely freedom in his discussion of the '*analogia relationis*'. Our freedom, he writes, is not an '*anaologia entis*', or something in us that is 'like God's being'. Rather, we are free like God only through the creaturely and bounded 'relation that God has established'.[70] We are 'in the image of God in being for God and neighbour, in its original creatureliness and limitedness'.[71] Accordingly, this means that to be created in the image of God does not mean to be free as God is free. It means simply reflecting and participating in God's own purposes in creating the free human being.

Moreover, Bonhoeffer claims that we are *imago Dei* only as bodily beings who are bound to the earth. Humankind 'is the image of God not in spite of but precisely in its bodily nature. For in their bodily nature human beings are related to the earth and other bodies; they are there for others and dependent upon others.'[72] This stands in contrast to Zizioulas's (and Reinders's) claim that being drawn towards the Trinity involves being drawn away from our natural and biological nature. Bonhoeffer explicitly affirms that 'human beings have their existence as existence on earth. They do not come from above; they have not by some cruel fate been driven into the world and been enslaved by it.'[73] Our existence is inextricably tied to the earth and even our salvation and redemption restore us to our status as creatures of the world.

In *Creation and Fall*, Bonhoeffer develops his account of relational and bodily freedom in a detailed exposition of the second Genesis narrative. He describes Eve as 'the limit given to Adam in bodily form'.[74] Adam's existence is for Eve as his concrete other, and vice versa. Moreover, Bonhoeffer maintains that it is in terms of Eve as concrete limit that Adam is the recipient of God's grace: 'This very revelation of the limit in bodily form, in the love he has for the other person, would have brought Adam into an even deeper knowledge of the grace of the creator.'[75] It is only in relation to the concrete other as bodily limit that we encounter God's grace and goodness. We are human beings precisely in and through such concrete relations.

---

70. DBWE 3: 65.
71. DBWE 3: 113.
72. DBWE 3: 113. As Bernd Wannenwetsch notes, 'it is precisely as bodily beings that humans experience their mutual dependency, both in the most pleasurable and the most painful way'. Bernd Wannenwetsch, 'Angels with Clipped Wings: The Disabled as Key to the Recognition of Personhood', in *Theology, Disability and the New Genetics: Why Science Needs the Church*, ed. John Swinton and Brian Brock (London: T&T Clark, 2007), 189.
73. DBWE 3: 77. As Bonhoeffer writes, 'humanity is derived from a piece of the earth ... From it human beings have their *bodies*.' DBWE 3: 76.
74. DBWE 3: 122.
75. DBWE 3: 118.

Again, there is an ethic entailed in this theological anthropology. If we are human beings or persons only as set in relation to a concrete other – and in relation to the concrete other as embodied limit – then this too entails an opportunity for attending to and serving this other. As Bonhoeffer writes in his *Ethics*, 'To live as a human being before God ... can only mean to be there not for oneself, but for God and for other human beings.'[76] To live before God (*coram Deo*) means that we do not have to pursue or secure our own meaning: we are free for God and free to serve the other human being.[77]

One way that Bonhoeffer develops this claim in *Ethics* is through his concepts of 'vicarious representative action' (*Stellvertretung*) and 'responsibility' (*Verantwortlichkeit*). To live as a human being before God means to follow Christ by acting for the other and in the place of the other. Our action and responsibility flow from and reflect Christ's prior action upon the cross. In other words, we are free to respond to and serve others because Christ has freed us from ourselves and for this other. As Bonhoeffer writes, 'Vicarious representative action and therefore responsibility is only possible in completely devoting one's life to another person.'[78] Christ frees us to respond and be responsible without expectation of reward or reciprocation.

The point here, however, is that we are not responsible for the other per se or in the abstract, but only for this particular other in his or her given situation: 'The attention of responsibility is directed to concrete neighbours in their concrete reality.'[79] We respond to the concrete neighbour as and where we encounter them, not in terms of their *telos* towards something higher. At the same time, this means that being responsible involves attending to actual human beings and not the idea of a human being. For Bonhoeffer, 'God loves the world. Not an ideal human, but human beings as they are.'[80] With Christ, we do not embrace and serve others on the basis of what we think they should be or become, but simply as we find them.

This means that our action and responsibility for the other remains limited and bounded. Bonhoeffer states that 'action in accord with reality [in Christ] is limited by our creatureliness. We do not create the conditions for our action but find ourselves already placed within them ... Our responsibility is not infinite but limited.'[81] Our responsibility and service are limited in that they are defined and guided by our creaturely limits.[82] As creatures we respond to and are responsible

---

76. DBWE 6: 400.

77. On this sense of being free for service to the other, see Martin Luther, 'The Freedom of a Christian', in *Luther's Works, Volume 31: Career of the Reformer I*, trans. Helmut T. Lehmann, ed. Harold J. Grimm (Philadelphia: Fortress Press, 1957), 307–26.

78. DBWE 6: 259.

79. DBWE 6: 259.

80. DBWE 6: 84.

81. DBWE 6: 267.

82. As Paul makes this point in Ephesians, 'we are what he has made us, created in Christ Jesus for good works, which God prepared beforehand to be our way of life' (Eph. 2.10).

for the ones who God has set before us. As Bernd Wannenwetsch makes this point, 'every individual is to respond in his life at the very place in which he finds himself placed'.[83] Accordingly, Bonhoeffer writes that responsible action is not 'unbounded or frivolous [*übermütig*]', but 'creaturely and humble [*demütig*]'.[84] 'The transcendent', as he puts it in a later 'Outline for a Book', 'is not the infinite unattainable tasks, but the neighbor within reach in any given situation'.[85] We encounter God in our everyday tasks and responsibilities, not in terms of any ecstatic transformation out of or away from these tasks.

To be clear, in *Creation and Fall* and *Ethics* Bonhoeffer recognizes the difficulties with embracing the limit of the other human being after the fall. After Adam and Eve's fall into sin, we still experience the other as a concrete limit, but no longer as the means of God's grace. Rather, we now experience and encounter the other primarily as judgement: 'Adam has transgressed the boundary, and now hates his limit'.[86] With Adam, we strive to control this other who presents a threat and limits us. Bonhoeffer puts this sharply: 'One thing is quite certain, namely that at the point where love for the other is obliterated, a human being can only hate the limit. A person then desires only, in an unbounded way, to possess the other or to destroy the other'.[87] While God continues to encounter us through the other human being, we now experience this limit as a curse. Insofar as we desire to live without limits (*sicut Deus*), we experience the limit of this other as standing against us.

For Bonhoeffer, we are to learn to embrace the limit of other human being in Christ. Indeed, he holds that it is in Christ that we rediscover creation and our creaturely relationality.[88] This means that genuine human relationships and community are mediated by Christ. In *Life Together*, Bonhoeffer observes that 'without Christ we would not know other Christians around us; nor could we approach them … Christ opened up the way to God and one another.'[89] After the fall, we recognize and embrace the other human being as God's gift and grace through the mediation of Christ.

However, even when we recognize the other in Christ, it is significant that we still do so only as creatures: life in Christ 'means to assume the place assigned to us as creatures', as Wannenwetsch puts it.[90] In Christ, we are to embrace and

---

83. Bernd Wannenwetsch, '"Responsible Living" or "Responsible Self"? Bonhoefferian Reflections on a Vexed Moral Notion', *Studies in Christian Ethics* 18, no. 3 (2005): 131.

84. DBWE 6: 269.

85. DBWE 8: 501.

86. DBWE 3: 127.

87. DBWE 3: 99.

88. As Bonhoeffer writes, 'It is because we know of the resurrection that we know of God's creation in the beginning, of God's creating out of nothing.' DBWE 3: 35.

89. DBWE 5: 33.

90. Bernd Wannenwetsch, 'Christians and Pagans: Towards a Trans-Religious Second Naivete or How to Be a Christological Creature', in *Who Am I? Bonhoeffer's Theology Through His Poetry*, ed. Bernd Wannenwetsch (London: T&T Clark, 2009), 190.

attend to the other as a concrete and creaturely limit. This indicates that even when Christ overcame sin and the fall, he did so in a way that re-established (rather than replaced or abolished) the creaturely limit that is integral to human beings and all human relationality. In other words, Bonhoeffer explicitly rejects the kind of deification or theosis that is central for Zizioulas's trinitarian notion of personhood. As he writes in his *Ethics*, 'God changes God's form into human form in order that human beings can become, not God, but human before God'.[91] God's work in Christ restores and redeems fallen human beings to their status as creatures, that is, beings set in relation to one other as concrete limits. Even more pointedly, he insists that 'human beings are not transformed into an alien form, the form of God, but into the form that belongs to them, that is essentially their own'.[92]

Implications for disability theology and practice

What are the advantages of Bonhoeffer's insistence on the specifically creaturely form of our relationality and redemption? How can a theological anthropology and ethic that more clearly insist on the other as an embodied, concrete limit help us to better understand and negotiate our friendships and relationships with those with profound disabilities?

First, Bonhoeffer's theology more clearly requires that we attend to the concrete situations and particular needs of our friends. As we have seen, God has created us by setting us in relation to a concrete and embodied other which means that we are to attend to this other in his or her givenness. More specifically, we are to attend to this other in terms of his or her specific limitations, not in terms of an ecstatic transformation away from these. 'The human being is a bodily being and remains so in eternity as well. Bodiliness and being human [*Menschsein*] belong indivisibly together.'[93]

Second, Bonhoeffer's firmer emphasis on the other as concrete limit allows for a clearer recognition of how our relationships with others, especially those with profound disabilities, are themselves limiting. Bonhoeffer's theology recognizes the pain that is inherent in all human relationships after the fall, which we cannot ourselves mitigate or overcome: 'What we shrink back from with pain and hostility, namely, real human beings, the real world, this is for God the ground of unfathomable love.'[94] After the fall, we invariably try to control others and shrink back from others because of how they challenge and limit us. Bonhoeffer recognizes the deeply painful aspects of human community, and yet he does so without giving this the final word: 'While we exert ourselves to grow beyond our

---

91. DBWE 6: 96.
92. DBWE 6: 96.
93. DBWE 6: 96.
94. DBWE 6: 84.

humanity, to leave the human being behind us, God becomes human; we recognize that God wills that we be human, real human beings.'[95]

Finally, I suggest that Bonhoeffer's theology provokes an understanding of our relationships and friendships that is more realistic and ultimately more sustainable. As we have seen, he maintains that God has indeed set us in relation to one another as a grace and blessing, but we no longer directly recognize or experience other people in this way. This is why our friendships and responsibility must be grounded in Christ, and not a recognition or embrace of the other directly or apart from Christ: 'Our living as real human beings, and loving the real people next to us is ... grounded only in God's becoming human, in the unfathomable love of God for us human beings.'[96] On our own terms we remain unable to recognize and respond to others in the ways that we should. While we may catch occasional glimpses of God's grace in the concrete other, this is more often the exception than the rule. Following Bonhoeffer, we hold in faith that Christ is present in the limit of the other even when we cannot recognize this to be the case. It is this kind of Christian friendship – grounded upon the other as concrete limit rather than in an anticipation of community in the Trinity – that better enables us to attend to others and improve their lives and situations over the long haul.

Conclusion

The approach to a theological anthropology and ethic displayed by Reinders and several other disability theologians provides an important alternative to secular and cultural conceptions of personhood. A theological account of human being as relational and gifted by God properly challenges and expands our understanding of what it means to be human. Moreover, this anthropology provides a basis for an ethic of hospitality and friendship. All of the theologians I have in mind are themselves deeply attentive to and engaged with the concrete situations of their friends in precisely the right ways.[97]

Nonetheless, in this chapter I have expressed concerns with a tendency to model human personhood on the Trinity and understand human relationality in terms of a teleological metaphysics. My basic concern is that this subtly undermines and displaces an ethic of friendship that attends to others in their concrete givenness. By modelling relational personhood and Christian friendship on the Trinity, Reinders, for instance, potentially obfuscates how our relational personhood is constituted by the other as bodily limit.

---

95. DBWE 6: 84.
96. DBWE 6: 87.
97. For Reinders, this is apparent through his rich descriptions of his own friendships and engagements with Kelly and Ronald. Reinders, *Receiving the Gift of Friendship*, 19–23, 354–6. Also see his extraordinarily rich and concrete discussions in the chapter 'Stories We Live By', in *Disability, Providence, and Ethics* (Waco: Baylor University Press, 2012), 167–90.

In Bonhoeffer's theology, we find resources for an anthropology and ethic that avoids this potential idealization or abstracting of the other. While Bonhoeffer similarly develops an account of relational personhood as gifted by God, his theology more clearly insists upon the concrete and embodied particularity of the other human being and thus attends to the ways in which we are limited through such relationships. Ultimately, it is this creaturely anthropology that can provide a better basis for attending to and actively caring for others, for taking action and responsibility in the world.

Chapter 7

ENCOUNTERING GRACE AFTER THE FALL:
BONHOEFFER'S 'NATURAL LIFE' AS A RESPONSE
TO GERALD MCKENNY ON BIOTECHNOLOGY

In his 2018 book *Biotechnology, Human Nature, and Christian Ethics*, Gerald McKenny explores the role and status of human nature for ongoing work in Christian and philosophical ethics. More specifically, he identifies and reflects upon four different ways in which Christians and others have understood nature as having normative significance, especially in relation to negotiating recent challenges presented by biotechnology and biotechnological enhancement. How should Christians understand and appeal to nature when responding to attempts to extend the human lifespan, for example? Or how should Christians respond to the emergence of other technologies and therapies that could significantly alter human nature or enhance abilities beyond the normal range?

In the first approach that McKenny outlines in *Biotechnology*, nature is understood as having normative significance simply in its givenness. Accordingly, this implies that what is natural should be respected rather than altered or enhanced through biotechnology. Labelling this position 'NS1',[1] McKenny identifies it with thinkers as diverse as Oliver O'Donovan, Michael Sandel and Jürgen Habermas.[2] In the second approach, nature is normative as a ground for human flourishing and rights (NS2). Proponents of this view share a basic concern that the alteration of natural capacities and traits by means of biotechnology might imperil distinctively human goods and rights. Drawing upon Aristotelian philosophy, its advocates include Francis Fukuyama, Martha Nussbaum and Leon Kass. In the third approach, nature is normative due to its malleability or susceptibility to intervention and alteration (NS3). For those who take this approach, the very indeterminacy, open-endedness and malleability of human nature invites and even requires ongoing enhancement. Unlike the previous positions, proponents of NS3 often embrace and advocate for the enhancement and alteration of human nature

---

1. 'NS' is McKenny's shorthand for 'normative status'.
2. Locating this position theologically, McKenny suggests that NS1 is in some respects anticipated by Augustine's theology. See Gerald McKenny, *Biotechnology, Human Nature, and Christian Ethics* (Cambridge: Cambridge University Press, 2018), 34–6.

through biotechnology.³ Fourth and finally, nature has normative significance in that it equips or prepares us for life with God (NS4). 'According to NS4', as McKenny summarizes, 'our creaturely nature suits or equips us for a particular form of life with God that was God's purpose in creating us'.⁴ Each of these different ways of understanding the normative status of human nature facilitates a different response to the challenges presented by biotechnology.

In this chapter, my interest is primarily in McKenny's presentation of NS4, his own preferred option, which he constructs through careful readings of Kathryn Tanner and Karl Barth. In the first section, I outline the main features of McKenny's NS4, remaining close to the relevant chapter of *Biotechnology*. I also review some weaknesses which McKenny himself identifies with Tanner's and Barth's versions of NS4.⁵ In the second section, I set out Bonhoeffer's reflections on human nature in his unfinished 'Natural Life' manuscript, suggesting how 'Natural Life' can be read as a version of NS4. Finally, I conclude by briefly reflecting on some advantages of this Bonhoefferian version of NS4, as compared with the versions found in Tanner and Barth.

McKenny's NS4: Human nature as the condition for imaging God

In McKenny's account,⁶ NS4 is the view that human nature has normative status because God has created and determined human beings with this particular nature in order to equip them for relationships with God and one another.⁷ Furthermore, this view implies that human nature as it stands is sufficient and good: 'With respect to its status as God's creation, human nature is good insofar as it suits human beings for the life with God for which God has determined them.'⁸ If we have been created and determined by God as the particular creatures that we are, then this implies that there is no inherent need to pursue alterations or enhancements that fundamentally alter or enhance the nature that we have.

3. Theologically, this position finds a precedent in Irenaeus and various Patristic theologians. Its modern subscribers include Ted Peters and Philip Hefner. In McKenny's account it also has resonances with some aspects of Kathryn Tanner's theology. McKenny, *Biotechnology*, 137–42.

4. McKenny, *Biotechnology*, 147.

5. In what follows, I assume a certain level of familiarity with McKenny's project. My summary of his sophisticated presentation of NS4 is necessarily brief.

6. Of the four options that McKenny explores in *Biotechnology*, NS4 is the most explicitly theological in that its point of departure is Christology. Indeed, at the end of his chapter on NS4, McKenny suggests that this may, in fact, be a weakness, as I outline later in this chapter.

7. As McKenny succinctly puts this, 'Normative status therefore attaches to human nature (which with its present traits and powers is to be understood as in some sense the good and finished work of God) as the condition for the particular form of life with God for which God has created us.' McKenny, *Biotechnology*, 148.

8. McKenny, *Biotechnology*, 148.

McKenny develops his account of NS4 using theological language of *imago Dei*: 'God created human beings to reflect something of God: life with God ... is lived in that reflection; and their creaturely nature equips human beings to live with God in this way.'[9] As beings created in God's image, humans have a 'unique dignity' that extends to and encompasses their biological nature.[10] Specifically, he follows Paul (citing Rom. 8.29; 2 Cor. 4.4; Col. 1.15) in opting for a Christological interpretation of *imago Dei*: 'to be in the image of God is in some way to conform to Jesus Christ'.[11] McKenny's two main interlocutors for constructing his account of NS4, Kathryn Tanner and Karl Barth, both understand the *imago Dei* in terms of this Pauline conformation to Christ.

For Tanner, this conformation is mainly understood in terms of the 'plasticity' of human nature.[12] Human nature is normative or has ethical significance simply in its capacity to be reformed and remade. As McKenny summarizes, 'it is the almost unlimited capacity of human nature to be shaped by intentional human action ... that equips humans to receive God's image and be remade by it'.[13] It is because human beings have been created with a highly flexible or malleable nature that we are able to be remade into Christ's image through the work of the Spirit.

In terms of her Christology, Tanner understands Christ as God's image with reference to his divine nature, namely Christ as the second person of the Trinity. Christ 'shares the divine nature and thus images God as "the perfect manifestation of all that the first person is"'.[14] We in turn attain or enter into this image, then, by being drawn into Christ's divinity. As McKenny summarizes, we image God 'by participating in what we are not', namely God.[15] This indicates the 'deificationist orientation' of Tanner's Christology and related anthropology.[16]

On this basis McKenny suggests there are continuities between Tanner's position and the view he outlined in an earlier chapter in *Biotechnology* as NS3 (that human nature has normative significance in its susceptibility to being transformed into something else entirely).[17] He suggests, however, that despite this proximity, Tanner finally remains within the parameters of NS4: 'Tanner's position ... expresses the principle that our nature is equipped for enjoyment of life with God by virtue of the creaturely characteristics it now has, even as, by virtue of the plasticity of these characteristics and powers, it is susceptible to work of the Spirit,

---

9. McKenny, *Biotechnology*, 150.
10. McKenny, *Biotechnology*, 149.
11. McKenny, *Biotechnology*, 150.
12. McKenny's engagement focuses on Kathryn Tanner's *Christ the Key* (Cambridge: Cambridge University Press, 2009).
13. McKenny, *Biotechnology*, 152.
14. McKenny, *Biotechnology*, 152.
15. McKenny, *Biotechnology*, 153.
16. McKenny, *Biotechnology*, 157.
17. Note that McKenny also discusses Tanner's theology in his chapter on NS3. McKenny, *Biotechnology*, 122–3.

which takes our nature beyond what is natural to it.'[18] Because our nature opens us to God's work in the Spirit 'by virtue of the characteristics it now has', Tanner's position draws back from the view of nature entailed in NS3's pursuit of radical transformation.

In developing his account of NS4, McKenny gives more sustained attention to Karl Barth's theology.[19] While similarly holding that our nature equips and determines us for life with God, Barth is even clearer that 'human nature as created by God is already suited to the enjoyment of life with God and need not undergo any working over to be made fit for it'.[20] As compared with Tanner, Barth is even clearer that our nature is sufficient for this enjoyment as it stands. Following Barth, McKenny argues that we are conformed to the image of God in Christ *in* – and not simply *through* – the nature we already possess as God's creatures.[21] This means that 'life with God does not take us beyond our created state'.[22]

This difference relates to how Barth and Tanner each understand Christ as *imago Dei*. Barth also holds that it is Christ who is the image of God in the true sense, and that we in our place image God in conformity to Christ.[23] In contrast to Tanner, however, he insists that 'it is in his *humanity*, and thus in his *creaturely nature*, that Christ is the image of God'.[24] In his humanity or human nature, Christ repeats and reflects *ad extra* who God is in Godself. Specifically, Barth holds that Christ does this through his love for his fellow human beings: 'What characterizes Jesus' humanity for Barth is his absolute and unconditional being for his fellow humans, which accomplishes in time God's absolute and unconditional being for humanity that is God's eternal resolve, and thereby fulfils the covenant of grace.'[25]

This is also what gives human nature its normative status. For Barth, Christ's 'being for his fellow humans … in time' presupposes and attests to the 'natural characteristics that make it possible for Christ to be with us and for us'.[26] In other words, these natural characteristics have significance because Christ's concrete love and service of others presupposes and requires them. This is Barth's counterintuitive move in his anthropology: we are to understand the significance

18. McKenny, *Biotechnology*, 154.

19. McKenny is focusing in particular on Barth's *Church Dogmatics: III/2*, ed. G. W. Bromiley and T. F. Torrance (London: T&T Clark, 1960).

20. McKenny, *Biotechnology*, 157.

21. As McKenny clarifies, 'Barth holds, in contrast to Tanner, that our nature participates in the image of God just as it is, without having to be worked over by the Holy Spirit in such a way that it is no longer natural with respect to its created state or condition.' McKenny, *Biotechnology*, 162.

22. McKenny, *Biotechnology*, 172.

23. As McKenny summarizes, 'Jesus Christ is the proper image of God: His is the one in whom God is God with and for humanity. Other human beings image God as those whom God is with and for in Jesus Christ.' McKenny, *Biotechnology*, 170.

24. McKenny, *Biotechnology*, 164. Emphasis added.

25. McKenny, *Biotechnology*, 164.

26. McKenny, *Biotechnology*, 174.

of human nature not directly or in itself, but by looking to Christ.[27] God from eternity has created all human beings with the particular nature that we have in service to Christ as God's image in time.

This creaturely nature also anticipates and makes possible our own conformity to Christ as God's image. As McKenny writes, it is what enables us to 'live in a way that conforms to God's being with and for us in Christ'.[28] In a more limited and conditional way, therefore, we too are able to express the same concrete love that Christ has for others. As beings created with the same human nature as Christ, we too can witness to God's image in Christ through acts of love and service.

In reflecting on this nature that is attested to in Christ, Barth largely refrains from speaking in terms of specific natural powers and capacities (e.g. reason, will, etc.). Instead, Barth presents our creaturely nature in terms of three aspects: 'relationality, as a composite of body and soul, and as temporal'.[29] God has created and determined humans as relational, as integrated and as temporal beings in anticipation of Christ's concrete work of love. Furthermore, these broad aspects of human nature can be viewed as 'signs' of how God has prepared us to participate in this work. Recognizing that God in Christ has embraced and works through human nature frees us to similarly embrace the aspects of the nature that we have been given.[30] Looking to Christ allows us to recognize, for example, that a bounded lifespan is one way that God frames and directs our concrete love and service of others.[31]

With respect to biotechnology, McKenny suggests that NS4 does not provide principled grounds for opposing enhancement and alteration. Even Barth's position, he reflects, 'could accommodate ... many of the possibilities that biotechnology might bring about'.[32] What NS4 does provide, however, is a place from which to evaluate specific technologies and their anticipated effects:

27. This is part of what sets NS4 apart from NS1. For Barth and Tanner, even as our nature attests to God's purposes, it is not intelligible in itself or directly. In other words, we are able to understand nature as normative only by seeing it in relation to God's work in Christ.

28. McKenny, *Biotechnology*, 165

29. McKenny, *Biotechnology*, 160.

30. Nonetheless, at this end of his chapter McKenny suggests that a limitation with Barth's version of NS4 is that his three 'characteristics of human nature (relationality, body-soul composition and temporality)' remain at a general and abstract level. And Barth himself provides little reflection on 'the concrete functions or the rational, volitional and sensible capacities that are the "stuff" of human nature'. As a result, McKenny observes, Barth leaves it 'unclear how these concrete aspects of our concrete nature signify its meaning and purpose'. McKenny, *Biotechnology*, 182.

31. That is, in a way that frees us from needing to resist or overcome a bounded lifespan through the pursuit of life-extending technologies and therapies.

32. McKenny, *Biotechnology*, 174. For McKenny, it is conceivable that certain enhancements and alterations may even serve and enhance our creaturely relationality, integration and temporality.

> The crucial claim is that the point of our creaturely nature is to equip us to image God by attesting to God's being with and for us in actions as creatures. The question posed to biotechnology, then, is this: In acting to determine the possibilities of our creaturely nature, are we instantiating (in our creaturely nature as well as our actions towards it) that point or some other one?[33]

Following Barth, the question is whether a proposed alteration or enhancement will actually help us to better attest to God's image in Christ.

At the end of his presentation of NS4, McKenny draws attention to some limitations or 'flaws' in the versions that he has drawn from Tanner and Barth.[34] On the one hand, he suggests that even while Tanner's version remains within the parameters of NS4, there is still an 'insufficient affirmation of the goodness of our nature in its present state, with the possibilities that are inherent in it apart from the work of the Holy Spirit'.[35] In other words, Tanner's version is limited due to the fact that 'the normative significance of our creaturely nature consists entirely in its capacity to be transformed into something else'.[36]

On the other hand, McKenny suggests that Barth's version 'risks the opposite error'.[37] Barth celebrates the goodness of human nature in its current condition in a way that leaves little room for the 'eschatological transformation of our nature into the divine likeness'.[38] As McKenny elaborates it, Barth tends to understand the life to come, our resurrected nature, in terms of an affirmation or restoration of the nature that we already possess.[39] As McKenny succinctly states, Barth's view of resurrection 'comes perilously close to the notion of resurrection as a kind of resuscitation'.[40]

---

33. McKenny, *Biotechnology*, 176.
34. McKenny, *Biotechnology*, 180–3.
35. McKenny, *Biotechnology*, 181.
36. McKenny, *Biotechnology*, 180.
37. McKenny, *Biotechnology*, 181.
38. McKenny, *Biotechnology*, 180.

39. For more on Barth's anthropology and understanding of resurrection, see the rich essay by Donald Wood, '"This" Ability: Barth on the Concrete Freedom of Human Life', in *Disability in the Christian Tradition: A Reader*, ed. Brian Brock and John Swinton (Grand Rapids: Eerdmans, 2012), 391–426.

40. McKenny, *Biotechnology*, 181. McKenny also suggests that a limitation with NS4 (at least as compared with NS1, NS2 and NS3) is that the 'Christological grounds appear to confine NS4 to those who accept that human nature is the creaturely condition for a form of life with God that is given to us in Jesus Christ'. Put differently, NS4 seems to exclude all those who lack specifically Christian convictions and commitments, or at least seems to render this version incomprehensible and inaccessible to those without such commitments. Yet McKenny briefly reflects that even with its Christological grounds NS4 is not 'entirely esoteric'. Without providing details, he speculates that those familiar with NS2 and NS3 may still be able to account for its differences in ways that 'ignore' or 'place less emphasis on' revelation. See McKenny, *Biotechnology*, 183.

Nonetheless, the very fact that NS4 can 'accommodate positions with opposite shortcomings' means that, in McKenny's judgement, 'the vices of these two positions do not nullify the virtues of NS4'. McKenny concludes that NS4 itself is 'broad enough to include the range of theological positions that fall between Tanner's and Barth's positions'.[41] Indeed, early in his account of NS4 he makes clear that his own use of Tanner and Barth is 'exemplary' rather than exhaustive.[42] This leaves space for reflecting and expanding upon McKenny's NS4 by drawing in other voices.

Bonhoeffer's 'Natural Life'

In the winter of 1940, Bonhoeffer drafted a manuscript, 'Natural Life' [*'Das Natürliche Leben'*[43]], as part of an intended work on theological ethics (edited and published posthumously by Eberhard Bethge as *Ethics*).[44] Bonhoeffer worked on 'Natural Life' while staying at Ettal Abbey in Bavaria, making use of the abbey's extensive library.[45] As with all of the *Ethics* manuscripts, he composed 'Natural Life' in the context of National Socialism and during the Second World War.[46] He left Ettal in February 1941, never finding an opportunity to return to and complete this text.

Running to fifty-five pages in the most recent German edition,[47] 'Natural Life' is one of the longest manuscripts of *Ethics*. It contains reflections on how to situate and approach nature or natural life theologically, as well as detailed discussions of specific ethical topics, including euthanasia, suicide, marriage rights, birth control and forced sterilization. In these discussions Bonhoeffer goes into a level of concrete detail that is notably absent from most of the other manuscripts of *Ethics*. Furthermore, it is not always clear how 'Natural Life' fits with some of his wider claims and ideas, even while fairly closely following and building upon

---

41. McKenny, *Biotechnology*, 183.

42. McKenny, *Biotechnology*, 152.

43. In this section, I follow the DBWE translators in rendering '*das natürliche Leben*' as 'natural life', but it might also perhaps be rendered as 'natural *living*'. This would capture the more dynamic sense of how God encounters and works with human beings in the midst of their everyday living.

44. That is, DBWE 6.

45. Bonhoeffer, 'To Hans-Werner Jensen', 26 December 1940, DBWE 16: 112.

46. Indeed, given the central concern with bodily life and natural rights, 'Natural Life' can be read as partly responding to the racism and eugenic programmes of the Nazi regime. See Bernd Wannenwetsch, 'My Strength Is Made Perfect in Weakness: Bonhoeffer and the War over Disabled Life', in *Disability in the Christian Tradition*, ed. Brock and Swinton, 354–60 (Grand Rapids: Eerdmans, 2012).

47. Dietrich Bonhoeffer, 'Das natürliche Leben', in *Ethik*, ed. Ilse Tödt, et al. DBW 6, 163–217 (Munich: Gütersloher Verlagshaus, 1992).

the preceding manuscript: 'Ultimate and Penultimate Things'. 'Natural Life' ends abruptly with a few scattered remarks following a subheading: 'The Natural Rights of the Life of the Spirit'.

While there has been limited secondary scholarship on 'Natural Life',[48] one trend has been to read the manuscript as an attempted recovery of the natural law tradition.[49] In a rich essay, Jens Zimmermann has exemplified this approach. In particular, Zimmermann positions Bonhoeffer as anticipating a subsequent Catholic (and now also Protestant[50]) return to natural law.[51] In Zimmermann's reading, Bonhoeffer 'clearly assumes a "natural order of the world", woven into the fabric of God's creation, to which human beings ought to conform'.[52] Furthermore, he continues, 'in granting fallen reason the power to discern creational directives for human flourishing, Bonhoeffer establishes the natural as common ground for public moral reasoning'.[53] Following this natural law reading, reason provides us with access to nature as a set of moral prescriptions or directives. For all that this

---

48. Some of the main engagements include Adam C. Clark, 'The Creator Sovereign in Christ: Dietrich Bonhoeffer and Protestant Natural Law Retrieval', PhD Dissertation, University of Notre Dame, 2017; William F. Connor, 'The Natural Life of Man and Its Laws: Conscience and Reason in the Theology of Dietrich Bonhoeffer', PhD Dissertation, Vanderbilt University, 1973; Steven Van der Heuvel, *Bonhoeffer's Christocentric Theology and Fundamental Debates in Environmental Ethics* (Eugene: Pickwick Publications, 2017), 22–72; Robert Vosloo, 'Body and Health in the Light of the Theology of Dietrich Bonhoeffer', *Religion and Theology* 13, no. 1 (2006): 23–7; Heinz Eduard Tödt, *Authentic Faith: Bonhoeffer's Theological Ethics in Context* (Grand Rapids: Eerdmans, 2007), 142–50; Ralf K. Wüstenberg, Stefan Heuser and Ester Hornung, eds, *Bonhoeffer and the Biosciences: An Initial Exploration* (Pieterlen: Peter Lang, 2010); Jens Zimmermann, 'Recovering the Natural for Politics: Bonhoeffer and the Natural Law Tradition', in *Dietrich Bonhoeffer, Theology and Political Resistance*, ed. Lori Brandt Hale and W. David Hall, 27–48 (Lanham: Lexington, 2020).

49. This trend is partly in reaction to readings of Bonhoeffer that have emphasized his proximity to Barth. An example can be seen in Robin Lovin, *Christian Faith and Public Choices: The Social Ethics of Barth, Brunner, and Bonhoeffer* (Minneapolis: Fortress Press, 1984), 168–72. While not discussing 'Natural Life' directly, Jordan Ballor has recently argued for a reading of Bonhoeffer as a natural law theologian. Jordan Ballor, 'Christ in Creation: Bonhoeffer's Orders of Preservation and Natural Theology', *Journal of Religion* 86, no. 1 (2006): 1–22.

50. Zimmermann mentions a 'spate of publications' in the 1990s that 'indicated a renewed interest among Protestants in natural law theory'. Zimmermann, 'Recovering the Natural for Politics', 28. As an example, he refers to Stephen J. Grabill, *Rediscovering the Natural Law in Reformed Theological Ethics* (Grand Rapids: Eerdmans, 2006).

51. In the conclusion to his essay, Zimmerman draws a parallel between Bonhoeffer and Jacques Maritain. Zimmermann, 'Recovering the Natural for Politics', 42.

52. Zimmermann, 'Recovering the Natural for Politics', 29.

53. Zimmermann, 'Recovering the Natural for Politics', 33.

kind of reading has to offer, approaching 'Natural Life' as a version of NS4 provides insights into some less recognized aspects of Bonhoeffer's account of natural life.[54]

Bonhoeffer begins his manuscript by positioning it as an attempt to recover a concept of nature or the natural for Protestants. He notes that the concept of the natural has 'fallen into disrepute in Protestant ethics', which has in turn led to a loss of the 'relative differences within the human and the natural'.[55] The result, Bonhoeffer reflects, is that Protestant Christians no longer have the 'ability to give clear guidance on the burning questions of natural life'.[56] Bonhoeffer aims to recover a concept of nature, then, in a way that might assist with negotiating these burning questions and providing concrete ethical guidance.

In recovering this concept, Bonhoeffer is clear that nature or natural life can only properly be understood and approached from God's revelation. Much like Tanner and Barth, Bonhoeffer holds that nature or natural life is not intelligible and does not have normative status in itself.[57] Rather, it has significance only because of who God is and what God has done: 'The concept of the natural must be recovered from the Gospel.'[58] For Bonhoeffer, we recognize and affirm nature as having normative significance on the basis of God's word.

Bonhoeffer too develops this claim Christologically: 'Only through *Christ's* becoming human do we have the right to call people to natural life and to live it ourselves.'[59] In the incarnation, God has disclosed and affirmed human nature or natural life as a place of God's own presence and work. And this means that all those who follow Christ are called to attend to God's presence and work in natural life: 'Because Jesus Christ is the reconciliation of God and the world', as one commentator recently put it, 'one cannot look to Christ without looking to the natural life that he has taken upon himself'.[60] Like Tanner and Barth, Bonhoeffer approaches nature or natural life from the standpoint of being conformed to Christ.

It is significant, however, that at this point Bonhoeffer avoids using language of *imago Dei*. This indicates a major difference from the two versions of NS4 that were outlined by McKenny in *Biotechnology*. Even while holding that it is

---

54. Following McKenny's classification, Zimmermann is largely locating Bonhoeffer's 'Natural Life' as a version of NS1 (nature has normative significance in its givenness prior to and apart from human action or intervention). While this reading captures important aspects of Bonhoeffer's position, I worry that it underplays what is at stake with Bonhoeffer's situating of nature as postlapsarian, as well as the fluid and dynamic ways in which he understands reason in relation to natural life. For a reading that comes closer to what I propose later in the text, see Clark, 'The Creator Sovereign in Christ'.

55. DBWE 6: 171.

56. DBWE 6: 172.

57. That is, the position McKenny labels as NS1 in *Biotechnology*.

58. DBWE 6: 173.

59. DBWE 6: 174. Emphasis added.

60. Banman, *Reading in the Presence of Christ*, 170.

Christ who allows for recognizing and attending to natural life as normative, Bonhoeffer carefully distinguishes between this normativity and the goodness of God's creation. In contrast to Barth, he insists on keeping the normativity of nature separate from our status as God's creatures and covenant partners.[61]

This difference is most readily apparent in Bonhoeffer's consistent positioning of natural life as postlapsarian: 'Through the fall, "creation" became "nature". The unmediated relation to God of the true creation becomes the relative freedom of natural life.'[62] In other words, because of the fall, we no longer possess the same kinds of relationships with God and one another that we had in the primal state. This is why language of *imago Dei* can no longer accurately describe what we are as human beings.[63] Bonhoeffer is using the concept of nature or natural life only in relation to the *new* space or situation in which human beings live and exist after the fall. Specifically, he uses this concept for describing how God continues to uphold and preserve (*erhalten*) human beings as fallen creatures.

In an earlier book, *Creation and Fall*, Bonhoeffer had provided detailed reflection on how God continues to care for the first human beings after the fall. Here he reflects at length on how God continues to work with and care for a sinful humanity: 'God accepts human beings for what they are, as fallen creatures. God affirms them in their fallenness … God's action accompanies humankind on its way.'[64] Accepting these first human beings as fallen creatures, God upholds and preserves Adam and Eve by ordering their lives: 'By making cloaks for human beings God shows them that it is their wickedness that makes this necessary … God's way of acting to preserve the world is to affirm the sinful world and to show it its limits by means of order.'[65]

This anticipates how Bonhoeffer understands and presents human nature or natural life as postlapsarian in *Ethics*. After the fall, God acts to preserve and order human beings through the very form of natural, bodily existence itself: 'God wills and gives life a form [*Gestalt*] in which it can live, because left to its own resources it can only destroy itself.'[66] Accordingly, the concept of nature or natural life is naming a particular form of God's preserving work. It is describing one way in

---

61. Bonhoeffer, 'We speak of the natural as distinct from the created, in order to include the fact of the fall into sin.' DBWE 6: 173.

62. DBWE 6: 173.

63. References to the *imago Dei* are almost entirely absent from *Ethics*. When it does appear, it is being used to draw a contrast with what human beings become after the fall. See comments to this effect in the manuscript 'God's Love and the Disintegration of the World', DBWE 6: 301.

64. DBWE 3: 139.

65. DBWE 3: 139.

66. DBWE 6: 178. Elsewhere in *Ethics* Bonhoeffer treats history as a way in which God works to order and preserve human beings. See, 'Heritage and Decay', *Ethics*, 103–33.

which God has chosen to impede and limit our continuing attempts to flee from God and one another.[67]

With respect to Christ, this means that God's presence and preserving work in the form of natural life has a kind of 'penultimate' (*vorletzten*) significance.[68] It is one way that God preserves and orders human life *for Christ*, without directly being part of God's ultimate work of reconciliation and redemption *in Christ*.[69] As Bonhoeffer himself writes, 'the natural is that form of life preserved by God for the fallen world that is directed toward justification, salvation and renewal through Christ'.[70] Natural life has a kind of anticipatory or preparatory status with respect to God's ultimate work of reconciliation in Christ, even while natural life is not itself necessary or foundational for this work.[71]

What does this mean for human thinking and action? Following the fall, with their newfound knowledge of good and evil,[72] human beings now have a relative freedom to think and act in ways that either embrace or aim to overcome God's preserving work through natural life. Within the relative freedom of postlapsarian

---

67. Bonhoeffer holds that God preserves fallen human beings through a kind of impulse or 'basic will' that is embedded in the very form of natural life: 'Life itself tends towards the natural'. DBWE 6: 176. For Bonhoeffer, this form of life thus provides guidance or exerts normative claims in ways that ultimately exceed our attempts to organize or understand them: 'The natural cannot be organized but is simply there'. DBWE 6: 177.

68. Hans Ulrich has observed that Bonhoeffer 'understands the natural primarily in its directedness to Christ, and thus in the ways in which it is preserving and preparing shared human living for Christ'. See Hans Ulrich, 'The Form of Ethical Life', in *The Oxford Handbook of Dietrich Bonhoeffer*, ed. Michael Mawson and Philip G. Ziegler, 302 (Oxford: Oxford University Press, 2019).

69. Bonhoeffer provides more detailed reflection on this relationship between God's penultimate and ultimate work in his preceding manuscript, 'Ultimate and Penultimate Things'. 'From a Christian perspective', he writes, 'the fallen world becomes understandable as the world preserved and maintained by God for the coming of Christ, a world in which we as human beings should live a "good life" in given orders'. DBWE 6: 165. As Christians we are called to recognize God's preserving work in these given orders, including in the form of natural life. We are called to embrace and attend to what God is providing in this place.

70. DBWE 6: 174.

71. Bonhoeffer writes: 'The natural does not compel the coming of Christ, nor does the unnatural make it impossible; in both cases the real coming is an act of grace. Only through the coming of Christ is the natural confirmed in its character as penultimate and the unnatural definitively exposed as the destruction of the penultimate. DBWE 6: 173. At the same time, however, in *Ethics* Bonhoeffer also affirms the ways in which God's ultimate work in Christ takes up and affirms natural, bodily life: 'Jesus Christ the human being – that means that God enters into created reality, that we may and should be human beings before God.' DBWE 6: 157.

72. On the knowledge of good and evil, see Bonhoeffer, 'God's Love and the Disintegration of the World', DBWE 6: 299–303.

life, Bonhoeffer insists, 'there is a difference between its right use and its misuse; there is therefore a relative openness and a relative closedness for Christ'.[73] In other words, there is a difference between attending to God's preserving work in the form of nature and attempting to live and exist apart from this form. In 'Natural Life' Bonhoeffer presents and develops these two alternatives as 'the natural' and 'the unnatural'.[74]

Beginning with the latter, he identifies two unnatural ways of relating to life in particular: vitalism and mechanization (*Vitalismus und Mechanisierung*). He describes the former as a kind of 'absolutizing of life' or treating it 'as an end in itself'.[75] Vitalism is an attempt to construe life or the pursuit of life as the ultimate good.[76] By contrast, Bonhoeffer describes mechanization as the construal of human life as simply a means to an end. Here natural life becomes sacrificed to something higher. As Bonhoeffer states (in the context of National Socialism), 'the individual is understood only in terms of usefulness [*Nutzwert*] to the whole, the community only in terms of its use to an all-controlling institution, organization or idea'.[77] In the case of mechanization, human life exists solely for the service of something beyond itself, and thus in a way that subverts and displaces natural life as God's chosen place of preserving work.

While Bonhoeffer construes vitalism and mechanization as unnatural, he nonetheless insists that they are both still based on partial truths. In the case of vitalism, 'it arises from the false absolutizing of an insight that is essentially correct, that life, both individual and communal, is not only a means to an end, but an end in itself'.[78] Theologically speaking, vitalism on some level still recognizes natural life as a place of God's presence, even while failing to attest to how it is preserving or preparing human beings for something else: for Christ. By contrast, mechanization tries too quickly to move beyond the given form of natural life to achieve something higher. Ultimately, Bonhoeffer suggests that vitalism and mechanization equally 'express ... despair about natural life, an enmity to life, a weariness of life, an incapacity for life'.[79] On their own terms both these responses fail to attend to natural life as a place where God is upholding and preserving human beings.

---

73. DBWE 6: 172.

74. DBWE 6: 176.

75. DBWE 6: 179.

76. In *Creation and Fall*, Bonhoeffer describes this as 'essentially a desperate, an unquenchable, an eternal thirst that Adam feels for life'. DBWE 3: 143. Bonhoeffer's discussion of vitalism helpfully diagnoses the thirst underlying the more recent pursuit of technologies that might radically extend the human lifespan. See Mark O'Connell, *To Be a Machine: Adventures among Cyborgs, Utopians, Hackers, and the Futurists Solving the Modest Problem of Death* (London: Granta, 2017), 179–93.

77. DBWE 6: 179.

78. DBWE 6: 178.

79. DBWE 6: 179.

Against these unnatural responses, how are we to embrace and attend to natural life? 'How is the natural recognized?'[80] On the one hand, Bonhoeffer maintains that in a 'formal' sense (*formale Bestimmung*) the natural 'can only be recognized by looking at Jesus Christ'.[81] As we have already seen, and in alignment with NS4, he holds that we can understand the purpose of natural life as a place of God's preserving work only with reference to Christ.[82]

On the other hand, Bonhoeffer suggests that we recognize specific claims or 'content' of the natural (*die inhaltliche Bestimmung des Natürlichen*) in a different way: through reason.[83] 'With respect to the content of natural life, human "reason" [*Vernuft*] is the organ for recognizing the natural'.[84] Bonhoeffer presents this use of reason as a kind of 'grasping' (*erfassen*) or 'perceiving' (*vernehmen*) of what has been naturally 'given' (*Gegebene*).[85] Here it is worth noting that this use of reason remains close to the ground. Contra the natural law reading of Bonhoeffer, as outlined earlier in the text, reason is not a capacity for deriving prescriptions or directives from nature, which we then adhere to or enact.[86] Rather, reasoning is a more dynamic, open-ended grasping of the significance of natural life within a given situation.[87]

---

80. DBWE 6: 174.

81. DBWE 6: 174. As Bonhoeffer continues, this is because 'the natural is determined by the preserving will of God and by its orientation towards Jesus Christ'.

82. That is, what natural life is in its anticipation of and orientation to Christ's coming.

83. Bonhoeffer endorses reason as the means by which human beings are to discern natural life and its content. Nonetheless, he is also careful to insist that 'reason is not a divine principle of cognition and order in human beings, superior to the natural. Rather, it is part of this preserved form of life' and 'completely embedded in the natural.' DBWE 6: 174. He also makes clear that even while reason allows us to recognize the content of the natural (and also natural rights), it does not allow us to discern God's work in and through that content. DBWE 6: 184.

84. DBWE 6: 174.

85. DBWE 6: 174. It is worth noting that there is no specifically Christian ground for using reason in this way. For Bonhoeffer, *all* human beings are capable of discerning the content of God's preserving work in natural life, even when they do not name it as such.

86. Bonhoeffer's position is not an attempt to understand nature or creation as providing moral order, that is, in the sense of Oliver O'Donovan's *Resurrection and Moral Order: An Outline for Evangelical Ethics* (Grand Rapids: Eerdmans, 1986). McKenny engages O'Donovan in detail in the second chapter of *Biotechnology*, 25–69. For a penetrating critique of this aspect of O'Donovan's work, see Sam Tranter, *Oliver O'Donovan's Moral Theology* (London: T&T Clark Bloomsbury, 2020).

87. Of course there are many understandings of natural law that are dynamic and open-ended in ways that resonate with this aspect of Bonhoeffer's approach. See, for example, Stephen Pope, 'Reason and Natural Law', in *The Oxford Handbook of Theological Ethics*, ed. Gilbert Meilaender and William Werpehowski, 148–67 (Oxford: Oxford University Press, 2007).

This leads to Bonhoeffer's detailed reflections on natural rights (*Rechte*). In his manuscript, he insists that using reason to grasp the content of natural life involves discerning and protecting the rights of natural life: 'The natural … becomes rights with respect to human beings. The rights of natural life are the glory of God the Creator in the midst of the fallen world.'[88] Much of Bonhoeffer's manuscript is occupied with outlining specific rights and then reflecting on how these can help with negotiating pressing ethical questions and challenges. We attest to God's presence and work in human nature by affirming and upholding the natural rights of others. These reflections on rights are integral to Bonhoeffer's specific version of NS4.[89]

When he first turns to considering rights, Bonhoeffer clarifies that they need to be held in tension with certain obligations or 'duties' (*Pflichten*) that similarly proceed from natural life.[90] Indeed, it is by holding rights and duties together that natural life is concretely affirmed vis-à-vis the extremes of vitalism and mechanization: 'In the context of natural life … life as an end in itself is expressed in rights [*Rechte*], and life as a means to an end is expressed in duties.'[91] Affirming both rights and duties is therefore a way of avoiding these unnatural responses. Nonetheless, Bonhoeffer suggests that procedurally rights should be given a certain priority over duties: what is 'given to life' by God precedes the obligations that are then 'demanded of it'.[92]

If rights are about affirming and protecting natural life, this takes place as the protection of the bodily life of individuals.[93] Bonhoeffer is primarily interested in the rights of the specific, individual body over against attempted encroachments by collectives or institutions: 'The most primordial right of natural life is the protection of the body from intentional, injury, violation and killing.'[94] With echoes of Kant, he asserts that 'the human body never becomes simply a thing

---

88. DBWE 6: 180.

89. To some extent this emphasis on rights brings Bonhoeffer's version of NS4 into proximity with the position McKenny outlines as NS2 (that nature has normative significance as a ground for rights and human flourishing). However, locating natural rights in terms of God's *preserving* work results in a more constrained and less teleological account of rights.

90. In an important essay, Michael DeJonge has emphasized the importance of duties for Bonhoeffer's approach, even while this aspect of his text is underdeveloped. See Michael P. DeJonge, 'Respecting Rights and Fulfilling Duties: Bonhoeffer's *Formed Life* in Bioethical Perspective', in *Bonhoeffer and the Biosciences: An Initial Exploration*, ed. Ralph K. Wüstenberg, Stefan Heuser and Ester Hornung, 109–22 (Pieterlen: Peter Lang, 2010).

91. DBWE 6: 180. Put differently, it is by discerning and protecting natural rights that we avoid construing life either as an end in itself or as a means to an end.

92. DBWE 6: 180.

93. Bonhoeffer writes: 'Each individual brings a natural right into the world at birth.' DBWE 6: 183.

94. DBWE 6: 186.

that might fall under the unbounded power of another person, to be used only as a means to that person's end'.⁹⁵ All of the natural rights that Bonhoeffer outlines proceed from this initial need to protect and preserve bodily living.

Furthermore, protecting and supporting the integrity of individual bodies involves making space for the 'joys' and freedom of bodily life. Because God upholds and preserves the natural life of the individual person as an end in itself, 'there is a right to bodily joys without subordinating them to a further, higher purpose'.⁹⁶ This plays out in a number of Bonhoeffer's discussions of specific rights. He insists that a natural right to housing, for example, is not simply about 'protection against bad weather and the night' but facilitates and provides a 'space in which human beings may enjoy the pleasures of personal life'.⁹⁷ Later he insists that a right to marriage is grounded in the bodily freedom or 'free decision of each individual' over against all external factors or pressures.⁹⁸ These and other rights attest to God's work as it preserves and upholds the integrity and freedom of human beings in their natural, everyday living.

In his account, Bonhoeffer outlines a number of rights when critiquing encroachments and affirming the joys and freedoms of natural life. In some places he insists on a particular right unequivocally. For example, without mentioning the T4 programme explicitly, he opposes the idea of euthanasia simply in that it 'comes from the false presupposition that life consists only in its social utility'.⁹⁹ Against this presupposition, Bonhoeffer is adamant that all 'life created and preserved by God possesses an inherent right' irrespective of its usefulness.¹⁰⁰

In most other cases, however, his discussions are more fluid and his judgements less definitive. Indeed, Bonhoeffer's reasoning about natural rights displays a certain tentativeness. In an extended reflection on suicide (*Selbstmord*), he insists that the very freedom of bodily life is what makes this act possible which means that it cannot be judged 'before the forum of morality' but only by God.¹⁰¹ Elsewhere he affirms the 'right of developing life' while suggesting that responsible reason

---

95. DBWE 6: 214.

96. DBWE 6: 186.

97. DBWE 6: 187. What Bonhoeffer has in mind here is perhaps evident in a later manuscript of *Ethics*, 'The Christian and the Ethical as a Topic', in which he celebrates 'eating, drinking, sleeping, as well as conscious decision making and acting, working and resting, serving a purpose and just being without purpose, meeting obligations and following inclinations, striving and playing, abstaining and rejoicing'. DBWE 6: 365–6. Rights are about protecting and making space for this kind of natural, everyday living.

98. DBWE 6: 204.

99. DBWE 6: 204.

100. DBWE 6: 193. On similar grounds, Bonhoeffer affirms the rights and dignity of disabled persons or 'persons severely retarded from birth'. DBWE 6: 195.

101. That is, judged as a failure of faith that life (even in extreme difficulties) is a place of God's work and preserving presence.

can support the use of contraception. Indeed, he suggests that limiting family size might itself be a kind of 'natural' attempt to create a 'sort of breathing space for human nature' within growing populations.[102]

The point here is that Bonhoeffer is not so much appealing to rights in the abstract or as absolute. Rather he deploys natural rights language as part of his reasoning or discerning of the content and claims of natural life amidst pressing challenges. Indeed, he allows his understanding of rights to itself be shaped by these challenges and contexts. In this sense his reasoning about rights involves a continual openness to what is being given through the form of nature in a specific context. If discerning and protecting natural rights is about attesting to God's preserving work in natural life, then this may look very different in different times and places.

This relates back to Bonhoeffer's fundamental framing of natural life and natural rights as postlapsarian. Because rights can only ever attest to nature or natural life as a place of God's preserving work (not to the goodness of creation per se), they are reflective of and 'rooted in sin that is also at work in the natural'.[103] Bonhoeffer is clear that rights and the freedoms they support have at best a 'relative correctness';[104] they attest to God's work in ways that remain ambiguous and incomplete.

Conclusion: Assessing Bonhoeffer's version of NS4

In 'Natural Life' Bonhoeffer's central claim is that human nature or natural life has normative status because of how God preserves fallen human beings for Christ. After the fall, God uses the form of natural life to uphold and order human living in preparation for and anticipation of Christ. And we in our place attest to this preserving and ordering work by discerning and protecting natural rights.

Bonhoeffer's account of natural life clearly qualifies as a version of McKenny's NS4. As with the other two versions that McKenny outlines, Bonhoeffer holds that our human nature or natural life equips us for life with God, even if in a penultimate and less direct sense. Furthermore, Bonhoeffer holds that there is a certain sufficiency or adequacy of human nature or natural life for this task. Christ comes to and encounters us as fallen human beings, meaning that we do not need to strive to become more or other than what we are for this encounter.

---

102. DBWE 6: 208. When discussing birth control, Bonhoeffer also acknowledges tensions between different natural rights: the right to bodily communion, the right to reproduction and the right to control over one's own body. He finally concludes that 'the facts here are not so clear' and that 'we need to make room for the freedom of a conscience responsible to God'. DBWE 6: 210. In other words, Bonhoeffer proceeds in a way that leaves significant room for differing, even conflicting opinions.

103. DBWE 6: 182.

104. DBWE 6: 182.

Without needing to endorse every detail of Bonhoeffer's account, his understanding of human nature in terms of God's preserving work offers something distinctive as compared with the versions of NS4 drawn from Barth and Tanner. Bonhoeffer's version would seem to overcome or at least mitigate the two main shortcomings that McKenny identifies with these other versions. Bonhoeffer's positioning of natural life as a place of God's preserving work, as well as his attentiveness to the dangers of mechanization and vitalism (as making nature either a means to an end or an end in itself) allows him to stake out a 'plausible' version of NS4 between Tanner's and Barth's positions.[105]

On the one hand, Bonhoeffer's position seems to avoid Tanner's understanding of human nature as having normative status only in its capacity to be transformed into something else. By situating natural life as postlapsarian, he avoids the 'deificationist orientation' of Tanner's theology.[106] As we have seen, Bonhoeffer maintains a firm distinction between the normativity of nature (as penultimate) and God's ultimate and transformative work in Christ. He thereby distinguishes between our nature as fallen creatures and any transformation that we might undergo through God's work in Christ. As compared with Tanner, this means that he is better able to affirm the integrity and value of natural life as such. Natural life has integrity precisely as a place of God's preserving work.

On the other hand, by situating natural life as penultimate, Bonhoeffer avoids the main limitation McKenny associates with Barth's version of NS4. By understanding nature or natural life as a place of God's preserving work (not in terms of the goodness of creation per se), Bonhoeffer leaves more room for a final, eschatological transformation that will take us beyond our present state. In other words, he avoids coming so close to 'the notion of resurrection as a kind of resuscitation'.[107] By maintaining a distinction between natural life and our status as creatures and covenant partners, Bonhoeffer anticipates a more decisive break between this life and the life to come.[108]

Finally, what is at stake with Bonhoeffer's version of NS4 for negotiating and responding to challenges presented by biotechnology and enhancement? What does his specific account of nature and natural life have to offer with respect to these recent challenges? Without providing a basis for principled or outright opposition to the alternation or enhancement of nature, Bonhoeffer's version of NS4 arguably facilitates a more critical and cautious posture towards biotechnology.[109] Or, at

---

105. McKenny, *Biotechnology*, 181.
106. McKenny, *Biotechnology*, 157.
107. McKenny, *Biotechnology*, 181.
108. Similarly, Bonhoeffer's language of preservation leaves more room for acknowledging the presence of sin in the midst of nature and natural life as we experience it. As compared with Barth, Bonhoeffer gives greater emphasis to the deep ambiguities and conflicts that rend human nature and natural living in the here and now.
109. Does McKenny's care and 'even-handedness' when treating so many different positions in *Biotechnology* lead him to a position on biotechnogy that is too measured?

least, Bonhoeffer's account of natural life encourages close, sustained attention to how the pursuit of alteration and enhancement may be bound up with continuing (unnatural) attempts to resist and overcome bodily life and its claims.[110] Against the desire to escape nature and become more or other than what we already are, Bonhoeffer's specific version of NS4 encourages us to attend closely to natural life as a place of God's presence. In particular, his theology presses us to discern and uphold natural rights as a way of affirming and protecting natural, bodily existence and living.

See comments to this effect in Robert Song, 'Review of Gerald Mckenny's *Biotechnology, Human Nature and Christian Ethics*', *Theology* 123, no. 1 (2020): 46–7.

110. Whereas Barth encourages us to embrace aspects of our creaturely nature (i.e. relationality, integration and temporality) as good, Bonhoeffer focuses on our continuing attempts to flee from God's presence and work in natural life. Put differently, Bonhoeffer's version of NS4 encourages more direct attention to the (unnatural) impulses that are driving the current pursuit of biotechnological enhancement and alteration.

Chapter 8

SHOULD WE LIVE FOREVER? REFLECTING ON LIFE EXTENSION TECHNOLOGIES WITH BONHOEFFER AND KARL BARTH

In December 2016, the *Guardian* featured an article with the following headline: 'Ageing Process May Be Reversible, Scientists Claim'.[1] This brief article documents some results from experiments carried out upon mice at the Salk Institute in La Jolla, California. It summarizes research that utilized new forms of gene therapy, with the result that 'after six weeks of treatment, the animals looked younger, had straighter spines and better cardiovascular health, healed quicker when injured, and lived 30% longer'.[2]

The claims of the researchers who conducted the study are for the most part careful and restrained. They make it clear that it will be a decade or longer before this therapy could be extended to human beings, they make no claim that ageing and age-related diseases can on this basis be overcome entirely, and they reiterate that their primary concern is with improving health – with extending the healthspan in ageing and combatting age-related diseases – rather than with extending the lifespan per se.

Nonetheless, the article also makes clear the potential and dramatic impact of their findings. The researchers insist that we are increasingly coming to understand the internal genetic mechanisms that underlie and determine ageing processes. Within the coming decades, they speculate, it seems likely that therapies and technologies will be developed that can significantly delay, and possibly partially reverse, ageing processes in human beings, allowing us all to live much longer, healthier lives.

This headline and research is, of course, indicative of a much broader phenomenon: the rise of technologies and related discourses concerned with, or more implicitly contributing to, the extension of the human lifespan.[3] The concern of this present chapter, therefore, is in how we should respond to such technologies

---

1. Hannah Devlin, 'Ageing Process May Be Reversible, Scientists Claim', *Guardian*, 16 December 2016, https://www.theguardian.com/science/2016/dec/15/ageing-process-may-be-reversible-scientists-claim.

2. Devlin, 'Ageing Process May Be Reversible'.

3. For an accessible overview of this discourse, see O'Connell, *To Be a Machine*, 179–93.

and discourses theologically. What insights and resources can theology provide for negotiating proposals and attempts to combat ageing and radically extend the human lifespan?

If these questions and the technologies prompting them are in one sense novel, theologians have devoted significant time to reflecting on questions of finitude and death. In this chapter, I engage with the work of two modern theologians: Karl Barth and Bonhoeffer. Barth and Bonhoeffer provide rich and nuanced reflections on finitude and the limit of death in the context reflecting on creation and creaturely life. In the main part of this chapter, I explicate their approaches, drawing attention to some important differences. In the conclusion, I return to the issue of extending human life.

Barth and the freedom of finitude

In recent years, a number of theologians and Christian ethicists have responded to life extension technologies by drawing on Barth's theology, especially his treatments of temporality in III/2 of the *Church Dogmatics*. This includes established scholars such as Gerald McKenny and Robert Song,[4] as well as emerging scholars like Autumn Ridenour, Ashley Moyse and Cambria Kaltwasser.[5] Much of this scholarship has engaged with III/2 of the *Church Dogmatics*, in which Barth provides an extended reflection on temporality as part of a wider account of human beings as God's creatures and intended covenant-partners.

Barth frames his discussion of temporality in III/2 as follows: 'Man [sic] lives in the allotted span of his present, past, and future life. He who was before him and will be after him, and who therefore fixes the boundaries of his being, is the eternal God, his Creator and Covenant-partner. He is the hope in which man may live in his time.'[6] For Barth, God from eternity has fixed or allotted

---

4. See Robert Song, 'Technological Immortalization and Original Mortality: Karl Barth on the Celebration of Finitude', in *Immortal God, Immortal Life: Theological Investigations into the Concept of Technology*, ed. Philip G. Ziegler (London: T&T Clark Bloomsbury, 2016), 187–209; Gerald McKenny, 'Biotechnology and the Normative Signifcance of Human Nature: A Contribution from Theological Anthropology', *Studies in Christian Ethics* 26, no. 1 (2013): 18–36. See also my engagement with McKenny's *Biotechnology, Human Nature, and Christian Ethics* (Cambridge: Cambridge University Press, 2018) in Chapter 7 of this book.

5. See Autumn Ridenour, *Sabbath Rest as Vocation: Aging Toward Death* (London: T&T Clark Bloomsbury, 2018); Ashley Moyse, *Reading Karl Barth, Interrupting Moral Technique, Transforming Biomedical Ethics* (London: Palgrave Macmillan, 2015); Cambria Kaltwasser, 'Karl Barth on Death', in *The Wiley Blackwell Companion to Karl Barth*, ed. George Hunsinger and Keith Johnson (Oxford: Wiley Blackwell, 2020), 217–28.

6. Karl Barth, *Church Dogmatics: III/2*, ed. G. W. Bromiley and T. F. Torrance (London: T&T Clark, 1960), 437.

the time of human beings so that they might be God's creatures and covenant-partners. Accordingly, how we exist within time is integral to how God has determined us for intentional, embodied relationships with both God and one another.

In this reflection, Barth gives particular attention to the time of human beings as an 'allotted' time.[7] God fixes the time of human beings precisely as limited. That we are born, grow old and will eventually die is therefore essential for who we are before God and in relation to one another. In short, Barth affirms a limited lifespan is something that comes from God, and which should ultimately be recognized and embraced as such.

It should be noted, however, that Barth and his followers are not hereby claiming that a limited lifespan is a self-evident good, something that can be straightforwardly embraced on its own terms. Rather, Barth acknowledges that we continually resist and strive against the limit of our finitude: 'Human life as such will always abhor the suggestion that once it was not and one day it will be no longer, and that it is really to consist in this fulfilment which has a beginning and end, and has duration only between these points.'[8] In other words, we resist the ways in which our finitude relativizes and undermines our personal and collective identity and projects.

Furthermore, Barth holds that this resistance to finitude is not wholly or straightforwardly negative. Our resistance to a limited lifespan is not simply the result of the fall, but at least indirectly reflects our very status as God's creatures and intended covenant-partners. Barth maintains that our quest for more life, on one level at least, might be seen to reflect that we have been intended for perfection in our relationships with God and one another. Prima facie, a limited lifespan would seem to undermine the achievement of such perfection: 'What but an unlimited, permanent duration can be adequate for the fulfilment of this determination?'[9] That we are created and intended for perfection, therefore, would seem to require, or at least be assisted by, radically longer lives. As Gerald McKenny glosses this point, 'Life with God and our fellow humans is abundant life, and its very abundance seems to entail endless duration and unlimited time for perfection.'[10]

Yet despite this provisional endorsement, Barth and McKenny conclude that more time would not finally give us what we need: 'Even if it were an unlimited time, this could only mean the possibility of a constant reaching out to this perfection.'[11] More time, even unlimited time, would not allow us to achieve our intended creaturely perfection. For Barth, this is because time itself is not the problem that

---

7. Barth, *Church Dogmatics: III/2*, 554.
8. Barth, *Church Dogmatics: III/2*, 555.
9. Barth, *Church Dogmatics: III/2*, 556.
10. McKenny, *Biotechnology, Human Nature and Christian Ethics*, 167.
11. Barth, *Church Dogmatics: III/2*, 561.

we think it is.¹² We may well wish to live beyond our allotted lifespans, but any hope that this would lead to our fulfilment is illusory.¹³ As Robert Song osbserves, 'what human beings actually want is not everlasting time but deep fulfilment, and for such fulfilment additional time is finally of no benefit.'¹⁴

Indeed, Barth insists that the allotted time that we experience as a problem can, in fact, be ultimately embraced as a blessing and gift. Specifically, Barth holds that we can recognize a limited lifespan as a blessing, and not simply encounter it as a limit per se, once we recognize that it is *God* who has determined and limited life in this way: 'It makes all the difference whether we conceive our life as one which is abstractly limited or limited by God.'¹⁵ Accordingly, the problem with our desire to overcome a limited lifespan is that it misconstrues what time as such is. This desire and pursuit for more life construes time as *simply* something abstract and limiting, without recognizing God's hand and presence in this limiting. So, although we may be unable to directly and straightforwardly embrace finitude as something good, Barth holds that we can begin to do so once we recognize God's role in allotting time. We can begin to recognize and embrace our allotted time as integral to how God has created and prepared us for covenantal relationship.

In this context, Barth gives particular attention to some of the ways in which allotted or limited time makes us vulnerable, thereby opening and directing us to God and others. He insists that finitude is integral to our creaturely relationality and dependence. In other words, God in God's grace has given each of us allotted time or a limited lifespan as a way of reminding us of what we actually are: limited, relational beings who are meant to be dependent on God and one another. As Barth pointedly writes, 'man is not God, but a needy creature of God. He does not have his existence and nature autonomously, but as they are given by God.'¹⁶

This raises the question of *how*, exactly, we are to begin to recognize and embrace our allotted time as having come from God. How can we begin to move from our natural desire and quest for more life to the recognition that a limited lifespan is a gift and grace? For Barth, unsurprisingly, Jesus Christ is the key to this recognition. We come to recognize and embrace our allotted time through God's own work and revelation in Christ. In Christ and by looking to Christ, we can

---

12. As Barth continues, 'in relation to what he really asks for ... man would still be no better on the presupposition of the reality of this notion of infinite time than in the allotted span in which he actually has to live'. Barth, *Church Dogmatics: III/2*, 561.

13. Barth writes: 'If it [life] were without beginning or end it would always lack and seek this satisfaction.' Barth, *Church Dogmatics: III/2*, 562.

14. Song, 'Technological Immortalization and Original Mortality', 194.

15. Barth, *Church Dogmatics: III/2*, 563. Barth continues: 'The whole picture changes if we are not concerned abstractly and generally with the limitation of our life, but with the God who limits it; if we are not concerned abstractly and generally with allotted time, but with the reality of the God who allots it.'

16. Barth, *Church Dogmatics: III/2*, 525.

begin to recognize what we actually are as human beings, including as temporal beings who live with limited lifespans.[17]

Following Barth, this is because God in Christ has freely embraced an allotted time, and in so doing disclosed the nature and meaning of time as such. Specifically, that *God* took on a particular allotted time means that this time becomes the centre and meaning of all time.[18] The presence of the eternal God in the lifespan of Jesus as a first-century Jew endows time as such with eternal significance: 'This is the hidden meaning of all time, even of all other time.'[19] What is at stake with this claim? For Barth, this means that we should no longer try to understand time as abstract, as a horizon, but only with reference to Christ in his time. And this further means that we can properly understand our own allotted, particular time in relation to Christ's life: 'time as its historical form has its meaning in the particular time which God once took for the execution of this purpose, for establishing His covenant with man'.[20]

In summary, for Barth, as for McKenny, Song and others, we naturally and on our own terms experience our limited and allotted time as an abstract limit that stands over against us. By looking to Christ, however, Barth holds that we can begin to recognize and embrace this same limit as a sign of God's grace. We can recognize that God has given us an allotted time in order to remind us that we are *God's* creatures, and to free us from our futile attempts to secure our own meaning and fulfilment.

Bonhoeffer and the fall into finitude

In the turbulent months of early 1933, Bonhoeffer delivered a lecture course on the opening chapters of Genesis. His exposition displays Barth's influence,[21] but also has some notable theological differences. First, as compared with Barth, Bonhoeffer more firmly insists that our creaturely limits and finitude are implicated by the event of the fall. Second, this means that Bonhoeffer presents a different account of how God is present and at work in a finite life. While he still recognizes finitude as ultimately coming from God, he more closely identifies it with God's curse and judgement.

---

17. Don Wood summarizes this point: 'We are because he is ... we know ourselves as the ones we really are insofar as we know him as the one he is.' Wood, 'This Ability', 395.

18. Barth writes: 'It is the Creator of all reality distinct from himself who, taking flesh of our flesh, also took time, at the heart of what we think we know as time.' Barth, *Church Dogmatics: III/2*, 455.

19. Barth, *Church Dogmatics: III/2*, 456

20. Barth, *Church Dogmatics: III/2*, 456.

21. On Barth's impact on Bonhoeffer's early theology, see Mawson, *Christ Existing as Community*, 13–38.

In a central section in these lectures, Bonhoeffer reflects at length on Genesis 2:8-17: the two trees at the centre of the garden and God's promise to Adam that if he should eat from the tree of knowledge then he will surely die. Unpacking these verses, Bonhoeffer presents God's prohibition or limit as, paradoxically, God's blessing and grace to Adam: 'The prohibition means nothing other than this: Adam, you are who you are because of me, your Creator; so now be what you are.'[22] By giving Adam a concrete boundary or limit in the form of this prohibition, God recognizes and affirms Adam as a dependent creature. Even when God pronounces that transgressing this limit will lead to Adam's death, 'Adam understands this prohibition and the threat of death only as a renewed gift, as the grace of God.'[23]

Bonhoeffer goes on to claim, however, that what God had pronounced to Adam in the garden is what actually came to pass. Rather than suggesting that God relented following Adam and Eve's transgression, he holds that these first human beings did indeed come to die in the way that God had predicted: 'What does it mean to be dead? It does not mean the abolition of one's being a creature. Instead, it means no longer being able to live before God, but having to live before God … . It means receiving life from God no longer as grace coming from the centre and the boundary of one's own existence but as a commandment that stands in one's way.'[24] With the transgression of God's limit and prohibition, the first human beings lose their centre in God and thus lose themselves. Only the language of death does justice to the extent of this loss. With their transgression, as Bonhoeffer describes later in the lectures, Adam 'has ingested [*hineingegessen*] death into himself. Adam is dead before he dies.'[25]

However, this situation of '*living* death' means that the serpent's promise to Eve in Genesis 3 has also come to pass: 'You will not die at all. Instead God knows that on the day you eat from it your eyes will be opened, and you will be like God and know what good and evil is' (Gen. 3.4-5). With the transgression of God's boundary and prohibition, the first human beings continue to live, now with their newfound knowledge of good and evil. Indeed, part of God's judgement is precisely that these human beings *do* continue to live, even as those who have ingested death.

And this means that the serpent's promise is made part of God's Word and judgement. The nature of the fall is presented in Scripture through the juxtaposition of God's prohibition and the serpent's promise. Bonhoeffer reflects: ' "You will not die at all." "You shall die." These two statements mark the cleavage that now splits the world apart for Adam.'[26] After the fall, human beings are suspended between these two conflicting statements about who they are – living towards death, living as those already dead. As Bonhoeffer continues, 'The serpent was right: You will

22. DBWE 3: 85.
23. DBWE 3: 87.
24. DBWE 3: 90.
25. DBWE 3: 135.
26. DBWE 3: 113.

be like God; you will by no means die, that is, die the death that means ceasing to exist. But the Creator was also right: On the day that you eat from it you shall die, that is, die the death that means being *sicut deus*.'[27]

This account of the fall in terms of the serpent's promise and God's prohibition and judgement indicates Bonhoeffer's different understanding (than Barth) of the nature of limited time and finitude. For Bonhoeffer, the problem is not so much that we have forgotten that our allotted time is God's gift and a sign of God's grace. Rather, with the fall we have become imprisoned by life; we now experience our living and our having to live as a burden. When Adam ingested death into his life, death itself becomes central to life, including to our quest for more life: 'It is ... essentially a desperate, an unquenchable, an eternal thirst that Adam feels for life. It is essentially a thirst for death; the more passionately Adam seeks after life, the more completely he is ensnared by death.'[28]

Furthermore, Bonhoeffer's account of postlapsarian life as a living death – suspended between God's judgement and the serpent's promise – leads to differences in his Christology. If Barth understands God's entry into finite time in Christ as affirming an allotted lifespan, Bonhoeffer instead emphasizes God's presence in Christ in the very midst of conflicted, sinful human life.[29] Indeed, Christ's action on the cross enters into and discloses the contradiction of a humanity living in the midst of death. With Christ's death, Bonhoeffer concludes, 'the trunk of the cross becomes the wood of life [*zum Holze des Lebens*], and now in the midst of the world, on the accursed ground itself, life is raised up anew. ... What a strange paradise is this hill of Golgotha, this cross, this blood, this broken body. What a strange tree of life, this trunk on which the very God had to suffer and die.'[30]

---

27. DBWE 3 135.

28. DBWE 3: 143. In his later 'Natural life' manuscript for *Ethics*, Bonhoeffer presents this despairing pursuit of more life as vitalism: 'Vitalism inevitably ends in nihilism ... It is movement without end, without goal, movement into nothingness. It does not rest until it has drawn everything into this annihilating movement.' DBWE 6: 178. On this manuscript see the previous chapter.

29. For Bonhoeffer, God works with human beings precisely within their new conflicted situation: 'God accepts human beings for what they are, as fallen creatures. God affirms them in their fallenness. ... God's action accompanies humankind on its way.' For Bonhoeffer, God does not seek to overcome the fall, at least this side of the eschaton. As he writes: 'humankind remains in the twilight, and God affirms it in this, its new *sicut-deus*-world, by upholding and preserving it there'. For Bonhoeffer, this understanding of God as present and at work in the midst of human sin – upholding human beings and disclosing to them their sin – is exemplified by God's providing for them after the fall: 'By making cloaks for human beings God shows them that it is their wickedness that makes this necessary ... God's way of acting to preserve the world is to affirm the sinful world and to show it its limits by means of order.' DBWE 3: 139–40.

30. DBWE 3: 146.

Conclusion

What do Barth and Bonhoeffer have to offer with respect to technologies and discourses aiming to radically extend the human lifespan? On the one hand, as we have seen, Barth's theology in *Church Dogmatics* III/2 provides clear grounds for attending to and embracing our finitude or allotted time as integral to how God has determined us for embodied and dependent relationships. That we are born, grow old and die is a sign of God's goodness and grace. Our finitude thus reminds us who and what we properly are. And if we are also destined for perfection beyond our own limited lifespan, this will only be on God's terms and in God's own time.

Returning to our opening example, Barth's theology provides theological grounds for resisting, or at least for not actively pursuing, proposals and attempts to radically extend the human lifespan. Such proposals and attempts are misguided in that they misunderstand what time and finitude actually are. They express and are governed by a false and sinful understanding of finitude as an abstract limit that stands against us, rather than seeing time as something given and taken on by God. Embracing our allotted time as God's gift, therefore, frees us from the need to pursue radically longer lives.

While similar to Barth in many respects, Bonhoeffer gives greater emphasis to the situation of human beings as *fallen* creatures. He more closely links both life and death to our postlapsarian situation. The fall means that death has entered into life itself; life and its limits can now only be understood as suspended between God's prohibition and the serpent's promise. After the fall, living and dying both stand against us in ways that leave us in an impossible and irresolvable situation.

In terms of responding to life extension technologies and discourses, it is thus less clear that Bonhoeffer provides resources for outright resistance. Or at least Bonhoeffer seems less hopeful that we are able to recognize and embrace our finitude as a sign of God's goodness and grace. At the same time, Bonhoeffer provides a rich diagnosis of a conflict underlying our pursuit of more life. To repeat an earlier quote: 'It is … essentially a desperate, an unquenchable, an eternal thirst. … It is essentially a thirst for death; the more passionately Adam seeks after life, the more completely he is ensnared by death.'[31] Yet for Bonhoeffer, even in the midst of this contradiction and futile pursuit, Christ as the crucified one is present and at work.

---

31. DBWE 3: 143.

PART III

A COMMUNITY OF THE CROSS

Chapter 9

'ONLY THE SUFFERING GOD CAN HELP': BONHOEFFER AND JÜRGEN MOLTMANN ON DIVINE PASSIBILITY

In the last fifty years, many theologians have shifted away from traditional doctrinal emphases on the impassibility and immutability of God, instead seeking to understand and speak of God as suffering in and with creation. This is apparent across a range of theologians with diverse commitments and agendas: Protestant systematic theologians such as Eberhard Jüngel and Robert Jenson,[1] Catholics like Hans Urs von Balthasar and Jean Galot,[2] political theologians,[3] liberation and post-colonial theologians,[4] feminist theologians,[5] open theists,[6] process

---

1. See Eberhard Jüngel, *God's Being Is in Becoming: The Trinitarian Being of God in the Theology of Karl Barth*, trans. John Webster (Edinburgh: T&T Clark, 2001), 98–103; Robert Jenson, *Systematic Theology, Volume 1. The Triune God* (Oxford: Oxford University Press, 2012), 123–45.

2. Hans Urs von Balthasar, *Mysterium Paschale*, trans. Aiden Nichols, O.P. (Grand Rapids: Eerdmans, 1996), 89–147; Jean Galot, *Dieu Souffre-t-il?* (Paris: P. Lethielleux: 1976). On Galot, see also E. L. Mascall, *Whatever Happened to the Human Mind? Essays in Christian Orthodoxy* (London: SPCK, 1980), 87–93.

3. Dorothee Sölle, *Suffering*, trans. Everett Kalin (Minneapolis: Fortress Press, 1984), 121–50; Jürgen Moltmann, *The Crucified God: The Cross of Christ as the Foundation and Criticism of Christian Theology*, trans. R. A. Wilson and John Bowden (Minneapolis: Fortress Press, 1993), 200–90.

4. Kazoh Kitamori, *Theology and the Pain of God* (London: SCM Press, 1966).

5. Elizabeth Johnson, *She Who Is: The Mystery of God in Feminist Theological Discourse* (New York: Crossroad Publishing Company, 1992), 246–71; and Catherine LaCugna, *God For Us: The Trinity and the Christian Life* (New York: HarperCollins, 2000), 209–42.

6. John Sanders, *The God Who Risks: A Theology of Divine Providence* (Downers Grove: InverVarsity Press, 2009), 173–248; and Clark Pinnock, *Most Moved Mover: A Theology of God's Openness* (Grand Rapids: Baker and Paternoster, 2000).

theologians[7] and many others. Describing this situation in 1988, Paul Fiddes noted that 'whatever the popular view outside of academic theological circles, inside … the idea that God suffers hardly needs to be argued any longer'.[8]

One of the foremost proponents of this turn has of course been the German theologian Jürgen Moltmann. In the *Crucified God* (published in German in 1972) and *Trinity and the Kingdom* (in 1980), Moltmann presents a trinitarian theology of the cross, one which makes the cross constitutive for the very being and identity of God. Moreover, Moltmann insists that only an idea of God as suffering does justice to God's passionate love for and involvement with the world. For Moltmann, recognizing suffering as bound up with God's love facilitates greater openness to God's presence in the midst of human suffering and despair. On this basis, a theology of divine passibility provides the basis for Christian hope and action in the midst of worldly suffering and evil.

Contesting this turn to divine suffering, other theologians responded by defending traditional emphases on divine impassibility and immutability. In *Does God Suffer?*, for example, the Dominican Thomas Weinandy insists that God in Godself, in God's inner mystery and perfection, is necessarily incapable of suffering and change: 'To say that God suffers, even in a very restricted sense would, I fear, inevitably cause confusion and misunderstanding.'[9] While recognizing the pastoral concerns driving Moltmann's theology, Weinandy nonetheless insists that 'a passible God is actually less personal, loving, dynamic and active than an impassible God'.[10] Indeed, he suggests that maintaining a clear distinction between God's impassible divinity and Christ's human suffering is necessary for having a God who is ultimately able to overcome and redeem suffering in the world. As Gilles Emery makes this point, 'the immutability that is proper to God guarantees precisely the transcendence and the perfection of his free action'.[11]

In light of this turn and ensuing debate, my interest in this chapter is in how Bonhoeffer uses language of divine suffering in his late theology. In ways that resonate with Moltmann, Bonhoeffer famously proclaims in a letter from prison that 'only the suffering God [*der leidende Gott*] can help'.[12] Indeed, Moltmann and other proponents of divine passibility have often drawn on and appealed to

---

7. A. N. Whitehead and David Ray Griffin, eds, *Process and Reality: An Essay in Cosmology* (New York: The Free Press, 1978), 342–52.

8. Paul S. Fiddes, *The Creative Suffering of God* (Oxford: Oxford University Press, 1988), 1.

9. Thomas Weinandy, *Does God Suffer?* (Edinburgh: T&T Clark, 2000), 170.

10. Weinandy, *Does God Suffer?*, 26.

11. Gilles Emery, 'The Immutability of the Love of God and the Problem of Language Concerning the "Suffering God"', in *Divine Impassibility and the Mystery of Human Suffering*, ed. James F. Keating and Joseph Thomas White (Grand Rapids: Eerdmans, 2009), 29.

12. Bonhoeffer, 'To Eberhard Bethge', 16 July 1944, DBWE 8: 479. Bonhoeffer continues: 'It is not a religious act that makes one Christian, but sharing in God's suffering in the worldly life.' DBWE 8: 480.

Bonhoeffer in support of their position.[13] Nevertheless, in what follows I draw attention to some of the subtle yet important differences between how Bonhoeffer and Moltmann understand God's suffering.

Bonhoeffer's lectures on Christology

Scholars have long recognized the deeply Christological nature of Bonhoeffer's prison theology, including his statements about the suffering God.[14] Christians are those 'pulled along into the – messianic – suffering of God in Jesus Christ', as Bonhoeffer at one point writes.[15] To understand Bonhoeffer's use of this kind of language in his late theology, it will be useful to first turn to his more thoroughgoing treatment of Christology in some lectures from 1933.

In these lectures on Christology, Bonhoeffer develops his approach as a reflection on the Chalcedonian formula: 'One and the same Christ, Son, Lord, Only-begotten, acknowledged to be unconfusedly, unalterably, undividedly, inseparably in two natures.'[16] On the one hand, Bonhoeffer reads this formula as condemning various attempts to understand or conceptualize Christ directly. For Bonhoeffer, Chalcedon rules out attempts to conceptualize Christ's divinity and humanity by means of fixed or static philosophical concepts, that is, 'nature', 'person', and so forth. The basic problem with heresies such as Nestorianism or Monophysitism, for example, is that they begin with a fixed concept or preconceived idea of what is divine. They hold a particular idea of the divine and then proceed to approach or interpret Christ's humanity in ways that comport with this concept.[17] By beginning with a fixed idea of the divine, such heresies try to explain *how* Christ can be both divine and human, but they do so in ways that invariably compromise his full humanity.

On the other hand, Bonhoeffer maintains that the Chalcedonian formula is not in itself an attempt to establish or provide correct language for speaking about or understanding Christ, at least not straightforwardly. While this formula clearly

---

13. Moltmann, *The Crucified God*, 47. Also see Jürgen Moltmann, *A Broad Place: An Autobiography*, trans. Margret Kohl (Minneapolis: Fortress Press, 2009), 196.

14. Ernst Feil, *The Theology of Dietrich Bonhoeffer*, trans. Martin Rumscheidt (Minneapolis: Fortress Press, 1985), 90–5.

15. DBWE 8: 481. Just before asserting that 'only the suffering God can help', Bonhoeffer writes that '*Christ* helps us not by virtue of his omnipotence but rather virtue of weakness and suffering'. Emphasis added. DBWE 8: 47.

16. See Richard A. Norris Jr., ed., *The Christological Controversy: Sources of Early Christian Thought* (Philadelphia: Fortress Press, 1980), 159.

17. Bonhoeffer asserts that for the Monophysites, 'Christ is not an individual person; instead, he put on nature like a garment'. Bonhoeffer, 'Lectures on Christology', DBWE 12: 340–1. The Nestorians, by contrast, emphasize the necessary distance between Christ's divine and human natures.

affirms that Christ *is* both fully human and fully divine, it does not try to provide an explanation of *how* this is the case. Rather, in Bonhoeffer's reading, it simply advances a series of contradictory claims about Christ, thereby confounding or going 'beyond [its own] conceptual forms'.[18] In this way, he suggests, Chalcedon 'reveals the limitations of its own concepts' and indicates that in themselves 'these concepts are inappropriate and heretical forms'.[19] With this formula, concepts such as 'nature' and 'person' are juxtaposed and used in ways that stretch the ordinary meanings of these concepts to their breaking point.

This means that after Chalcedon the meaning and stability of ideas about divine and human natures can no longer be taken for granted. What Chalcedon affirms is that 'nothing can be known about [either] God or human being, until God has become a human being in Jesus Christ'.[20] In other words, we know who God is and what it means to be human only from Christ, and hence only by looking to Christ. Following Chalcedon, we can know and speak of the divine and human natures only in reference to their unity in Christ's person. Bonhoeffer's basic claim, therefore, is that if we attempt to speak of or know about God or human nature directly, otherwise than by looking to Christ, we move into abstraction and idealism.

It is on this basis that Bonhoeffer briefly criticizes attempts by Reformed theologians to understand the divine *logos* as existent outside of or alongside the incarnate Christ.[21] Such attempts try to go beyond or behind the Chalcedonian formula as it stands, that is, by referring to the divine nature apart from Christ's concrete personhood. According to Bonhoeffer, these are essentially attempts to hold back or protect a part of God from the concrete Christ. Against such attempts, he is adamant that 'the λόγος no longer exists otherwise than in the σάρξ. God is no longer other than the one who has become human'.[22] Similarly, he asserts that 'we should speak not of God becoming human [*das Menschwerden*] but of the God who became human [*der Menschgewordene*]'.[23] Whereas the former implies the possibility of knowledge of God prior to and apart from God's becoming this particular human being, the latter more clearly affirms that all knowledge of and speech about God begins and remains with Christ.

---

18. DBWE 12: 342.

19. In a later essay, Bonhoeffer reflects upon Chalcedon: 'Seldom was reason so willing to humiliate itself and surrender itself before the miracle of God as happened in these words.' Bonhoeffer, 'Meditation on Christmas', DBWE 15: 532.

20. DBWE 12: 352.

21. In his 1932 essay, 'Concerning the Christian Idea of God', Bonhoeffer writes: 'Since God is accessible only in his self-revelation, man can find God only in Christ. That does not exclude God's being elsewhere too, but he cannot and should not be grasped and understood except in Christ. God entered history and no human attempt can grasp him beyond this history.' Bonhoeffer, 'Concerning the Christian Idea of God', DBWE 10: 457.

22. DBWE 12: 344.

23. DBWE 12: 344.

9. 'Only the Suffering God Can Help'

For our interests, Bonhoeffer's reading of Chalcedon clearly distances him from Weinandy and other recent defenders of divine impassibility, namely, those who would insist on a clear distinction between the human and the divine natures of Christ in order to ensure God's freedom from creation. According to Bonhoeffer's logic, the problem with this move is that it again involves the attempt to speak of the divine nature prior to and apart from the person of Christ.[24] Theology should instead simply attend to God's revelation in Christ; it should not seek to speculate or speak about God (or humanity) otherwise or more directly.[25]

This leads to a further move that Bonhoeffer makes in his Christology lectures. In line with this reading of Chalcedon, Bonhoeffer endorses Luther's reading of the *communicatio idiomatum*: that what we know of Christ as a human being pertains to his divinity, and vice versa. This is encapsulated in Article VIII of the Formula of Concord: 'Everything human ... can be ascribed to and believed about God and everything divine ... can be ascribed to and believed about the human Christ.'[26] In endorsing this position, Bonhoeffer makes direct appeal to Luther: 'Luther spoke of the divinity and humanity of Jesus as if they were one nature' and 'felt it was important to see Christ's humanity as divinity'.[27] If Chalcedon means that we can only understand and speak of the divine and human natures in terms of their unity in Christ, then this in turn means we can only understand and speak of Christ's divinity with continual reference to his concrete humanity.

Bonhoeffer draws out the profound implications of this for theological language: 'If we are to describe Jesus as God, we would not speak of his being all-powerful or all-knowing; we would speak of his birth in a manager and of his cross.'[28] Accordingly, any knowledge of and speech about God proceeds

---

24. This sets Bonhoeffer apart from those who understand theology as properly beginning with the immanent Trinity. In his theology, Bonhoeffer consistently avoids speaking of trinitarian persons and relations. On this basis Christopher Holmes has suggested that Bonhoeffer's Christology is therefore in need of a 'trinitarian supplement', and that 'without such a supplement, Bonhoeffer's Christology is hamstrung'. Christopher R. J. Holmes, 'Bonhoeffer and Reformed Christology: Towards a Trinitarian Supplement', *Theology Today* 71, no. 1 (2014): 29. My worry with such a proposal is that it downplays the extent to which Bonhoeffer actively avoids (and not just neglects) appealing to the immanent Trinity. On this issue also see DeJonge, *Bonhoeffer's Theological Formation*, 106-14.

25. Bonhoeffer writes: 'The point of critical theology is to indicate the limits of every assertion [as they are found] in the actual reality of Jesus Christ.' DBWE 12: 352.

26. DBWE 12: 345. In his 1937 'Meditation on Christmas', Bonhoeffer again quotes Luther in relation to this formula: 'Wherever you can say, "Here is God", there you must also then say, "Christ the man is also there". And if you point out a place where God is and not the man, the person would already be divided ... No my friend, wherever you place God for me, there you must also place the humanity for me.' DBWE 15: 533.

27. DBWE 12: 346.

28. DBWE 12: 354.

from and depends on the life and death of Christ as a human being, meaning that concepts such as impassibility or immutability have limited value for theology. We know and speak of God in terms of Christ's concrete humanity, or, as Luther succinctly formulates this point: 'Christ alone, and no other God.'[29]

To be clear, Bonhoeffer maintains that the humanity of Christ does not provide a basis for knowing or speaking of God directly and unambiguously. This is because of the particular form of Christ's concrete existence as divine and human: 'This God-human [*Gott-Mensch*] is veiled in his existence as the humiliated one.'[30] When we look to the person of Christ in the Gospels, what we see is a humiliated human being, even a 'sinner among sinners'.[31] In Christ, God is at once revealed and hidden in suffering and crucifixion. In the final part of his lectures, Bonhoeffer thus describes this form as the stumbling block that frustrates and prevents any direct recognition of Christ for who he is.[32]

At the same time, however, Bonhoeffer insists that it is this hidden presence of God (and true humanity) under the form of Christ's suffering and humiliation that facilitates faith. By confounding our own attempts to directly recognize and understand Christ as the God-human, this form of suffering and humiliation allows for something deeper. As Bonhoeffer writes, 'Faith exists when I yield myself to God ... even and especially there where it goes against all visible appearances. Only when I give up having visible confirmation do I believe in God.'[33] Put differently, the form of Christ's suffering and humiliation helps us to relinquish our own preconceived notions of what God is or should be. This form means that we no longer have to rely upon our own concepts or ideas about God (i.e. concepts such as omnipotence, impassibility, etc.).[34] By attending to how God comes to us in Christ's humiliation and crucifixion, we allow God to begin to teach us who God actually is.

---

29. Martin Luther, 'On the Councils of the Church', in *Luther's Works, Volume 41*, 286. Along similar lines, in the Heidelberg Disputation Luther writes: 'None of us can talk adequately or profitably about God's glory and majesty unless we see God also in the lowliness and humiliation of the cross.' Martin Luther, 'Heidelberg Disputation', in *Luther's Works, Volume 31*, 52.

30. DBWE 12: 356.

31. DBWE 12: 356. Bonhoeffer's assertion in his lectures that 'Christ took on all the mortifying aspects of being human; otherwise he could not help us in our σάρξ' (DBWE 12: 356) anticipates the later claim in his prison letters that 'only the suffering God can help'. Bonhoeffer, 'To Eberhard Bethge', 16 July 1944, DBWE 8: 479.

32. DBWE 12: 355–60.

33. DBWE 12: 358.

34. Moltmann attributes the emergence of these concepts within Christianity to the influence of Platonic and Greek philosophy. See Moltmann, *The Crucified God*, 127–35.

Bonhoeffer's prison theology

The language of the suffering God is at the very heart of Bonhoeffer's prison theology. In a series of letters, poems and other fragments composed during his incarceration, Bonhoeffer famously proposes a form of 'religionless Christianity' that takes seriously the 'world come of age'.[35] Moreover, he begins to reflect upon the implications of such religionlessness and worldliness for theological language; for concepts such as 'repentance, faith, justification, and sanctification'.[36]

In this late theology, Bonhoeffer is once again critical of attempts to understand or approach God conceptually: 'How do we talk about God – without religion, that is, without the temporally conditioned presuppositions of metaphysics, the inner life, and so on?'[37] Accordingly, for Bonhoeffer, a religionless Christianity is one that no longer depends upon metaphysics or inwardness as prerequisites for faith. A religionless Christianity neither presupposes a 'religious a priori' in human beings nor insists upon God as a 'working hypothesis' for 'morality, politics, and the natural sciences'.[38] This kind of Christianity moves beyond many of the ways in which human beings have traditionally constructed and called upon God.[39]

Bonhoeffer's discussion of 'the world come of age' is similarly directed against conceptual approaches to God. In his analysis, one result of the progressive secularization of thought and culture – of God having been 'pushed out of a world come of age'[40] – is that modern Christianity has often problematically sought to retain a place for God in 'ultimate questions' and 'unsolved problems'.[41] Bonhoeffer suggests that this is again an attempt to determine God from the standpoint of our own needs and ideas. The resulting God is a *'deus ex machina'* who is to 'solve insoluble problems or provide strength when human powers fail'.[42] Bonhoeffer endorses the world come of age, therefore, as an opportunity for something

---

35. Bonhoeffer, 'To Eberhard Bethge', 30 April 1944. DBWE 8: 363. Bonhoeffer writes: 'How can Christ become Lord of the religionless as well? Is there such a thing as a religionless Christian? If religion is only the garb in which Christianity is clothed – and this garb has looked very different in different ages – what then is religionless Christianity?'

36. Bonhoeffer, 'To Eberhard Bethge', 5 May 1944. DBWE 8: 373.

37. Bonhoeffer, 'To Eberhard Bethge', 30 April 1944. DBWE 8: 364.

38. Bonhoeffer, 'To Eberhard Bethge', 16 July 1944. DBWE 8: 478.

39. Bonhoeffer endorses Barth's critique of religion: Barth 'led the God of Jesus Christ forward to battle against religion'. However, Bonhoeffer then insists that Barth himself did not go far enough. Barth effectively mobilized Christ against religious metaphysics and inwardness, but gave 'no concrete guidance' for 'the nonreligious interpretation of theological concepts'. Consequently, according to Bonhoeffer, Barth lapses into a 'positivism of revelation' by positing a new theological system or edifice in the place of religion. Bonhoeffer, 'To Eberhard Bethge', 8 June 1944. DBWE 8: 429.

40. Bonhoeffer, 'To Eberhard Bethge', 30 June 1944, DBWE 8: 450.

41. Bonhoeffer, 'To Eberhard Bethge', 29 May 1944, DBWE 8: 407.

42. Bonhoeffer, 'To Eberhard Bethge', 30 April 1944, DBWE 8: 366.

richer and deeper: 'The world that has come of age is no longer an occasion for polemics and apologetics' but should itself be understood 'from the Gospel and Jesus Christ'.[43]

In his letters, Bonhoeffer's discussions of religionlessness and the world come of age lead to and culminate in the language of the suffering God: 'One may say that the previously described development toward the world's coming of age, which has cleared the way by eliminating a false notion of God, frees us to see the God of the Bible, who gains ground and power in the world by being powerless.'[44] In particular, these developments help to release us from our dependence upon our own ideas about God, that is, in terms of power or immutability. These developments help us instead to attend to a biblical God who comes to us in and as the suffering and crucified Christ.[45]

Bonhoeffer reiterates this need to relinquish our own concepts and needs as a basis for approaching God in his brief 'Outline for a Book'.[46] He writes: 'Who is God? Not primarily a general belief in omnipotence.'[47] Rather, he continues, we know God in 'the Crucified One'.[48] As with the earlier lectures on Christology, this means that 'we must immerse ourselves again and again … in Jesus's life, his sayings, actions, suffering, and dying in order to recognize what God promises and fulfils'.[49] In Bonhoeffer's prison theology, knowing God in Christ entails attending to Christ as he comes to us in Scripture: 'The Bible directs people towards the powerless and suffering of God.'[50]

This shift from attempting to approach God on our own terms to recognizing the one who comes to us as Christ is at the centre of Bonhoeffer's short poem, 'Christian and Heathens'.[51] In the poem's first stanza, he writes: 'People go to God when they're in need, plead for help, pray for blessings and bread.' All people instinctively appeal to God on the basis of our own human needs and desires. In the second stanza, however, he disrupts and overturns this movement: 'People go to God when God's in need / find God poor, reviled, without shelter or bread / see God devoured by sin, weakness, and death / Christians stand by God in God's own pain [*Leiden*].'[52] A deeper encounter with God involves relinquishing our own

---

43. Bonhoeffer, 'To Eberhard Bethge', 8 June 1944, DBWE 8: 431.

44. Bonhoeffer, 'To Eberhard Bethge', 16 July 1944, DBWE 8: 479–80.

45. On the relationship between Christology and Scripture in Bonhoeffer's theology, see Chapters 2 and 3.

46. This outline was composed in August 1944 after the assassination attempt on Adolf Hitler had failed. Bonhoeffer provides brief notes and possible headings for three chapters.

47. Bonhoeffer, 'Outline for a Book'. DBWE 8: 501. As Bonhoeffer continues, 'That is not a genuine experience of God but just a prolongation of a piece of the world.'

48. DBWE 8: 501.

49. Bonhoeffer, 'To Eberhard Bethge', 21 August 1944, DBWE 8: 515.

50. Bonhoeffer, 'To Eberhard Bethge', 16 July 1944, DBWE 8: 479.

51. Bonhoeffer enclosed this poem with a letter to Bethge on 20 July 1944. For a rich discussion of this poem and its theology see Wannenwetsch, 'Christians and Pagans', 175–96.

52. Bonhoeffer, 'Christians and Heathens', DBWE 8: 460.

needs and concepts as a basis for approaching God. We now recognize and stand beside the God who comes to us in God's own pain and suffering. We stand beside the one who has been 'devoured by sin, weakness and death', embracing the one who suffers in and as the concrete Christ.[53]

Moreover, by disrupting and subverting our own concepts of divinity, for Bonhoeffer the suffering God frees us to properly be in the world. In light of God's suffering, 'our lives are *allowed* to be "worldly", that is, we are delivered from false religious obligations and inhibitions'.[54] That God is fully present in the world in Christ's suffering means that we too are freed to embrace the world and recognize its claims upon us. The suffering God releases us from our dependence on religion to secure meaning or redemption from beyond this world.[55] As Bonhoeffer makes this point in another letter, 'the Christian is not a *homo religiosus* but simply a human being, in the way Christ was a human being'.[56]

In his 'Outline for a Book', Bonhoeffer gives further clarity on what it means for God to release us into worldliness. If we know of God only in the suffering of Christ, then this means that 'our relationship to God is no "religious" relationship to some highest, most powerful and best being imaginable … transcendence. Instead, our relationship to God is bound up with a life of "being there for others" through participation in the being of Jesus'.[57] The God who suffers frees us to follow Christ by attending to the needs of those around us: 'the neighbour within reach in any given situation'.[58]

Following Bonhoeffer, this indicates what it means to be Christian. To be Christian involves relinquishing our own ideas about God and instead attending to God in God's own suffering presence. Bonhoeffer is clear, however, that this is not something that we ourselves achieve or enact. In his prison theology, he emphasizes the responsive nature of our participation in God's suffering. We are 'pulled along into the suffering of God' and 'pulled into walking the path that Jesus walks'.[59] We learn who God is only in the suffering of Christ, and we learn what it means to follow this Christ only in following him.

---

53. DBWE 8: 460.

54. Bonhoeffer, 'To Eberhard Bethge', 16 July 1944, DBWE 8: 480. Emphasis original. As Bonhoeffer immediately continues, 'it is not a religious act that makes one Christian, but rather sharing in God's suffering in the worldly life'.

55. Bonhoeffer writes: 'Unlike believers in the redemption myths, Christians do not have an ultimate escape route out of their earthly tasks and difficulties into eternity.' Bonhoeffer, 'To Eberhard Bethge', 25 July 1944, DBWE 8: 488.

56. Bonhoeffer, 'To Eberhard Bethge', 21 July 1944, DBWE 8: 485. As Bonhoeffer continues, 'I think Luther lived in this kind of worldliness.'

57. Bonhoeffer, 'Outline for a Book', DBWE 8: 501.

58. DBWE 8: 501.

59. Bonhoeffer, 'To Eberhard Bethge', 16 July 1944, DBWE 8: 480.

Finally, this means there is no clear pattern or stable model for being Christian or living by faith.[60] In one letter Bonhoeffer briefly reviews a number of examples of discipleship found in Scripture, including those of Zacchaeus, the shepherds, the centurion at Capernaum, Cornelius in Acts and others: 'The only thing they have in common', he reflects, 'is their sharing in the suffering of God in Christ. That is their "faith."'[61] We cannot learn what faith or sharing in God's own suffering means, therefore, in advance or in abstraction from following Christ's call.[62] As Bonhoeffer makes this same point in his earlier *Discipleship*: 'How should disciples know what their cross is? They will receive it when they begin to follow the suffering Lord. They will recognize their cross in communion with Christ.'[63]

In summary, Bonhoeffer's language of 'religionlessness' and 'the world come of age' is intended to disclose what it means to properly live before God and in the world, that is, without the support of traditional ways of conceptualizing or depending upon the divine. Religionless Christianity involves a willingness to have our notions of who and what God is interrupted and reshaped; it involves allowing God to come to us on God's own terms. In particular, it involves standing by and attending to the one who comes to us and is present in the world in the human suffering of Christ. And this means that we are Christians only by holding in faith that this one who suffers and dies for us really is God. We hold in faith that the one who has come to us in weakness and sin is the one who has saved us.

Moltmann's trinitarian theologia crucis

In order to bring further clarity to Bonhoeffer's language of God's suffering, it will be useful to draw some comparisons with Jürgen Moltmann's more recent and better-known account of divine passibility. Like Bonhoeffer, Moltmann makes Luther's *theologia crucis* the centre of his theology. In *The Crucified God*, he provides a rich and nuanced account of this *theologia crucis*, positioning it against both theistic and atheistic attempts to approach God or divinity apart from the cross.[64] Moltmann too insists that we can properly know and speak of God only

---

60. Bonhoeffer is clear that suffering as such does not provide a principle or method for sharing in God's suffering. It is only being drawn into God's suffering that provides the basis for faith and worldliness. Indeed, Bonhoeffer writes: 'If one has completely renounced making something of oneself ... then one takes seriously no longer one's own suffering but rather the suffering of God in the world.' DBWE 8: 482. God's presence and suffering in the world direct us away from ourselves and towards the suffering of God and others.

61. DBWE 8: 481.

62. Luther writes: 'The only reason they [Christians] must suffer is that they steadfastly adhere to Christ and God's word, enduring this for the sake of Christ.' Luther, 'On the Councils and the Church', 165-7.

63. DBWE 4: 89.

64. See Moltmann, *The Crucified God*, 207-27.

in the human suffering and humiliation of Christ: 'We see God most clearly in Christ's death upon the cross. God is not greater than he is in this humiliation.'[65] Like Bonhoeffer, he again frames this in terms of Luther's radical reading of the *communicatio idiomatum*: 'The divine being must encompass the human being and vice versa.'[66]

Moltmann also recognizes that this *theologia crucis* firmly places the human being into worldliness. He follows Luther, who 'sees in the cross God's descent to the level of our sinful nature and our death, not so that man is divinized, but so that he is de-divinized and given new humanity in the community of the crucified Christ'.[67] Moltmann thus endorses Luther's emphasis on God embracing human beings and thereby freeing them to properly be in the world. Moltmann's own theology of the crucified God is directed towards engagement with and action in the world.

Nonetheless, Moltmann departs from Luther (and Bonhoeffer) when he insists that this *theologia crucis* needs to be developed in a more explicitly trinitarian direction. Indeed, he criticizes Luther for failing to clearly distinguish between trinitarian persons and relations in his language of the suffering God: '[Luther] left out of his account the relationships in which this suffering and dying person of the Son is involved with the persons of the Father and the Spirit … his Christology was formed in terms of incarnation and the theology of the cross, but not always in trinitarian terms.'[68] In other words, Luther failed to identify the specific roles of the Son and the Father with respect to the work of cross. And Moltmann attributes this failure to Luther's reliance upon a Chalcedonian Christology.[69] Luther's language of the divine and human natures in Christ leads to paradoxical and convoluted ways of speaking of the suffering God: 'God died the death of the godless on the cross and yet did not die. God is dead and yet not dead.'[70]

Moltmann insists that more explicitly trinitarian language can bring clarity to this situation: 'The theological concept for the perception of the crucified Christ is the doctrine of the Trinity.'[71] Or, as he elsewhere writes, 'it is advisable to abandon the concept of God and to speak of the relationships of the Son and the Father and the Spirit at the point at which "God" might be expected to be mentioned'.[72]

---

65. Moltmann, *The Crucified God*, 205.
66. Moltmann, *The Crucified God*, 205.
67. Moltmann, *The Crucified God*, 213.
68. Moltmann, *The Crucified God*, 235. Consequently, Moltmann continues, Luther arrives 'at paradoxical distinctions between God and God: between the God who crucifies and the crucified God'.
69. Against Luther, Moltmann writes: 'We have not interpreted the death of Jesus as a divine–human event but as a trinitarian event between the Son and the Father.' *The Crucified God*, 245.
70. Moltmann, *The Crucified God*, 244.
71. Moltmann, *The Crucified God*, 240.
72. Moltmann, *The Crucified God*, 207.

Rather than using the language of God in relation to the cross, it would be better to think and speak in terms of the specific persons and relations of Father, Son and Holy Spirit.

On this basis Moltmann describes and locates the cross as a 'trinitarian event' between the Father, Son and Spirit. He employs trinitarian language to identify the distinct ways in which the particular persons of the Trinity each suffers in and through the cross: 'The Son suffers dying, the Father suffers in the death of the Son.'[73] The Father suffers by surrendering the Son to crucifixion, whereas the Son suffers by surrendering to the cross in obedience to the Father. The Father and Son are united in suffering and surrender, even while suffering and surrendering to one another in their own distinct ways.[74]

Moltmann's claim, therefore, is that attending to these more particular roles of trinitarian persons allows us to better recognize that God's suffering on the cross is ultimately God's love. It allows us to recognize that the suffering of the Father and the Son is not simply 'unwilling suffering', but instead an 'accepted suffering' precisely as the 'suffering of love'.[75] That the Father and the Son surrender to one another means that each willingly embraces their suffering for the sake of the other. By speaking of God as Trinity, we can better recognize that God's suffering is a 'freedom to suffer as a result of the otherness of the other'.[76] This loving surrender for the other precedes and defines the event of the cross, thereby redeeming this suffering and showing it to be meaningful.[77]

Moltmann gives somewhat less attention to pneumatology in his trinitarian *theologia crucis*, but the Holy Spirit too plays a crucial role. Specifically, the work of the Spirit is to open up and extend this event of God's suffering love to the world. The Spirit draws the world and all human history and suffering into the sacrificial love of the Father and the Son.[78] Through the Spirit, Moltmann writes, 'all human history, however much it may be determined by guilt and death, is taken up into this "history of God", i.e. into the Trinity, and integrated into the future of the "history of God".'[79] Through the work of the Spirit, God's trinitarian love encompasses all human history and provides a standpoint from which to interpret

---

73. Moltmann, *The Crucified God*, 243.

74. Moltmann writes: 'In the cross, Father and Son are most deeply separated in forsakenness and at the same time are most inwardly one in their surrender.' Moltmann, *The Crucified God*, 244.

75. Moltmann, *The Crucified God*, 230.

76. Moltmann, *The Crucified God*, 230.

77. As Moltmann writes, 'God allows himself to be forced out. God suffers, God allows himself to be crucified and is crucified, and in this consummates his unconditional love that is so full of hope.' Moltmann, *The Crucified God*, 248.

78. Moltmann writes: 'What proceeds from this event between Father and Son is the Spirit which justifies the godless, fills the forsaken with love and even brings the dead alive.' Moltmann, *The Crucified God*, 244.

79. Moltmann, *The Crucified God*, 246.

it. In this way the Spirit gives the cross its eschatological significance: 'The Trinity ... presses towards eschatological consummation, so that the "Trinity may be all in all", or put more simply, so that "love may be all in all".'[80]

All of this means that Moltmann's trinitarian *theologia crucis* is in the final instance a theology of hope.[81] The recognition that God's loving surrender precedes and redeems all human history and suffering provides a foundation for hope in the depths of our own experiences of suffering. As Moltmann writes, it is 'the ground for a love which is stronger than death and can sustain death. It is the ground for living with the terror of history and the end of history, and nevertheless remaining in love and meeting what comes in openness for God's future.'[82] A trinitarian theology of the suffering God, therefore, allows for recognizing the depth of worldly suffering while still retaining hope in its midst. This in turn provides a basis for human freedom and action in the world: 'Freedom in the light of hope is the creative passion towards the possible.'[83] For Moltmann, a theology of the suffering God provides the possibility for properly recognizing and responding to a suffering world.

Bonhoeffer, Moltmann and theological language

There are subtle yet important differences between Moltmann's explicitly trinitarian *theologia crucis* and Bonhoeffer's Chalcedonian Christology.[84] As we have seen, Moltmann positions his trinitarian *theologia crucis* as an attempt to bring clarity to Luther's convoluted and paradoxical ways of speaking of God's suffering. At this point Bonhoeffer stands much closer to Luther. Specifically, Bonhoeffer's insistence that Chalcedon places limits on attempts to understand or conceptualize God stands in contrast to Moltmann's pursuit of clarity. Bonhoeffer writes: 'God as human being and human being as God must be held together in our thinking at the risk of sacrificing the rationality of such an assertion.'[85] This insistence also underlies Bonhoeffer's reflections on Christ as a stumbling block in the final section of the 1933 Christology lectures; Christ's suffering and crucifixion is an offence to human thinking in a way that makes room for faith. For Bonhoeffer,

---

80. Moltmann, *The Crucified God*, 255.

81. See Jürgen Moltmann, *Theology of Hope: On the Ground and Implications of a Christian Eschatology*, trans. James W. Leitch (London: SCM, 1964). And see also Moltmann's more recent *Ethics of Hope*.

82. Moltmann, *The Crucified God*, 278.

83. Moltmann, *Trinity and the Kingdom*, 217.

84. To be clear, Bonhoeffer is not anti-trinitarian or against trinitarian theology. When he does use such language, however, it tends be about God as *creator*, *reconciler* and *redeemer*, not triune persons or relations as such. And he maintains the centrality of Christ even in discussions of God as creator or redeemer.

85. DBWE 12: 340.

the point is not to better interpret or conceptualize God's suffering in Christ, but rather (as quoted earlier) to 'yield to God ... even and especially there where it goes against all visible appearances'.[86]

On this basis Bonhoeffer also gives more attention to the structure and form of Christ's person as *'pro-me'* or *'pro-nobis'*.[87] That Christ as the God-human is a paradox or stumbling block for human thinking means we have no independent vantage point with respect to Christ.[88] In his lectures, Bonhoeffer asserts that 'the being of Christ's person is essentially related to me ... The very core of his person is *pro-me*'.[89] We know and encounter Christ only as he comes to us and is related to us, not otherwise or more directly: 'I can never think of Jesus Christ in his being-in-himself, but only in his relatedness to me.'[90]

This commitment is apparent in Bonhoeffer's understanding of theological language as such. As we have seen, he maintains that theology cannot be, in the first instance, an attempt to understand or speak about God or Christ in the abstract, but only a kind of thinking and speaking that proceeds from the particular way that God comes to us in and as Christ. As Bonhoeffer writes elsewhere, 'theological thinking is not a construction a priori, but a posteriori'.[91] His basic point, then, is that we can only know of or speak about God by attending to how we ourselves are being formed by Christ.[92]

By contrast, Moltmann's attempt to understand the person of Christ primarily in relation to the Father (and Spirit) less clearly maintains this *pro-me* or existential structure. Moltmann's trinitarianism subtly shifts an emphasis away from theology as language *before* God (*coram Deo*), in its a posteriori attentiveness to Christ's call, to language *about* divine persons and relations. For Moltmann, the point seems to be to better understand Christ's suffering as the Son's loving surrender to the Father. In this way Moltmann's theology operates as a third-person discourse. Theology is the attempt to rightly speak about and understand God as Trinity, although in a way that also necessarily leads to engagement with and action in the world.

Finally, this demonstrates a difference at the level of anthropology. Moltmann's trinitarian *theologia crucis* displays greater confidence that human beings are able to know and speak of God. It displays more confidence that human beings

---

86. DBWE 12: 358.

87. That is, 'for me' or 'for us'. For more on Bonhoeffer on promeity, see Philip G. Ziegler, 'Christ for Us Today – Promeity in the Theologies of Bonhoeffer and Kierkegaard', *International Journal of Systematic Theology* 15, no. 1 (2013): 25–41.

88. In light of the encounter with Christ, 'the "who question" interrogates the very existence of the one asking it'. DBWE 12: 303.

89. DBWE 12: 314.

90. DBWE 12: 314.

91. Bonhoeffer, 'Concerning the Christian Idea of God', DBWE 10: 454.

92. On being formed by Christ, see Bonhoeffer's manuscript 'Ethics as Formation', in DBWE 6: 92–102.

are in a position to grasp the nature of God's suffering, as the sacrificial love of both the Father and the Son, and to then draw from this knowledge as a basis for interpreting and responding to reality. By contrast, Bonhoeffer's Christological approach places less confidence in human agency and reason; it consistently keeps an emphasis upon God's activity and on human beings as responding to or being drawn into this activity. For Bonhoeffer, the language of the suffering God thus marks the limits of attempts to theologically grasp or understand God. As he writes in an earlier essay, 'The real study of *theologia sacra* begins when, in the midst of questioning and seeking, human beings encounter the cross; when they recognize the endpoint of all their own passions in the suffering of God at the hands of humankind, and realize that their entire vitality stands under judgment.'[93]

Conclusion

At the beginning of this chapter, I indicated that my interest is in how Bonhoeffer uses the language of the suffering God in his late theology. My claim is that Bonhoeffer uses this language in ways that differ from Moltmann and other more recent advocates (and also opponents) of divine passibility.[94]

These differences are already anticipated in the main title of my chapter, 'How God Suffers', which itself has two possible meanings. The first and more common of these meanings follows the *interrogative* sense of the word 'how', as in questions like 'how *does* God suffer?' or 'how *is* God suffering?' According to this meaning, the title 'how God suffers' signals an intention to take a position on the questions at the heart of the recent debates about divine passibility. Is God capable of suffering? And what is at stake with this question for responding to suffering in the world?

As we have seen, these kinds of questions are central to Moltmann's trinitarian *theologia crucis*. For Moltmann, it is necessary for God to be capable of suffering. Indeed, he insists that 'a god who is incapable of suffering is a being who cannot be involved ... He cannot weep for he has no tears. But the one who cannot suffer cannot love either.'[95] It is only a God who suffers who is able to love.

---

93. This is the essay 'What Should a Student of Theology Do Today', DBWE 12: 433. Bonhoeffer continues: 'It is about responsible study and listening, becoming attentive to the Word of God, which has been revealed right here in this world; it is toning down one's self in the face of what is far and away the most important matter.' On this essay, see also Chapter 1.

94. As indicated earlier, Thomas Weinandy's driving question (the title of his book) is 'does God suffer?', and his interest is in the problematic implications of an affirmative response to this question. Moltmann and Weinandy thus pursue and explore the same basic question with respect to God, even while arriving at opposite answers.

95. Moltmann, *The Crucified God*, 222. Moltmann makes this same point more positively: 'The one who is capable of love is also capable of suffering, for he also opens himself to the suffering which is involved in love.' Moltmann, *The Crucified God*, 230.

There is, however, a second, less obvious meaning of the main title of this chapter, 'how God suffers'. This meaning is tied to the more emphatic sense of the word 'how', as found in exclamations such as 'how wonderful to see you' or 'how I wish things were different'. Following this minority report, the word 'how' would not so much signal a question or explanation, but rather it intensifies what follows. In light of an encounter with the crucified Christ, we exclaim or cry out, 'how God suffers!'

This indicates what Bonhoeffer seems to be pursuing with the language of the suffering God in his late theology. In other words, Bonhoeffer has little interest in speculation or debates about whether God is able to suffer, or even what suffering might mean for who God is. In his earlier Christology lectures, he rules out such questions explicitly. With 'how' language, he writes, 'the object [i.e. God] is defined, recognized and understood by means of its possibilities, by means of its "how"'.[96] Such questions about God proceed from and remain tied to our own conceptions and ideas about what is possible for God. Instead, Bonhoeffer proposes that we stand with God and attend to the one who has come to us (and is for us) in Christ's suffering and humiliation. For Bonhoeffer, the language of the suffering God affirms the cross as the beginning and end of all theological language.

---

96. DBWE 12: 303. Bonhoeffer continues: 'That we are always asking the "how" question shows we are chained to our own authority. It is the *cor curvum in se*.'

Chapter 10

THE SPIRIT AND THE COMMUNITY: PNEUMATOLOGY AND ECCLESIOLOGY IN ROBERT JENSON, REINHARD HÜTTER AND BONHOEFFER

If Luther achieved a certain notoriety with the claim that 'there is no sinner so great as the Christian church',[1] he was equally adamant that this *same* church is instituted by Christ and a work of the Holy Spirit. According to Luther, we are to have faith in the holiness of the existing church, even in spite of its apparent sinfulness.

Luther's approach to the church – as simultaneously holy and sinful – takes on renewed importance in light of recent ecclesial conflicts and scandals.[2] How are we today to attend properly to the realities of sin and the fallibility in the church, without making this the final word about what the church is? How are we to have faith that the existing church is, in fact, the body of Christ and a work of the Spirit, without thereby romanticizing the activities and relationships of its members?

These questions can be situated in relation to an increasing number of theologians and ethicists who have given renewed emphasis to the distinctive visibility and prophetic witness of the church in the world.[3] Positively, this ecclesial turn of recent decades has clearly succeeded in securing and conveying the church in its holiness (i.e. as 'set apart'). What is less clear, however, is

---

1. 'Non est tam magna peccatrix, ut Christiana ecclesia?' Martin Luther, 'Predigten des Jahres 1531', in *Luthers Werke: Kritische Gesammtausgabe* 34, no. 1 (Weimar: Hermann Bölaus Nachfolger, 1908), 276.

2. On church conflict and division, see Ephraim Radner, *A Brutal Unity: The Spiritual Politics of the Christian Church* (Waco: Baylor University Press, 2012).

3. This renewed emphasis on ecclesial visibility is apparent in the work of a wide variety of theologians. Some examples would include Stanley Hauerwas, *The Peaceable Kingdom: A Primer in Christian Ethics* (Notre Dame: University of Notre Dame Press, 1983); John Howard Yoder, *Body Politics: Five Practices of the Community before the Watching World* (Harrisonburg: Herald Press, 2001); William Cavanaugh, *Torture and the Eucharist: Theology, Politics, and the Body of Christ* (Oxford: Blackwell, 1998); James McClendon, *Systematic Theology: Ethics*, vol. 1 (Nashville: Abingdon Press, 2002); George Lindbeck, *The Nature of Doctrine* (Louisville: Westminster John Knox, 1984); Samuel Wells,

whether this turn has allowed for an adequate recognition of the church as sinful.

What is even more surprising is the relative neglect of these questions by some theologians who appeal to and draw on Luther directly.[4] In the first and second sections of this chapter, I indicate this in relation to two theologians in particular: Robert Jenson and Reinhard Hütter.[5] Jenson and Hütter strongly emphasize the visibility and holiness of the church by identifying the work of the Holy Spirit with either the communal spirit of the church (Jenson) or its core practices (Hütter). My concern, however, is that they both relinquish or diminish Luther's firmer insistence that the church is sinful. In the third section, I identify an alternative in the theology of Bonhoeffer. Bonhoeffer's early work on ecclesiology has deep resonances with Jenson and Hütter and includes much that is attractive in their work.[6] Nevertheless, I argue that Bonhoeffer provides an account of the work of the Holy Spirit that more clearly allows for a recognition of the church as at once holy and sinful.

The Holy Spirit as the Spirit of the community

Robert Jenson's magisterial two-volume *Systematic Theology*[7] consistently emphasizes the concrete visibility and witness of the church. In his reflections on ecclesiology, Jenson first sets out a general phenomenology of spirit as background to an account of the church as a community and polity:

God's Companions: Reimagining Christian Ethics (Oxford: Blackwell, 2006); Barry Harvey, *Can These Bones Live? A Catholic Baptist Engagement with Ecclesiology, Hermeneutics, and Social Theory* (Grand Rapids: Brazos Press, 2008) and John Milbank, *Theology and Social Theory: Beyond Secular Reason* (Oxford: Blackwell, 1990).

4. In an important essay, David Yeago traces this turn to visibility among Lutheran theologians to the struggles of the Confessing Church under National Socialism. David Yeago, 'The Church as Polity? The Lutheran Context of Robert W. Jenson's Ecclesiology', in *Trinity, Time, and Church: A Response to the Theology of Robert W. Jenson*, ed. Colin Gunton (Grand Rapids: Eerdmans, 2000), 208–14.

5. With regard to Hütter, my interest is primarily in his early work, within which he more directly aligned himself with Luther and Lutheran theology.

6. A number of Jenson's and Hütter's critics have raised concerns with how they emphasize Christ's presence or immanence in the church. For example, see Colin Gunton, 'Until He Comes: Towards an Eschatology of Church Membership', *International Journal of Systematic Theology* 3, no. 2 (2001): 190. I have sympathies with this line of critique, but my interest in this chapter is in demonstrating how Bonhoeffer provides a more viable version of this same kind of Christo-ecclesiology, that is, with a different account of the work of the Holy Spirit in relation to the church.

7. Robert W. Jenson, *Systematic Theology, Volume 1: The Triune God*; *Systematic Theology, Volume 2: The Works of God* (Oxford: Oxford University Press, 2001).

Every individual person has and is a spirit: this is his or her personal liveliness, as a 'wind' that stirs that to which he or she directs her personal energies. But also every community has a spirit, which is not a mere aggregate of members' spirits. So an athletic team can be composed of superior athletes and still regularly lose, if it lacks 'team spirit', if it has not become a community. A community's spirit is the liveliness that blows through it, the freedom in which it is more than the sum of its parts because each member moves in the liberating impetus of others. The relation between a community's spirit and that of some one or more individual persons varies from situation to situation.[8]

In this passage, Jenson presents the insight from social theory that there are social structures or entities transcending those individuals they encompass and that the study of these is essential for understanding human reality.

Jenson builds on this general insight with the claim that the spirit of one particular community, the church, can be identified as the Holy Spirit: 'It is the church's founding miracle that her communal spirit is *identically* the Spirit that the personal God is and has.'[9] Put differently, the spirit of the community of the church is the Spirit of God or the Holy Spirit *tout court*. This is not an isolated claim of Jenson's, and it is made throughout his treatment of the church.[10] At one point he quotes Luther as saying, 'It is the proper work of the Holy Spirit to make the Church,'[11] but then proceeds to specify that 'the Spirit does this by giving himself to be the Spirit of this community, by bestowing his own eschatological power to be her liveliness.'[12] In other words, God brings about the church as a community by gifting the Holy Spirit to it as its communal identity. There is a consistent and direct identification of the Holy Spirit as that which makes the church a community as such.[13]

The main consequence of God's gifting the Spirit to the church in this way is that it supplies this community with an eschatological orientation.[14] This gift of the

---

8. Jenson, *Systematic Theology 2*, 181.
9. Jenson, *Systematic Theology 2*, 181. Emphasis added.
10. Jenson writes that 'the spirit founds the church by giving himself to be her spirit' and that the 'spirit of the church is the Holy Spirit himself'. Jenson, *Systematic Theology 2*, 182. See also Robert W. Jenson, 'The Church as *Communio*', in *The Catholicity of the Reformation*, ed. Carl E. Braaten and Robert W. Jenson (Grand Rapids: Eerdmans, 1996), 1–12.
11. Jenson, *Systematic Theology 2*, 197.
12. Jenson, *Systematic Theology 2*, 197.
13. This, of course, is something of a departure from Luther's approach to the church. Mark Mattes writes of Jenson's break with 'the Lutheran affirmation that the church is an assembly of people shaped by the gospel's message and sacraments'. Instead, Mattes continues, 'Jenson believes that God expresses his identity to his creatures in and as a creature, the body of the church.' See Mark Mattes, 'An Analysis and Assessment of Robert Jenson's Systematic Theology', *Lutheran Quarterly* 14, no. 4 (2000): 478.
14. On Jenson's eschatology, see Carl Braaten, 'Eschatology and Mission in the Theology of Robert Jenson', in *Trinity, Time, and Church*, ed. Gunton, 298–311. For a critique of this

Spirit frees 'a community within this age to be appropriate for union with a person [Christ] risen into the eschatological future'.[15] Accordingly, 'the church exists in and by *anticipation*' of the kingdom,[16] or – in a more Hegelian parlance – as a 'moment in the coming of the Kingdom'.[17] In this way the Holy Spirit provides an orientation or *telos* for the church that defines it in its entirety. This orientation sets the church apart from all other human communities, which in turn gives the church its critical, prophetic edge with respect to them. One could ask at this point, what kind of eschatology is in play here? At one level Jenson is careful to maintain that the eschaton is not already realized in the church; the Spirit is orientating and drawing this community towards its future indwelling in the Trinity. By figuring eschatology primarily in terms of a positive orientation to this *telos*, however, there is little sense of the eschaton as more radically delimiting and disrupting the existing church.[18]

Although Jenson understands the church as the community of the Spirit – and thus as having an eschatological *telos* and prophetic distinctiveness – he still tries to develop this in ways that give emphasis to its concrete, empirical form. Therefore, one of the main ways in which he describes the church in his *Systematic Theology* is as a polity. Following Augustine, he describes the church as 'a *people* united in a common spirit, that is, a people who have become a community, a *polity*'.[19] This language of polity contributes to Jenson's treatment of ecclesiology in a variety of ways. In particular, this language contributes to his strong emphasis on ecclesial visibility. That the church is 'the polity of Christ' means that Christ's presence is 'not a private phenomenon, an invisible interiority'.[20] Rather, for Jenson, as a polity the church takes up space within the world. This remains the case in spite of its eschatological orientation or destiny. As David Yeago has noted on this issue, 'it is precisely as a *public* phenomenon – an outward "bodily" and "visible" community – that the church is an eschatological reality'.[21]

---

aspect of Jenson's work, see George Hunsinger, 'Robert Jenson's Systematic Theology: A Review Essay', *Scottish Journal of Theology* 55, no. 2 (2002): 161–200.

15. Jenson, *Systematic Theology 2*, 182.

16. Jenson, *Systematic Theology 2*, 171.

17. Jenson, *Systematic Theology 2*, 172.

18. Gunton writes that Jenson's 'over-realized eschatology … serves as a recipe for the clericalism and sacerdotalism which has historically militated, and still does militate, against the participation of the whole people of God in *koinonia* and mission'. Gunton, 'Towards an Eschatology of Church Membership', 197.

19. Jenson, *Systematic Theology 2*, 204. This language has parallels with how Jenson elsewhere describes the church as a 'culture'. Robert W. Jenson, 'Christ as Culture 1: Christ as Polity', *International Journal of Systematic Theology* 5, no. 3 (2003): 323–9.

20. Jenson, 'Christ as Culture 1', 329.

21. As Yeago continues: 'insofar as the church bears eschatological predicates, it is precisely as a public phenomenon, as a polity, that it does so'. Yeago, 'The Church as Polity', 203. I am indebted to Yeago's rich essay throughout my discussion of Jenson's ecclesiology.

In addition, this language of polity is central to Jenson's claim that the church necessarily possesses an institutional structure or form: 'As a polity, the church has a government.'[22] While at one level this simply means the church is to be an 'ordered' community (again in line with Luther), Jenson is not reticent to specify the particular structures of governance that such order should entail – namely, offices of bishops, priests and deacons. (I return to Jenson's account of offices later.)

This language of polity contributes to Jenson's account of the visibility of the church in terms of its sacraments, that is, baptism and the eucharist. Jenson describes baptism, for example, as a visible and public 'renunciation of the world' that takes place upon entry into the church.[23] He presents it as the 'visible sign' by which I can be 'assured that I belong to God's people'.[24] In a lengthy reflection on the eucharist, he similarly emphasizes its public and embodied character: 'The bread is Jesus' availability to those gathered, for them to see, touch, address, and even finally take into themselves.'[25] For Jenson, if the church is a specific, visible polity on the basis of its eschatological *telos*, this becomes available to us sacramentally: 'The eucharist promises: *there is* my body in the world, and you here eating and drinking commune in it. It promises: *there* is the actual historical church, and you are she.'[26] In other words, Jenson uses the language of polity, in relation to the sacraments, in order to draw out the visible, institutional and embodied nature of the church and its concrete life.

What is also significant, however, is how Jenson does *not* use this language of polity. He at no point uses this language to designate the church as a polity in a more familiar sense: that is, a community in which individuals and groups negotiate with one another politically. In this respect Jenson positions the church as unlike other human polities. Indeed, the whole point of the church's eschatological orientation is that it draws the church out of the *libido dominandi* which Jenson sees as underlying and defining all other polities: 'As *God's* polity, the church's great character is peace ... The church anticipates this eschatological peace in the imperfect but real concord of her members.'[27] Furthermore, the fact that this peace of the Christian community is gifted by the Spirit *ab extra* means, for Jenson, that it 'is unbreakable, even when the church is shaken by controversy or tortured by misused authority or rebellion, because it is constituted in the communal love of God'.[28] The gift of the Holy Spirit that makes the church a distinctive community places the church itself beyond the sphere in which power might conceivably be abused.

---

22. Jenson, *Systematic Theology 2*, 205.
23. Jenson, *Systematic Theology 2*, 188.
24. Jenson, *Systematic Theology 2*, 252.
25. Jenson, *Systematic Theology 2*, 219.
26. Jenson, *Systematic Theology 2*, 220. Emphasis original.
27. Jenson, *Systematic Theology 2*, 204. This has resonances with John Milbank. See Milbank, *Theology and Social Theory*, 380–438.
28. Jenson, *Systematic Theology 2*, 205.

To be clear, Jenson acknowledges that the existing church is not unequivocal in its expression of this eschatological *telos* or peace (as the qualifier 'imperfect' in the quote cited earlier indicates). He stipulates that 'the moral history of the church is not, as it were, pure'.[29] The existing church remains impure insofar as individuals fail to live up to this new eschatological identity: 'In this age the *libido dominandi* remains and survives baptism to appear in the church'.[30] The sinful individual remains even after he or she has been incorporated into the new community of the Spirit. The point, however, is that while Jenson is willing to acknowledge the presence of sin at this level, he cannot recognize the possibility that the church *as such* is (or could become) sinful.[31] Indeed, to a significant extent this recognition has already been ruled out by the identification of the communal identity of the church *as* the Holy Spirit. If the spirit of the church is the Holy Spirit *tout court*, then sin is only really possible as the failure of individuals (and not on a corporate or institutional level).[32]

One place where the implications of this become apparent, therefore, is in Jenson's discussion of ecclesial hierarchy and governance.[33] As we have seen, the language of polity allows him to draw out the need for order and governance in the Christian community. However, Jenson goes beyond a basic Lutheran emphasis on order in the church and insists that the church's eschatological orientation underwrites very specific forms of governance. We 'look to the future', he suggests, 'for a norm of development in the church's life'.[34] He holds that the authority of the office of the episcopate can be identified as such a norm and can be justified on these grounds:

> If the Spirit has been leading the church [towards its future], then if the episcopate has been in fact established in the history of the church, and if this establishment can dramatically have been the leading of the Spirit, then we must judge that the establishment *was* the leading of the Spirit. And, as we have just argued, given the scope of the decision made as the episcopate became established, if this particular decision was in its time proper it is also irreversible.[35]

---

29. Rather, as Jenson continues, 'it is simply other than the moral history of the communities around it'. *Systematic Theology* 2, 210.

30. Jenson, *Systematic Theology* 2, 205.

31. Jenson's earlier treatment of sin earlier in this volume (*Systematic Theology* 2, 133–52) seems to have limited bearing on his ecclesiology.

32. My concern is that this move makes the *libido dominandi*, or problems of sin in the church, external to ecclesiological reflection. With Jenson's approach there is no inherently theological basis for a kind of ecclesial governance that necessarily attends to, and is cognizant of, the *libido dominandi* and its effects. This means that there is no theological basis for delimiting the authority of the ecclesial hierarchy.

33. Jenson, *Systematic Theology* 2, 236–7.

34. Jenson, *Systematic Theology* 2, 239.

35. Jenson, *Systematic Theology* 2, 240. This comment is followed by Jenson's theoretical support for the notion of the papacy: 'But if the communion ecclesiology is anywhere close

10. The Spirit and the Community

If the episcopal office is in one sense historical, its real authority is finally secured by a *telos* (provided by the Spirit) that lies beyond history. It is thus secured without any necessary reference to a political or pastoral function.[36] Moreover, the authority of the episcopate is secured without reference to either political negotiations or problems of sin.

My concern, then, is that Jenson's direct identification of the Holy Spirit as the spirit of the Christian community cannot do justice to the concrete situation and realities of the church. While this direct identification may indeed secure ecclesial distinctiveness and holiness, it does so in a way that seems to displace the church as a genuinely and fully historical human entity. In particular, this direct identification seems to militate against the possibility of recognizing the church itself as flawed and sinful.

The Holy Spirit and the practices of the community

In *Suffering Divine Things: Theology as Church Practice*, Reinhard Hütter's central interest is in locating the discipline of theology in terms of the core practices of the church.[37] He begins by suggesting that there are two options for contemporary theology:

> In the present crisis of intellectual and spiritual orientation, theology has two choices. It can continue to take its orientation largely from a comprehensive concept of reason ... The other alternative would be an *explicitly pneumatological* as well as *ecclesiological* prolegomena to Christian theology.[38]

In pursuing the second option, Hütter makes a number of the same basic moves as Jenson. Drawing on *communio* theology,[39] he too understands the church in terms of a teleological orientation which is supplied by the Holy Spirit and available to us sacramentally: 'In the Lord's Supper and in the eschatological proclamation of the word associated with it, the eschaton has commenced as *opus inchoatum*,

---

to the truth, then plainly the "one church" of its slogans must have her own pastor.' Jenson, *Systematic Theology 2*, 242.

36. Jenson's defence of ecclesial hierarchy might be contrasted with John Webster's more cautious defence of the episcopate: 'An adequate doctrine of the church will maximize Christology and pneumatology (for it is Jesus Christ through Word and Spirit who "gathers protests and preserves") and relativize (but not minimize or abolish) ecclesial action and its ordered forms.' John Webster, 'The Self-Organizing Power of the Gospel', in *Word and Church: Essays in Christian Dogmatics* (Edinburgh: T&T Clark, 2001), 198.

37. My focus in this section is on Reinhard Hütter's *Suffering Divine Things: Theology as Church Practice* (Grand Rapids: Eerdmans, 2000).

38. *Suffering Divine Things*, 23.

39. Hütter draws on Zizioulas, *Being as Communion*.

qualifying both the present and the past from the perspective of the end.'[40] On this basis he strongly emphasizes the existing church as already on the way to the kingdom (rather than understanding it as also under judgement and radically delimited by the kingdom).[41]

Hütter similarly understands this *telos* as the basis of the existing church's communal spirit, distinctive identity and public witness. On the one hand, he writes that 'the fulcral pneumatological point … is that the Holy Spirit – as *Spiritus Creator* – creates this communion [of the church] and thus also its relationality'.[42] Any communion or relationality within the church is gifted to it by the Holy Spirit *ab extra*. On the other hand, he describes the church as a 'public of the Holy Spirit'.[43] He expands on this: 'The highly unique character of this public is to be understood entirely from the perspective of its soteriological telos.'[44] The *telos* of the church again provides the basis for its visible distinctiveness and witness in the world.

Where Hütter differs from Jenson, however, is by providing a more detailed account of how the Holy Spirit draws the church to its *telos* through the core practices of this community. Hütter situates this account of core practices between two extremes: a direct institutionalization of the Spirit in the church (represented by Catholicism and the theology of Erik Peterson),[45] on the one side, and underdetermined or general accounts of the Holy Spirit's work, on the other. In *Suffering Divine Things*, his primary concern is with the second of these excesses, which he associates with Protestant theology in particular. For instance, he identifies an underdetermined pneumatology of this kind in the theology of Karl Barth.[46] According to Hütter, Barth develops his theology 'within the framework of a pneumatologically conceived Christology according to which the Holy Spirit is Christ's mode of action'.[47] Hütter's concern with this approach is that 'the Holy Spirit is accorded no work of its own in relation to church doctrine'.[48] In other

---

40. *Suffering Divine Things*, 165.

41. Hütter writes: 'This is not the "anticipation" of something yet to come, but the pneumatic manifestation of the eschaton.' Quoting Zizioulas, he continues, 'by bringing the eschaton into history, the Spirit enables the church through its sacramental structures to lend presence to the eschaton in history and at the same time to point beyond history'. *Suffering Divine Things*, 120.

42. Hütter, *Suffering Divine Things*, 107.

43. See Hütter, *Suffering Divine Things*, 164–5.

44. Hütter, *Suffering Divine Things*, 165.

45. Erik Peterson, *Theological Tractates*, trans. Michael Hollerich (Stanford: Stanford University Press, 2012).

46. On this reading of Barth see Paul Hinlicky, *Paths Not Taken: Fates of Theology from Luther through Leibniz* (Grand Rapids: Eerdmans, 2009), 127–70.

47. Hütter, *Suffering Divine Things*, 113.

48. Hütter, *Suffering Divine Things*, 113.

words, his concern is that Barth's theology leaves it unclear how the Holy Spirit *specifically* works in and through the church.[49]

Hütter's response is to emphasize a deep and necessary connection between the Holy Spirit's work and the core practices of the church:[50] 'Without concrete mediation through the core practices of the church, including church doctrine, the activity of the Spirit becomes questionable.'[51] Appealing to Luther, he identifies and elaborates on these practices as visible signs of the Holy Spirit's work.[52] Indeed, he at one point goes so far as to describe the church's core practices as the 'unequivocal ... concrete incarnation'[53] of the Spirit and as the 'indispensable mediate forms ... through which the Holy Spirit guides the church to truth'.[54] It is through these practices, then, that the Spirit works to orientate the church to its *telos* and to sustain it as a visibly distinctive community: 'The core practices and *doctrina* demarcate this identity and circumscribe at the same time ... the specific spatial and temporal locale of the church.'[55]

While Hütter's account of ecclesial practices initially follows Luther, some specific ways in which he then develops this account are innovative.[56] For instance, Hütter suggests that these practices can be understood as '*enhypostatically* ... works of the Spirit'.[57] In order to integrate human and divine agency within ecclesial practices, Hütter appeals to language usually reserved for Christ. The church in its practices is understood as an 'enhypostatic' union of the divine and the human in the same way that Christ is divine and human. This move allows Hütter to maintain that the Holy Spirit is present in these practices without displacing their status as fully human practices: 'The core practices *qua* practices naturally always include the "presence" of human action.'[58] It is at this point, however, that some questions

---

49. Hütter elaborates: a 'general theory of communication and truth takes the place of ecclesiology by rendering unnecessary explicit and substantive reference to those particular procedures and practices that constitute the church and which must be proclaimed and taught in a binding fashion in the church'. Hütter, *Suffering Divine Things*, 20.

50. Hütter writes: 'one can alter slightly Kant's famous expression and say that pneumatology without ecclesiology is empty, ecclesiology without pneumatology is blind'. Hütter, *Suffering Divine Things*, 127.

51. Hütter, *Suffering Divine Things*, 127.

52. As one commentator summarizes, 'Only as the church attends to these practices as binding will it re-establish its public character and, with this, its vocation to witness'. John G. Flett, 'Communion as Propaganda: Reinhard Hütter and the Missionary Witness of the "Church as Public"', *Scottish Journal of Theology* 62, no. 4 (2009): 459.

53. Hütter, *Suffering Divine Things*, 176.

54. Hütter, *Suffering Divine Things*, 128.

55. Hütter, *Suffering Divine Things*, 165.

56. While this language of enhypostasis is restricted to a short discussion, it plays a crucial role for Hütter's account.

57. Hütter, *Suffering Divine Things*, 248.

58. Hütter, *Suffering Divine Things*, 249.

must be raised about Hütter's approach. Does this language of enhypostasis allow for properly maintaining the freedom and priority of the Spirit's work with respect to the church? Does Hütter's attempt to avoid Barth's 'underdetermined pneumatology' with an account of ecclesial practices begin to institutionalize the work of the Spirit in the church?

To be clear, Hütter himself insists that the existing church and the work of the Spirit are necessarily distinct: 'Although the mission of the church must thus be identified with the mission of the Holy Spirit ... this constitutes neither a reification of the Spirit nor an incorporation of the church into the deity as the fourth hypostasis'.[59] The main way he tries to maintain this distinction, however, is by emphasizing the 'receptivity' or 'pathos' of the church with respect to the work of the Spirit: 'The church remains strictly separate from the Holy Spirit', he writes, 'insofar as it [through its practices] perpetually *receives* what the Spirit creates in it and is thus *pathetically* determined by the spirit'.[60] In other words, Hütter frames this distinction as fundamentally one of giver and recipient. Does such a framing by itself ensure the integrity of the Spirit with respect to the church (or avoid the potential problem of institutionalization), as Hütter thinks it does? On this issue one of his critics has perceptively written:

> We need to know how the Holy Spirit, rather than being 'bound' to the church and its practices, can [also] *overcome* the effects of the churches upon their membership, and the membership upon their churches, so that in spite of the church as well as by its help we may be sanctified and brought closer to Christ.[61]

The problem, therefore, is that Hütter's account of the church as receiving the Spirit through its core practices, at least by itself, does not seem sufficiently to acknowledge how the Holy Spirit might be at work *even in spite of* the church and its practices. If the language of receptivity allows for a distinction of sorts, it is not finally clear that this is the right kind of distinction, or one that by itself ensures the Spirit's full freedom and integrity.[62]

On this basis it is also unclear that Hütter's approach can allow for recognizing the church as sinful. The basic emphasis on the Spirit as bound to and received in the church's core practices appears to imply that its work depends on the human enactment of these practices. This in turn appears to suggest that the church in

---

59. Hütter, *Suffering Divine Things*, 144.

60. Hütter, *Suffering Divine Things*, 144.

61. Nicholas M. Healy, 'Practices and the New Ecclesiology: Misplaced Concreteness?', *International Journal of Systematic Theology* 5, no. 3 (2003): 297.

62. John Swinton has written: 'When we don't know what to say, the Spirit prays on our behalf ... When we can no longer access God through our prayers, our meditations, or the Scriptures, we can be certain that God is with us in ways which, at least right now, we don't understand.' Swinton, *Dementia*. It is unclear that Hütter's emphasis on practices on its own terms allows for this more expansive vision of the Spirit's work.

its practices can never be sinful in such a way, or to such an extent, that no such enactment takes place. If the church were ever to be sinful in this way, then the Holy Spirit would simply no longer be present, and this community would no longer be the church.

This situation is only compounded by Hütter's use of enhypostasis language to frame how the Spirit relates to human action in ecclesial practices. By using language usually reserved for Christ, he models what is human about the church on Christ's humanity. This allows for recognizing the church and its practices as fully human in one sense, and it thereby allows for drawing out the concrete, embodied nature of such practices. The problem, however, is that if the church is human in the way that Christ is human, then this implies that the church, too, is human without sin. Hütter's appeal to the language of enhypostasis in relation to the church, along with his emphasis on the Spirit's work as bound to ecclesial practices, at least by themselves, subtly militate against a more thoroughgoing recognition of the church as a sinful, human community.

The Holy Spirit and the community's objective spirit

Thus far, I have suggested that Jenson and Hütter fail to formulate the relationship between the Holy Spirit and the existing church in ways that clearly allows for recognizing the church as at once holy and sinful. Specifically, they pursue the former in ways that seem to mitigate the latter. Bonhoeffer, while close to Hütter and Jenson in many respects, indicates an alternative way of framing this relationship.

It is worth acknowledging at the outset that Bonhoeffer is not ordinarily understood as having a developed pneumatology.[63] In his doctoral dissertation *Sanctorum Communio*, however, he provides a detailed (and largely neglected) treatment of the work of the Holy Spirit in relation to the church.[64] As we shall see, he is careful to articulate the work of the Holy Spirit in ways that attend to and maintain the human, even sinful, nature of the Christian community.[65]

---

63. See comments to this effect in David Höhne, *Spirit and Sonship: Colin Gunton's Theology of Particularity and the Holy Spirit* (Farnham: Ashgate, 2010), 23. In addition, see Christopher R. J. Holmes, 'The Holy Spirit', in *The Oxford Handbook of Dietrich Bonhoeffer*, ed. Michael Mawson and Philip G. Ziegler (Oxford: Oxford University Press, 2019), 168–78.

64. This relative neglect is apparent in the two major works that have taken *Sanctorum Communio* and its theology seriously: Clifford Green, *Bonhoeffer: A Theology of Sociality* (Grand Rapids: Eerdmans, 1972) and Joachim von Soosten, *Die Sozialität der Kirche: Die Theologie and Theorie der Kirche in Dietrich Bonhoeffers 'Sanctorum Communio'* (Munich: Chr. Kaiser, 1992).

65. For my more detailed engagement with Bonhoeffer's *Sanctorum Communio*, see Mawson, *Christ Existing as Community*.

One of Bonhoeffer's main interests in *Sanctorum Communio* is in what it means for the church to be the place of God's revelation as an 'empirical' or 'historical-empirical' entity.[66] Like Jenson and Hütter, Bonhoeffer insists that Christ is present to the world through the empirical or existing church: 'However questionable its empirical form may be, it remains the church in this very form.'[67] At the same time, however, he strives to retain Luther's firm insistence that the church is a community of sin: 'It is crucial that the sanctorum communio always has been a community of sinners and remains so.'[68] How does Bonhoeffer hold these two aspects of the church together?

To address this question, we need to begin with the phenomenology of spirit that Bonhoeffer sets out in an early chapter of *Sanctorum Communio* (chapter 3). Like Jenson (as quoted earlier), Bonhoeffer provides an account of individual persons and communities in terms of spirit. At the level of individuals, he maintains that the person as spirit is at once both 'open' and 'closed'. As open, the individual person is already related to others and formed by these relationships. Accordingly, all personal acts and intentions presuppose and require other human beings: 'self-conscious thinking and willing are possible and meaningful ... in reciprocal interaction with other minds'.[69] As closed, however, this same individual possesses a certain integrity or independence prior to and apart from its social relationships. Indeed, this relative integrity is necessary for genuine sociality; genuine sociality requires interactions between individual persons as independent and separate from one another. Individual persons must therefore be conceived of as equiprimordially social and individual, without either of these being dissolved into the other.

Next, Bonhoeffer provides an account of how the interactions between persons of this kind take on a certain 'objective' form apart from these interactions. (This parallels Jenson's description of the 'team spirit' of the athletic team.) Bonhoeffer develops this idea by drawing on Hegel's idea of objective spirit. Referring to Hegel, he defines objective spirit as an 'entity' or 'structure' that 'leads an independent life beyond individual persons, and yet is only real in and through them'.[70] He elsewhere describes an objective spirit as having an 'active will of its own that orders and guides the wills of its members who constitute it and participate in it, and that takes shape in specific forms, thereby providing visible evidence that it has a life of its own'.[71] Understanding human reality in all its depth and complexity is not possible solely in reference to individual persons; such an account requires

---

66. DBWE 1: 208–81.

67. DBWE 1: 211.

68. DBWE 1: 212.

69. DBWE 1: 69.

70. DBWE 1: 100. In spite of such appropriations from Hegel, Bonhoeffer's dissertation more broadly proceeds as a critique of idealism and Hegel's philosophy. See Mawson, *Christ Existing as Community*, 56–76.

71. DBWE 1: 209.

attending to the objective social structures that exist apart from and influence these individuals, even while still being generated by them.

While Bonhoeffer outlines this general phenomenology of spirit in his discussion of creation (chapter 3 of *Sanctorum Communio*), he then draws on this for his account of the church as the place of God's revelation and a fully human, sinful community (chapter 5). First of all, he claims that the interactions of the members of the Christian community generate its objective spirit. The objective spirit of the church in this sense remains historical and tied to a particular context: it is 'part of history'[72] and 'subject to the historical ambiguity of all *profane communities*'.[73] In addition, he uses the idea of objective spirit to maintain that the empirical church is an entity in its own right. The concept of objective spirit allows him to treat the empirical church as a sociological entity. So how does Bonhoeffer use this concept of objective spirit for a specifically theological account of church? How does he relate this concept of objective spirit to the claim that this existing church is in fact the body of Christ and is actualized by the work of the Spirit? Specifically, Bonhoeffer suggests that the main way in which the Holy Spirit actualizes Christ in and as the church – or constitutes the church in its visible, prophetic witness – is through the church's objective spirit. He writes: 'The Holy Spirit *uses* [*benutzen*] the objective spirit [of the church] as a vehicle for its gathering and sustaining social activity.'[74] Put differently, 'Christ and the Holy Spirit *make use of* the forms of the life of the objective spirit as they exist historically.'[75] In other words, the Holy Spirit not only works by drawing individuals into the church, but also through the church as a human social entity.

Moreover, it is the fact that the Holy Spirit continually uses the objective spirit of the church in this way that makes this community a witness to Christ in its concrete, sociological or empirical form. Bonhoeffer writes:

> The objective spirit is bearer and instrument of the spirit of the church of Christ; it has certain visible forms that the Holy Spirit produced and implanted into it … But the objective spirit does not bear these forms as one would carry a sack on one's back; rather it is itself sanctified through the load … This is of course true only insofar as the Holy Spirit does the carrying within it, for the objective spirit is not the Holy Spirit. The objective spirit … is *both instrument and end in itself*. It is both the object and the means of the Holy Spirit's work, in an interrelated fashion.[76]

The Christian community is continually being actualized as a visible witness to Christ in its own objective spirit through the sanctifying work of the Holy Spirit.

---

72. DBWE 1: 215.
73. DBWE 1: 216. Emphasis added.
74. DBWE 1: 215. Emphasis added.
75. DBWE 1: 215. Emphasis added.
76. DBWE 1: 216. Emphasis original.

The Holy Spirit uses, and indeed even implants itself within, the mutable and historically contingent spirit of the Christian community.

This brings us to the heart of the matter. Bonhoeffer takes care throughout his discussion to maintain a firm distinction between the Holy Spirit and the church's objective spirit.[77] He insists that the former comes to and works in the church from above, whereas the latter is generated from below: 'We have on the hand, the ever-changing, imperfect, sinful, objective human spirit; on the other hand, we have the Holy Spirit who bears this human spirit, and is eternally one and perfect.'[78] In other words, it is only the fact that the Holy Spirit freely bears or uses this objective spirit that makes the church, in its empirical and fallible form, integral to God's revelation.

What does this idea of the Holy Spirit coming to and using the objective spirit of the community make possible? First and foremost, it allows Bonhoeffer to acknowledge and attend to the sinfulness of the Christian community as a historical and fully human community in precisely the way that neither Jenson nor Hütter seem finally able to do. Instead, Bonhoeffer can maintain that the Holy Spirit is at work in the church 'in spite of all the sinfulness and imperfection of the individuals *and of the whole*'.[79] Specifically, it is possible for the church to be sinful in its objective spirit, without this ultimately being an impediment to the Spirit's work.

Second, that the Holy Spirit uses or works through an objective spirit that is generated from below implies a space of relative human freedom within the church. Bonhoeffer claims, for example, that both the church and its forms of governance have relative, although still genuine, authority over individual believers. This is the case because such offices of governance are grounded in the church's objective spirit and neither these offices nor those who hold them are ordained by God or the Holy Spirit directly. As Bonhoeffer (polemically) insists:

> In the Protestant church there is no theurgy, and no magical authority invested in the office or its bearers. The concept of the *priesthood of all believers* is merely another way of expressing this. The reality of the church-community, which has only one head, namely Christ, protects us from the idea of a spiritual-earthly head.[80]

This claim stands in stark contrast to Jenson's eschatological grounding of episcopal authority. By directly identifying the Holy Spirit as the spirit of the community, Jenson closes a space of relative human freedom that Bonhoeffer carefully keeps open with the concept of objective spirit.

Finally, Bonhoeffer's account of the Holy Spirit using the objective spirit allows for recognizing how certain 'sociological forms and functions' of the empirical

---

77. Bonhoeffer identifies the failure to do so with Hegel, who 'simply identifies the Holy Spirit with the corporate spirit of the church'. DBWE 1: 198.
78. DBWE 1: 215–16.
79. DBWE 1: 215. Emphasis added.
80. DBWE 1: 236.

church are integral to its holiness. Although the objective spirit of the church is not itself the Holy Spirit, it is still integral to how the Spirit works in this community. On this basis Bonhoeffer examines a number of the church's 'forms and functions' as ways in which the Holy Spirit actualizes Christ in the church; he provides analyses of such forms and functions as preaching, assembling for worship, the priestly office, the sacraments, and pastoral care.[81] In contrast to Jenson and Hütter, he insists that a theological approach to these forms (i.e. Hütter's practices) requires attending to their distinctly sociological or human dimension, that is, to the ways they contribute to the church's historical and objective spirit.

Two examples shall have to suffice. First of all, Bonhoeffer provides a rich and detailed discussion of the constitutive significance of the eucharist for the church. Like Jenson and Hütter, he insists that the true significance of this rite is only comprehensible if it is understood as 'God's gift for the people',[82] or in terms of the 'self-giving of Christ'.[83] A merely sociological approach alone cannot provide an adequate understanding of what the eucharist is. Nevertheless, Bonhoeffer then goes on to insist that the 'significance of administering the Lord's Supper is not fully grasped if it is not also understood as a human action before God'.[84] What it means to understand the Lord's Supper theologically, then, also involves attending to how it is administered and practised at the human, sociological level. Understanding the eucharist theologically involves attending to how the human actions surrounding the eucharist contribute to the objective spirit of the community.

Bonhoeffer provides a second example with baptism. He is again clear that this sacrament must be understood both as God's gift or a work of the Holy Spirit and as a human action or practice before God. The concept of objective spirit is therefore similarly essential for a theological understanding of baptism. Moreover, Bonhoeffer suggests that it is only with this concept of objective spirit that infant baptism in particular becomes intelligible for Protestants: 'Since the children do not themselves receive faith, even as *fides directa*, and the sacrament nevertheless demands faith, we must conclude that the subject that receives the sacrament in faith can only be the objective spirit of the church-community.'[85] In other words, the concept of objective spirit allows for the community (as a human and sinful entity) to stand in the place of those members who cannot stand on the basis of their own faith. It does so, however, without displacing the necessity of personal faith per se.[86] The point is that the objective spirit of the church is constituted (from below) by the interactions of individuals who personally possess such faith. The fact that the objective spirit achieves a relative integrity apart from such faith-bearing

---

81. DBWE 1: 226–50.
82. DBWE 1: 241.
83. DBWE 1: 242.
84. DBWE 1: 243.
85. DBWE 1: 241.
86. 'The act of baptism also calls for a confession of faith; this is why it must be made on behalf of the child who is baptized.' DBWE 1: 247.

individuals, however, means it is not necessary for *every* member who exists in terms of this spirit to have personal faith at the point of their baptism. Rather, it becomes possible for the community as such to 'pledge to raise and instruct the children in the Christian faith'.[87] The community is able to do this precisely as a flawed entity comprising of individual Christian sinners.

To be clear, Bonhoeffer's discussions of baptism and the eucharist still have a number of deep resonances with Jenson and Hütter. As we have seen, Jenson understands the sacraments as 'visible signs' of a distinctive *telos* and identity of the church. From within his approach, Bonhoeffer is at least broadly able to affirm this understanding: 'Here the church-community identifies itself as such by an obedient symbolic action in a *publicly visible form*, and ... God visibly recognizes it as such.'[88] Hütter more specifically identifies the sacraments as core practices through which the Spirit enters into the community. Bonhoeffer is again able to retain this basic emphasis: 'Sacraments are *acts of the community* ... they unite within themselves the objective spirit of the Church community and *the Holy Spirit who is operating through it.*'[89]

Nevertheless, Bonhoeffer's concept of objective spirit allows him to avoid some of the potential problems that arise for Jenson and Hütter. His insistence that the Holy Spirit constitutes the church in its public witness (Jenson) and is received through its practices (Hütter) *by way of the church's objective spirit* means that the Holy Spirit and its work are not so directly and unambiguously bound to given forms or practices. That the Holy Spirit uses and carries an objective spirit means that we can never definitively claim that the Spirit is present or visible at a given point or in a particular way. In other words, Bonhoeffer avoids Jenson's claim that the holiness of the church is directly visible in and secured by the sacraments. He also avoids Hütter's potential restricting of the Holy Spirit's work to the human enacting of core practices. Against Jenson and Hütter, the concept of objective spirit more clearly maintains the freedom of the Holy Spirit and its work with respect to the existing church. This in turn more easily allows for recognizing the church, in its concrete form and practices, as a flawed and sinful vessel. The point, however, is that Bonhoeffer's concept of objective spirit allows for this while still retaining a clear emphasis on the centrality of the sacraments to the work of the Spirit, that is, without retreating to what Hütter identifies as an 'underdetermined pneumatology'.

Conclusion

As suggested in the introduction, theologians and ethicists have in recent decades turned to ecclesiology in ways that have clearly, and importantly, emphasized the church's visible holiness and prophetic witness. They have done so, however, in

---

87. DBWE 1: 242.
88. DBWE 1: 244. Emphasis added.
89. DBWE 1: 240. Emphasis added.

ways that have tended to neglect the issue of how this same church is a community of sin. Bonhoeffer places this issue at the centre of his early ecclesiology: 'As a sinful community the church is nevertheless still holy, or rather ... in this world it is never holy without also being sinful.'[90] He does this by developing an account of how the Holy Spirit works in and through the objective spirit of the church. On this basis Bonhoeffer's theology can be distinguished from this more recent ecclesial turn. What, then, are the challenges that Bonhoeffer's theology presents to ongoing work in this area?

Following Bonhoeffer, Christians are called to recognize and attend to the sinfulness of the existing church. Problems of sin in the Christian community cannot adequately be understood with reference solely to individuals – that is, individual Christians failing fully to embrace or live up to their new ecclesial identity. Rather, sin and its effects be understood as permeating the structures, hierarchies and practices of the church on every level. Confessing sin before God involves attending to sin in all its forms; it requires attending to the complex ways in which the community and its practices may themselves be flawed and sinful.

That the church is on its own terms sinful further indicates that it is and remains a human community in the world. In other words, this indicates that there is no final basis for distinguishing the Christian community from other human polities. On the one hand, this suggests Christians should in most cases be adopting and implementing the same kinds of safeguards against power and its abuses as are found in ordinary politics – that is, so as to pre-empt and delimit (so far as humanly possible) the abuses resulting from the *libido dominandi*. On the other hand, this suggests Christians also should in most cases be willing to recognize themselves as under those regulations and laws governing ordinary polities. This side of the eschaton, the Christian community is unable to avoid attending to such worldly matters.

However, none of this means that Christians should relinquish the claim that the existing church is in fact a holy and prophetic witness. The point is that Christ and the Holy Spirit are working in and through the church even as a community of sin. The existing, sinful church is in fact the church of Christ and the Spirit, not 'merely as a manifestation of the non-real, ideal church of the future'.[91] The existing church is a distinctive and visible witness in the world, to a significant extent at least, *by means of* the Spirit convicting it of its sin.

The recognition that the church can itself be sinful implies the need for maintaining a clearer distinction between the church and the kingdom. A deeper recognition of sin in the church implies that there can be no smooth transition (or *telos*) extending from this sinful community to the kingdom. Against Jenson and Hütter, the kingdom is not already significantly embodied and visible in the church's own communal identity and practices, at least not in such a way that the church will bypass God's final judgement and the negation of its current form.

---

90. DBWE 1: 214.
91. DBWE 1: 211.

Bonhoeffer is adamant that God's 'judgment and grace apply to all individual persons within the church-community ... *and to the collective person of the church-community*'.[92] It is only with God's final judgement that the church's objective spirit and the Holy Spirit will be made one.

Finally, this indicates that the church in its holiness and witness, ultimately at least, remains a matter of faith and hope. In this age the church is rarely a distinctive or prophetic community in ways that are directly visible or unambiguously evident. Rather, Christians can only confess in faith that this existing, sinful community is in fact the body of Christ and a work of the Spirit: 'We *believe* that it [the church] is the body of Christ, Christ's presence in the world, and that according to the promise God's Spirit is at work in it.'[93] The church is a community of those who have faith and hope in God's promise. As Bonhoeffer proclaims, 'The church is *impalpabilis, insensibilis*, as Luther said; it must be believed ... It is only in faith that I perceive the church. And the experiences [and practices] of community that necessarily arise can only be seen by faith as manifestations of the church.'[94]

---

92. DBWE 1: 287. Emphasis added.
93. DBWE 1: 280. Emphasis added.
94. DBWE 1: 279.

Chapter 11

THE POLITICS OF JESUS AND THE ETHICS OF CHRIST: ON WHY BONHOEFFER IS NOT AN ANABAPTIST

In the *Politics of Jesus*, John Howard Yoder frames his approach to Christian discipleship as follows: 'My presentation emphasizes what was denied before: Jesus as teacher and example, not only as sacrifice.'[1] By contrast, in *Discipleship*, Bonhoeffer had earlier insisted that 'Jesus calls to discipleship, not as a teacher and a role model, but as Christ, the Son of God.'[2] What is at stake with this difference?

In recent decades, theologians and Christian ethicists have given significant attention to the role and importance of community and discipleship for Christian ethics. There has been a renewed emphasis on the concrete church as the place through which Christians witness to and engage the world. In particular, many theologians have pursued and developed this emphasis through rich, detailed accounts of the formative practices, virtues, character, habits and narrative that sustain and are sustained by the church as a community. Stanley Hauerwas, James McClendon, Mark Thiessen Nation, Glen Stassen and others have variously demonstrated the ways these are integral to the distinctive identity of this community.[3] One of the most important and widely acknowledged influences

---

1. John Howard Yoder, *The Politics of Jesus*, 2nd edn (Grand Rapids: Eerdmans, 1994), 226.

2. DBWE 4: 57.

3. Stanley Hauerwas, *Performing the Faith: Bonhoeffer and the Practice of Non-violence* (Grand Rapids: Brazos Press, 2004); McClendon, *Systematic Theology*; Mark Thiessen Nation, 'Discipleship in a World Full of Nazis: Dietrich Bonhoeffer's Polyphonic Pacifism as Social Ethics', in *The Wisdom of the Cross: Essays in Honor of John Howard Yoder*, ed. Stanley Hauerwas, Chris K. Heuber, Harry J. Hueber and Mark Thiessen Nation (Grand Rapids: Eerdmans, 1999); Mark Thiessen Nation, 'The First Word Christians Have to Say about Violence Is "Church": On Bonhoeffer, Baptists and Becoming a Peace Church', in *Faithfulness & Fortitude: In Conversation with the Theological Ethics of Stanley Hauerwas*, ed. Mark Thiessen Nation and Samuel Wells (Edinburgh: T&T Clark, 2000); Mark Thiessen Nation, Anthony G. Siegrist and David P. Umbel, *Bonhoeffer the Assassin: Challenging the Myth, Recovering His Call to Peacemaking* (Grand Rapids: Baker Academic, 2013). Other examples of this kind of theological approach include Wells, *God's Companions*; Harvey,

behind these thinkers and their vision is the Anabaptist theologian John Howard Yoder.[4]

Many of those who were influenced by Yoder, however, have also drawn upon and appealed to Bonhoeffer. The latter is seen to provide a precedent and resources for this same theological vision. Hauerwas, for example, writes that 'I am sure that Bonhoeffer's *Discipleship*, which I read as a student many times in seminary, was the reason some years later John Howard Yoder's *The Politics of Jesus* had such a profound influence on me.'[5] More recently, Mark Thiessen Nation has provided comprehensive readings of Bonhoeffer's theology along these lines.[6]

Bringing Yoder and Bonhoeffer together in this way seems to make sense. Bonhoeffer certainly makes claims that resonate with themes and concerns in Anabaptist theology, especially in his 1937 *Discipleship*. Like Yoder, Bonhoeffer places the concrete Christian community at the centre of his theology. Both theologians maintain a clear distinction between the church and the world, seeing the cross as central to their accounts of community and discipleship. The most obvious convergence, however, is the deep commitment to peace and non-violence that Yoder and Bonhoeffer share. In Bonhoeffer's words, Christ's disciples are to 'renounce violence' and remain 'silent in the face of hatred and injustice'.[7]

Nonetheless, in spite of these convergences, my interest in this chapter is ultimately in setting out some real and deep theological differences between Yoder and Bonhoeffer, as well as reflecting on what is at stake with these. First, I outline Yoder's understanding of discipleship and community, as found in his 1972 *The*

Can These Bones Live; Glen Stassen, *A Thicker Jesus: Incarnational Discipleship in a Secular Age* (Louisville: Westminster John Knox, 2012).

4. This chapter was written in 2013, before I became aware of Yoder's long history of sexual abusing. Accordingly, my critique here focuses on the limitations of Yoder's theology. Others have reflected on the potential connections between Yoder's theology and abusing. See, for example, the article by David Cramer, Jenny Howell, Jonathan Tran and Paul Martens, 'Scandalizing John Howard Yoder', *The Other Journal*, 2014, https://theotherjournal.com/2014/07/scandalizing-john-howard-yoder/.

5. Hauerwas writes, 'It is not accidental that my account of Bonhoeffer as a political theologian makes him an ally of John Howard Yoder. Bonhoeffer, like Yoder, sought to recover the visibility of the church amid the ruins of Christendom from the beginnings to the end of his life.' Hauerwas, *Performing the Faith*, 55.

6. Nation, Siegrist and Umbel, *Bonhoeffer the Assassin?* See also Nation, *Discipleship in a World Full of Nazis: Recovering the True Legacy of Dietrich Bonhoeffer* (Eugene: Cascade, 2022).

7. DBWE 4: 108. In addition, Bonhoeffer seems to come close to Yoder when he makes the Sermon on the Mount the centre of his account of Christian discipleship. He similarly resists a Weberian construal of the sermon as an 'absolute ethic' that cannot be incorporated into a responsible political existence. See Max Weber, 'Politics as Vocation', in *Weber: Selections in Translation*, ed. W. G. Runciman, trans. Eric Matthews (Cambridge: Cambridge University Press, 1978), 217–18.

Politics of Jesus. Second, I briefly review Yoder's direct engagement with Bonhoeffer in a 1987 lecture, 'The Christological Presuppositions of Discipleship'.[8] In this lecture, Yoder himself recognizes some key differences between Bonhoeffer's theology and his own. Third, I turn to Bonhoeffer, focusing on his account of Christian formation and community in *Discipleship*[9] and drawing attention to some differences to Yoder's account. In light of these differences, I conclude with some reflections on the broader challenges Bonhoeffer's theology poses to contemporary Christian ethics.

Yoder and the politics of Jesus

In *The Politics of Jesus*, one of Yoder's central claims is that the actions and teachings of Jesus, as presented by the synoptic gospels, provide a basis for the political form of the contemporary Christian church. He insists that Jesus provided a 'model of radical political action', one which was adopted by the early Christian church and is available to be adopted by Christians today.[10]

Yoder begins, therefore, by outlining some ways in which contemporary theologians and Christians have failed to understand the Jesus of the gospels as politically and ethically relevant. He identifies this in Catholic appeals to the natural law, for example, as well as in liberal Protestant understandings of the Gospels as about spiritual values or as displaying an interim ethic.[11] In these ways 'Jesus himself ... is not finally normative for ethics' and 'some kind of a bridge or transition into another realm or mode of thought' is pursued.[12] Yoder identifies a similar evasion in dogmatic understandings of Jesus: the view that Jesus came to earth 'to give his life for the sins of humankind'.[13] His concern is that this too draws attention away from the deeply political nature of Jesus' ministry. It provides a way of thinking about Christ and the Christian life that is not directly grounded in Jesus' earthly ministry and teachings.[14]

In developing an alternative, Yoder insists that Jesus directly displays a viable political agenda in the gospels: 'His deeds show a coherent, conscious

---

8. John Howard Yoder, 'The Christological Presuppositions of Discipleship', in *Being Human, Becoming Human: Dietrich Bonhoeffer and Social Thought*, ed. Jens Zimmermann and Brian Gregor (Eugene: Pickwick Publications, 2010).

9. Bonhoeffer is typically considered to be closest to Yoder's theology in *Discipleship*.

10. Yoder, *The Politics of Jesus*, 2.

11. That is, the liberal claim that Jesus' early followers did not need a coherent politics or ethics because they erroneously believed in his imminent return.

12. Yoder, *The Politics of Jesus*, 8.

13. Yoder, *The Politics of Jesus*, 7.

14. Yoder summarizes: 'Jesus knew he had to die, for reasons unrelated to his social humanity. Therefore, the social humanity of how that necessity came to be carried out is unimportant.' Yoder, *The Politics of Jesus*, 99.

social-political character and direction, and his words are inseparable therefrom.'[15] Furthermore, Yoder insists that the gospels are only properly understood when read along these lines. In chapter 2 of *The Politics of Jesus*, he illustrates this through a systematic treatment of the gospel of Luke.[16] Moving from the Annunciation to the temptation in the desert, from Jesus' ministry in Galilee to his crucifixion, Yoder draws out the social and political aspects of all that Jesus said and did. He summarizes: 'Jesus was ... the bearer of a new possibility of human, social, and therefore political relationships. His baptism is the inauguration and his cross is the culmination of that new regime in which his disciples are called to share.'[17]

At this point it is worth noting Yoder's reliance on developments in modern New Testament studies.[18] Yoder draws out Jesus' significance by locating him in his first-century context.[19] Accordingly, Jesus presents a 'particular social-political-ethical option' in this first-century world.[20] Jesus came to demonstrate a distinctive way of being and acting in the world, one which is historically and visibly different to other contemporary options.[21] On this basis Yoder frequently contrasts the particular political option of Jesus with other first-century political options: the quietist 'withdrawal into the desert' of the Essenes, the establishment responsibility of the Sadducees and the violent revolutionary action advocated by the Zealots.[22]

Yoder further draws out and develops the distinctive political option of Jesus throughout *The Politics of Jesus*. He identifies this historical-political option, for example, in Jesus' declaration of the year of Jubilee and economic retribution (chapter 3); in his willingness to abandon earthly security (chapter 4); in his opposition to oppressive and exclusionary social practices and finally in his consistent embrace of suffering or renunciation of violence (chapter 8). In all these ways, Jesus announced and inaugurated 'a new social reality ... an alternative to the structures that were there before.'[23]

---

15. Yoder, *The Politics of Jesus*, 112.

16. Yoder consciously selects Luke on the basis that it is usually considered the least political among the gospels. Yoder, *The Politics of Jesus*, 54.

17. Yoder, *The Politics of Jesus*, 52.

18. He writes, 'If we may be freed by self-critical scholarly objectivity no longer to have to assume that the authority of the Bible resides in its saying things that we agree with, we may be free as well to hear more clearly what it really says.' Yoder, *The Politics of Jesus*, 214.

19. To be clear, Yoder's interest is not in recovering a historical Jesus who stands behind or apart from the gospels. See Yoder, *The Politics of Jesus*, 54. His move to contextualization comes closer to the third quest of the historical Jesus. See N. T. Wright, *Jesus and the Victory of God* (London: SPCK, 1996), 78–82.

20. Yoder, *The Politics of Jesus*, 11. Emphasis added.

21. Yoder provides a more detailed treatment of the various first-century political options in *The Original Revolution: Essays on Christian Pacifism* (Waterloo: Herald Press, 1971), 18–27.

22. Yoder, *The Politics of Jesus*, 36.

23. Yoder, *The Politics of Jesus*, 33.

For Yoder, the distinctiveness of Jesus' option, as it appears in his life and ministry, culminates in and is summarized by the cross. At one level, the fact of the crucifixion confirms the political nature of this ministry: 'Jewish and Roman authorities were defending themselves against a real threat. That the threat was not one of *armed*, violent revolt [i.e. the Zealots], and that it nonetheless bothered them to the point of their resorting to irregular procedures to counter it, is a proof of the political relevance of nonviolent tactics.'[24] If Jesus' ministry had simply been spiritual or religious (i.e. apolitical), then there is no historically coherent reason he would have been crucified. At a deeper level, the cross expresses what is particular about Jesus' politics. That Jesus was willing to submit to this crucifixion, rather than resorting to violent revolt, discloses the nature of his ministry as one of servanthood, forgiveness and love. In other words, the cross represents 'the political alternative to both insurrection and quietism'[25] and shows that 'the alternative to how the kings of the earth rule is … servanthood.'[26]

For Yoder, the cross also provides the point of continuity between the ministry of Jesus and the early church.[27] Throughout his ministry, Jesus 'calls into being a community of *voluntary* commitment, willing for the sake of its calling to take upon itself the hostility of the given society.'[28] Jesus' teachings and actions open up a space for others actively to adopt his politics, thereby embracing the suffering that this inevitably entails. The result is that, 'the New Testament church sees … participation in the suffering of Christ … as guiding and explaining her attitude to the world.'[29] For the early Christian community, the experience of the option of Jesus is represented by the symbol of the cross: 'His people will encounter in ways analogous to his own the hostility of the old order.'[30]

This means that the early Christian community is necessarily distinctive within the world and is a visible witness to Jesus' distinctive politics. On the one hand, the early Christians' embrace of Jesus' option provides the basis for a new commonality. A common vision and identity results from the shared embrace of this option and all that it entails. On the other hand, the fact that this is a particular historical-political option implies that the common vision and identity of the disciples will

---

24. Yoder, *The Politics of Jesus*, 49. As Yoder elsewhere makes this point: 'Herod cannot be seeking to kill Jesus for heresy or prophecy; sedition would be the only possible charge.' Yoder, *The Politics of Jesus*, 37. On the political nature of the crucifixion see E. P. Sanders, *Jesus and Judaism* (London: SCM Press, 1985), 294-318.

25. Yoder, *The Politics of Jesus*, 36.

26. Yoder, *The Politics of Jesus*, 39.

27. Yoder emphasizes this continuity over against attempts to separate the politics of Jesus from Paul and the early church. See especially chapter 9 of *The Politics of Jesus*.

28. Yoder, *The Politics of Jesus*, 37.

29. Yoder, *The Politics of Jesus*, 95.

30. Yoder, *The Politics of Jesus*, 96.

again be a distinctive one. It will be distinctive and visible in that this community actively embodies one particular option over against others.

This leads to the issue of how the early Christian disciples – and by implication Christians today – are to go about taking up Jesus' option and forming this visible community. Yoder describes this process using the language of participation, imitation and discipleship. The Christian is actively and willingly to take up the option of Jesus by imitating him, or at least those actions and activities that led to the cross.[31] The early Christians participated in the option of Jesus by taking up a particular concrete, political stance: 'If we may posit ... that the apostles had and taught at least a core memory of their Lord's earthly ministry in its blunt historicity, then this centering of the apostolic ethic upon the disciple's cross evidences a substantial, binding, and sometimes costly social stance.'[32] The early Christians came together to adopt such a costly stance, one which set them at odds with the world, and ensured the visibility of their witness.

It is worth noting the predominance of active language in Yoder's conception of discipleship and community. For instance, he stresses 'imitation' in ways that imply a human capacity to imitate.[33] If Jesus is indeed the bearer of a 'new possibility of human, social, and political relationships',[34] then the task of the disciples is to actualize or realize this new possibility as a new community.[35] Human beings are faced with the decision of whether or not to follow Jesus by actively taking up this possibility (a decision which is already implied in the language of a 'political option'). Yoder's language thus implies that human beings have an independent standpoint from which to consider and respond to Jesus and his option.[36] This anthropology is elsewhere apparent in his characterization of Jesus as foremost a 'teacher and example'.[37]

On this basis Yoder appears to reject any forensic conception of justification, whereby 'God declares, on the ground of the work of Christ which no person

---

31. Yoder stipulates that Christians are not to imitate every aspect of the historical person of Jesus, a mistake he identifies with the mendicant tradition, which 'centred its attention upon the outward form of Jesus' life; his forsaking domicile and property, his celibacy or his barefoot literacy'. Yoder, *The Politics of Jesus*, 130. Rather, Christians are to embrace only that kind of politics that leads to the cross.

32. Yoder, *The Politics of Jesus*, 127.

33. See Yoder, *The Politics of Jesus*, 132–3.

34. Yoder, *The Politics of Jesus*, 52.

35. This idea that Jesus initiated something within his lifetime which the community then takes over following his death has broadly Hegelian overtones. See G. W. F. Hegel, *Lectures on the Philosophy of Religion: One-Volume Edition, The Lectures of 1827*, ed. Peter Hodgson (Berkeley: University of California Press, 1988), 464–70.

36. Yoder writes, 'the disciple *chooses* not to exercise certain types of power'. Emphasis added. Yoder, *The Politics of Jesus*, 154.

37. Yoder, *The Politics of Jesus*, 226. Yoder explicitly contrasts his own position with traditional notions of 'Jesus as sacrifice'.

could have accomplished for himself or herself, that he or she shall henceforth be considered a new person, forgiven and restored to fellowship.'[38] In contrast, he insists justification is primarily 'a social phenomenon centering in the reconciliation of different kinds of people.'[39] Justification involves the active and visible recognition and overcoming of social differences and exclusions within the new community.[40] Put differently, it involves actively realizing the social and political options that Jesus made possible.

Following from this, Yoder seems to reject any conception of sin as original or inherited. He positions sin as primarily a failure to recognize and realize this option offered in Jesus.[41] He writes:

> What then was Paul's understanding of sin? When he does speak of himself as a serious sinner at all, this is not because of his existential anguish under the righteousness of God in general, but very specifically because, not having recognized that the Messiah had come in Jesus, he had persecuted the church and fought the opening of God's covenant to the gentiles.[42]

In other words, Paul's sin consists of his initial failure to recognize Jesus and his significance, and of his subsequent failure to enact the inclusivity that Jesus' example requires. This conception of sin also appears in some of Yoder's comments on the Sermon on the Mount, where he rejects the view that the Sermon presents an unattainable standard: 'The "perfection" to which Jesus calls his hearers ... is not flawlessness nor impeccability, but precisely the refusal to discriminate between friend and enemy.'[43] Yoder's position appears to be that human beings, on their own terms, are able to follow these teachings and attain the standard that Jesus sets. There is nothing that inherently prevents the disciples from achieving Jesus' perfection for themselves.

Yoder concludes *The Politics of Jesus* with a brief discussion of the apocalyptic material in Scripture. He claims this material provides a 'resource' for the

---

38. Yoder, *The Politics of Jesus*, 213.
39. Yoder, *The Politics of Jesus*, 226.
40. According to Yoder, 'the word "justification" ... should be thought of in its root meaning, as a verbal noun, an action, "setting things rights"'. Yoder, *The Politics of Jesus*, 224.
41. In an earlier essay, Yoder writes that 'The Gospel does not say anything about sin as an unavoidable phenomenon in human existence; it says "Repent!" which, being interpreted, does not mean "continue to sin, but sorrowfully", but "STOP IT". The Church's not being the Church cannot be discussed in the indicative; "Repent and be the Church" is the only thing to say.' John Howard Yoder, 'Light to the Nations', *Concerns* 9 (1961): 18.
42. Yoder, *The Politics of Jesus*, 217.
43. Yoder, *The Politics of Jesus*, 225. Yoder rejects the view that the 'Sermon's intent is ... to prepare people for grace by crushing them under the demand of an unattainable Godlikeness.' Yoder, *The Politics of Jesus*, 116.

'perception of the meaning and course of history'.[44] The apocalypses, he continues, 'are about how the crucified Jesus is a more adequate key to understanding what God is about in the real world of empires and armies and markets than is the ruler in Rome, with all his supporting military, commercial and sacerdotal networks'.[45] Attending to this vision, therefore, frees Christians from needing to manage society on God's behalf,[46] and allows them to embrace the non-violent option of Jesus. It is worth noting that the stress is upon the apocalyptic as having already been realized through the option of Jesus: 'The gap between the present and the promise was not fundamental.'[47] For Yoder, there is a basic continuity between the present visible Christian community and the future kingdom of God.[48]

Yoder's reading of Bonhoeffer

Before turning to Bonhoeffer's theology, it will be useful to examine how Yoder explicitly positions himself with respect to Bonhoeffer. In *The Politics of Jesus*, Yoder makes only two passing references to him. First, in a footnote in his chapter on discipleship, he asserts that 'when Dietrich Bonhoeffer uses the term "discipleship" it carries a different shade of meaning. The accent falls less on sharing the Master's way or nature, and more on unquestioning willingness to obey.'[49] Second, in a later chapter, Yoder distinguishes his own theology of the cross from Bonhoeffer's language of 'breaking through to the cross' in confession, and related claim that sharing in Christ's death involves the 'shameful death of the sinner in confession'.[50] By Yoder's reckoning, such language displays a dangerous, existential or inward turn that again obfuscates the more material and political nature of the crucifixion.

---

44. Yoder, *The Politics of Jesus*, 231.
45. Yoder, *The Politics of Jesus*, 246.
46. See Yoder, *The Politics of Jesus*, 240.
47. Yoder, *The Politics of Jesus*, 241. This emphasis on a realized eschatology is elsewhere apparent in *The Politics of Jesus*: 'The jubilee which Jesus proclaims is not the end of time, pure event without duration, unconnected to either yesterday or tomorrow. The jubilee is precisely an *institution* whose functioning within history will have a precise, practical, limited impact.' Yoder, *The Politics of Jesus*, 104.
48. As Yoder writes, it is not the case that 'that to which we look forward is a radically different kind of world from the world in which we now live, but rather that it lies further in the same direction in which we are being led'. Yoder, *The Politics of Jesus*, 241. Hauerwas and others sometimes display a similar approach to the apocalyptic material. See, for example, Stanley Hauerwas, 'On Being a Church Capable of Addressing a World at War: A Pacifist Response to the United Bishops' Pastoral', in *The Hauerwas Reader*, ed. John Berkman and Michael Cartwright (Durham: Duke University Press, 2001), 436–48.
49. Yoder, *The Politics of Jesus*, 113.
50. Yoder, *The Politics of Jesus*, 130.

In a 1987 lecture (first published in 2010), Yoder engages Bonhoeffer's theology more extensively, focusing particularly on his account of discipleship.[51] Yoder's constant refrain in this lecture is that Bonhoeffer's Christology and related account of discipleship lack concrete, historical content: 'How does the Christ of Bonhoeffer's call to discipleship relate to the lifestyle of the man named Jesus?'[52] He elsewhere complains that Bonhoeffer 'makes no effort to illuminate what discipleship means for the disciple by reference to any events in the pre-passion ministry of Jesus'.[53] For Yoder, the problem is that Bonhoeffer fails to take the concrete, historical humanity of Jesus seriously. He thus reiterates his own position as 'an ethic for which the concrete humanity of Jesus, in his social decisions, provides the model'.[54]

The primary way that Yoder frames this difference between Bonhoeffer and himself is in terms of differing accounts of the incarnation, which he respectively labels 'Jesulogical' and 'logological'.[55] On the one hand, Yoder designates his own approach 'Jesulogical' in that it stresses that God became incarnate as a particular man, the first-century Jew named Jesus, who at that time and place made a series of particular decisions. On the other, he designates Bonhoeffer's Christology 'logological' in that it focuses on the fact of the son of God becoming human.[56] What is implied in such a Christology, in Yoder's judgement, is that the disciple needs to believe in, and be encountered by, this Christ, but need not overly concern himself or herself with the historical particularities of who Jesus actually was. Yoder's concern is that Bonhoeffer's Christ is not based on 'the words or the earthly works of Jesus', and that these words and works do not therefore 'contribute the ethical substance' of discipleship.[57]

Although Yoder clearly recognizes some fundamental differences between Bonhoeffer's theology and his own, he nevertheless concludes his lecture by suggesting a remedy. First, he suggests that a more Jesulogical or Anabaptist approach to Christ and discipleship may not even have occurred to Bonhoeffer: 'It

---

51. Yoder, 'The Christological Presuppositions of Discipleship'.

52. Yoder, 'The Christological Presuppositions of Discipleships', 134. Yoder continues: 'Is it some serious sense of a sharing in the sober social reality of the Messiah's cross through that instrumentality of his body, i.e. of a community projecting into its present the meaning of his past servanthood?'

53. Yoder, 'The Christological Presuppositions of Discipleships', 140.

54. Yoder, 'The Christological Presuppositions of Discipleships', 134.

55. Yoder, 'The Christological Presuppositions of Discipleships', 144.

56. Yoder's 'logological' reading of Bonhoeffer's Christology misses his sharp rejection of theoretical approaches to the incarnation and emphasis on Christ's promeity. For example, in his earlier Christology lectures, Bonhoeffer insists, 'it is impossible to ask how God can enter into time – as if such an isolated God could exist! The only question that makes sense is who is present, who is with us here and now?' Bonhoeffer, 'Lectures on Christology', DBWE 12: 313.

57. Yoder, 'The Christological Presuppositions of Discipleships', 143.

probably never came into his mind.'⁵⁸ Second, he proposes that Bonhoeffer's theology might be redeemed and deepened by moving it in this direction: 'To move in this direction would not be to despise the logological questions, but only to subordinate speculation about the incarnation to the fact of the incarnation.'⁵⁹ In other words, Yoder holds that some of Bonhoeffer's insights and questions might be taken up and reworked on the basis of a more robustly Jesulogical approach.

In broad terms, I would suggest that this is what followers of Yoder such as Hauerwas, McClendon, Nation, Stassen and others have sought to do. Such figures have sought to read Bonhoeffer's theology on the basis of broadly Anabaptist commitments, thereby emphasizing select aspects of his theology while downplaying others. While there is value in such an approach and what it draws from Bonhoeffer, this strategy neglects a number of crucial aspects of Bonhoeffer's theology. It is to these that we now turn.

Bonhoeffer and the ethics of Christ

Whereas for Yoder discipleship involves human beings actively taking up a political option presented by the historical person of Jesus, in his 1937 *Discipleship* (*Nachfolge*), Bonhoeffer gives a very different account of how Christ calls his disciples and what this call entails.⁶⁰ Furthermore, he provides a different account of the relationship between Christ's call and concrete Christian community.

One of Bonhoeffer's central claims in *Discipleship* is that the present or living Christ calls and gathers his disciples to himself directly. He had already developed this emphasis in his 1933 lectures on Christology: 'As the Crucified and Risen One, Jesus is at the same time the Christ who is present now … He is to be understood as present in time and space. *Nunc et hic.*'⁶¹ In other words, we can know Christ only because he is present and living, and thus able to encounter us today.⁶² In *Discipleship*, Bonhoeffer similarly insists that, 'Jesus Christ is not dead but alive and still speaking to us today through the testimony of scripture.'⁶³

---

58. Yoder, 'The Christological Presuppositions of Discipleship', 150. Yoder writes: 'Bonhoeffer does not focus upon these issues and reject the Anabaptist response to them; they simply have not yet come to a head in his thinking.' Yoder, 'The Christological Presuppositions of Discipleship', 141.

59. Yoder, 'The Christological Presuppositions of Discipleship', 151.

60. Ernst Feil has drawn attention to the centrality of Christology for *Discipleship*. Feil, *The Theology of Dietrich Bonhoeffer*, 78.

61. DBWE 12: 310.

62. Moreover, in these lectures Bonhoeffer insists that only this living Christ provides access to the Jesus of history (and not the reverse): 'It is the Risen One who himself creates faith and makes possible our access to the historicity of Jesus … Through faith, history is recognized by eternity, not by itself or from within itself.' DBWE 12: 330.

63. DBWE 4: 201.

Bonhoeffer's emphasis on the living Christ affects how we are to approach and interpret Scripture. In Yoder's theology, as we have seen, Scripture's role is primarily to present the life and teachings of the historical person of Jesus. The gospels and letters of Paul present a particular historical-political option of Jesus and the early church. In contrast, Bonhoeffer holds that the 'living Christ in judgment and grace encounters us in scripture and is himself the key to interpreting it'.[64] Bonhoeffer's interest is not so much in how human beings should properly read Scripture, or find Jesus in Scripture, but rather in how the living Christ comes to us through Scripture, opening and interpreting it for us.[65] In another essay from this period, Bonhoeffer writes that 'the only method of contemporization is thus the substantive [*sachliche*] textual exposition [of the Holy Scriptures] as the witness of Christ, and such exegesis has the promise of the presence of Christ'.[66]

For Bonhoeffer, this means that we should not try to 'identify ourselves directly with those called by Jesus' in the gospels.[67] We should not try to put ourselves in the place of the first disciples or follow Jesus in the same way that they did. Bonhoeffer explicitly insists that the first disciples do not provide a direct model for our own discipleship: 'It is never a question of our having or taking on the same identity as the disciples or other people in the New Testament.'[68] Rather, he continues, 'the only issue is that *Jesus Christ and his call* are the same, then and now'.[69] The biblical disciples do not provide a model for discipleship. Rather, the living Christ calls us to himself through the witness of these disciples.[70]

This suggests that discipleship cannot be adequately understood with the language of 'option' or 'possibility'. For Bonhoeffer, following Christ is not an option that we somehow adopt or realize. In an earlier essay, he insists that 'the concept of possibility has no place in theology and no place in theological anthropology'.[71] He elaborates on why this is the case:

> The concept of possibility rationalizes reality. It determines every reality according to the manner of a logically existing thing. That is, it fixes it, makes

---

64. DBWE 4: 82.

65. For a more detailed account of Bonhoeffer's approach to Scripture, see Chapter 2, 'As a Whole and in Its Parts'.

66. Bonhoeffer, 'Contemporizing New Testament Texts', DBWE 14: 421–2. Earlier in this same essay, Bonhoeffer writes that 'the movement is not from the word of Scripture to the present but rather from the present to the word of Scripture, where it then abides! ... Those who find this incomprehensible have not yet grasped the presupposition that the present can be found only where Christ and the Holy Spirit speak.' DBWE 14: 418–19.

67. DBWE 4: 82.

68. DBWE 4: 203.

69. DBWE 4, 203. Emphasis added.

70. Bonhoeffer writes, 'those who are called in scripture themselves belong to the word of God and to the proclamation of the word'. DBWE 4: 82.

71. DBWE 10: 403.

it universally accessible. (In this way, it is possible to place the point of unity of self-understanding into one's own ego through rationalization). For theological anthropology, this means that the human being is conceived with certain possibilities in relation to God, to which he can withdraw at any given time.[72]

The language of possibility is problematic in that it requires a kind of human being that exists prior to and apart from its relationship to God. It assumes a human being who is able to adequately position himself or herself with respect to God's call.

In *Discipleship*, Bonhoeffer famously insists that genuine discipleship can only involve an 'immediate response' or 'simple obedience' on the part of the Christian: 'The call goes out, and without any further ado the obedient deed of the one called follows.'[73] If discipleship cannot be understood as a human possibility or option, then it is not something that disciples actively choose for themselves: 'In simple obedience disciples do the will of the Lord who bids them do something extraordinary, and they know in everything only that they can do nothing else, that they are, therefore, doing what is simply a matter of course.'[74] Put differently, Bonhoeffer maintains the priority of Christ's call over against any human ability to respond to or interpret this call. Indeed, as Bernd Wannenwetsch has summarized, 'Christ's calling is authoritative in that it generates the need, wish, and will to follow the command – while at times explicitly rejecting the human need, wish, and will to follow him as insufficient.'[75]

This further means that discipleship cannot be adequately understood as an active imitation or emulation of Christ. It cannot be understood primarily through the language of virtue, performance or habituation. 'To be conformed to the image of Jesus Christ', Bonhoeffer writes, 'is not an ideal of realizing some similarity with Christ which we are asked to attain. It is not we who change ourselves into the image of God.'[76] 'Rather', he continues, 'it is the image of God, the form of Christ, which seeks to take shape within us'.[77] Discipleship does not involve disciples actively imitating Christ, but rather passively receiving Christ and being formed by Christ. Bonhoeffer elaborates on this point in a later manuscript from his *Ethics*: 'Formation occurs by being drawn into the form of

---

72. DBWE 10: 403.

73. DBWE 4: 57. Furthermore, Bonhoeffer is critical of independent attempts to understand or mediate this call through reason: 'How is this direct relation between call and obedience possible? It is quite offensive to natural reason. Reason is impelled to reject the abruptness of the response. It seeks something to mediate it; it seeks an explanation.' DBWE 4: 57.

74. DBWE 4: 150.

75. See Wannenwetsch, 'Christians and Pagans', 184.

76. DBWE 4: 284.

77. DBWE 4: 284. Bonhoeffer elsewhere writes in *Discipleship*, '"You *are* the salt" – not "you should be the salt"! The disciples are given no choice whether they want to be salt or not.' DBWE 4: 111.

Jesus Christ ... This does not happen as we strive to become like Jesus ... but as the form of Jesus Christ himself so works on us that it molds us, conforming our form to Christ's own.'[78]

Bonhoeffer does clearly admit in *Discipleship* that those wishing to become disciples should take a 'first step towards Christ', one which 'puts the follower into the situation of being able to believe'.[79] This first step is integral to Bonhoeffer's famous distinction between cheap and costly grace, and it has received significant attention in the secondary literature.[80] As Bonhoeffer puts it, such a step of human obedience is necessary in order that 'faith does not become pious self-deception, cheap grace'.[81] What has received less attention, however, is Bonhoeffer's careful stipulation that this step by itself 'remains a dead work of the law, which can by itself never lead to Christ'.[82] He is clear that it is only in light of Christ's call that we can even recognize whether this was even a step in the right direction: 'There is nothing in the situation as such to indicate which kind it is.'[83] Christ calls and claims the disciple in a way that takes account of this first human step, but Christ's call in no way requires or depends on this step.[84]

For Bonhoeffer, all genuine Christian discipleship depends on Christ alone, and remains independent of all human striving, because of sin. Following Luther, Bonhoeffer holds that attempts to interpret and negotiate Christ's call are implicated in a kind of self-assertion that emerged with the Fall: 'Even in their most pious ways and deeds, persons cannot stand before God, because they are always basically seeking themselves.'[85] In other words, the problem of sin and its effects goes all the way down. As compared with Yoder, Bonhoeffer is clearer that sin is not something that human beings are in any sense able to move beyond or

---

78. Bonhoeffer, 'Ethics as Formation', DBWE 6: 93. Later in this same essay Bonhoeffer describes the church as the place 'where Jesus Christ's taking form is proclaimed and where it happens'. DBWE 6: 102.

79. DBWE 4: 62.

80. In discussing this 'first step', Paul Spanring, for example, describes Bonhoeffer's position as involving 'a volitional commitment to following Jesus'. Paul Spanring, *Dietrich Bonhoeffer and Arnold Köster: Two Distinct Voices in the Midst of Germany's Third Reich Turmoil* (Eugene: Pickwick, 2013), 215.

81. DBWE 4: 64.

82. DBWE 4: 65. Bonhoeffer is clear that such a step, while required, is in no way foundational for faith: 'If we take the first step with the intention of putting ourselves into the situation of being able to believe, then even this ability to believe is itself nothing but works. It is but a new possibility for living within our old existence and thereby a complete misunderstanding. We remain in unbelief.' DBWE 4: 65.

83. DBWE 4: 63.

84. This first step has the status of the 'penultimate' with respect to Christ. See Bonhoeffer's essay 'Ultimate and Penultimate Things', DBWE 6: 146–70.

85. DBWE 4: 49.

negotiate through their own efforts: 'The sinner's very life is enmeshed in sin to such an extent that deliverance from sin can be brought about for the sinners only through their death.'[86]

This also means that justification depends entirely on God's work in Christ, and that any righteousness resulting from Christ's work (ultimately at least) remains with Christ. As Bonhoeffer insists, 'the justification of sinners consists in God alone being righteous and sinners being totally and utterly unrighteous, rather than in granting sinners their own righteousness alongside that of God'.[87] It is Christ's righteousness that allows for reconciliation with God. Christ overcomes the problem of human sin by standing in the place of human beings.[88] For this reason, justification cannot initially be understood in social and political terms, or as the active overcoming of social discrimination.[89] For Bonhoeffer, Christ does not indicate the way out of sin, or exemplify and present a new possibility for humanity. Rather, Christ himself is the way; it is in Christ that we stand reconciled before God.

This indicates why everything that is entailed in genuine discipleship proceeds from Christ. In contrast to Yoder, Bonhoeffer maintains that true discipleship has no fixed, identifiable material or social content in itself: 'What is said about the content of discipleship? Follow me, walk behind me! That is all … It is truly not a program for one's life.'[90] Following the call of Christ is necessarily a leap of faith or a step into the unknown. In contrast to Yoder, it does not involve adopting or taking up a determined social or political programme. Discipleship involves being drawn away from all such programmes and into Christ.[91]

---

86. DBWE 4: 255. In the lecture 'The Anthropological Question in Contemporary Philosophy and Theology', Bonhoeffer writes: 'If sin and faith are among the possibilities of human beings, then the complete incomprehensibility, inexcusability, and infinity of the fall is rationalized into a comprehensible action of immanent possibilities. Here sin loses the weight of infinity, the result being that forgiveness and the wiping out of sins can be understood only as the actualization – albeit from God – of human possibilities.' DBWE 10: 404.

87. DBWE 4: 256.

88. This means that right standing before God is bestowed on human beings entirely 'as a free gift'. DBWE 4: 257. Bonhoeffer continues, 'Jesus gave them [his disciples] the *gift* of justification … and forgiveness of sins.' DBWE 4: 209. This differs significantly from Yoder's understanding of justification in terms of an active pursuit of social reconciliation. To be clear, however, this is not to deny how, for Bonhoeffer, this reconciliation then flows from the work of Christ into his community.

89. To be clear, for Bonhoeffer an embodied, political reconciliation is still at the centre of God's work of justification. But this is in a way that is less reductive and predetermined than it is for Yoder. On the social implications of Bonhoeffer's understanding of justification, see Verhagen, *Being and Action* Coram Deo.

90. DBWE 4: 58.

91. That is, drawn away from fixed positions or ideologies that are set in advance.

The specific way that Christ calls his disciples away from worldly programmes and claims them is through suffering: 'Just as Christ is only Christ as one who suffers and is rejected, so a disciple is a disciple only in suffering and being rejected, therefore participating in crucifixion.'[92] Here Bonhoeffer's position seems to be close to Yoder's, in that both insist that genuine Christian discipleship involves suffering and the cross. However, Bonhoeffer goes on to stipulate that even this suffering does not provide material content for discipleship: 'There is no general form of suffering that the disciples enter into or embrace. Rather, the living Christ gives to each disciple his or her own suffering: How should disciples know what their cross is? They will receive it when they begin to follow the suffering Lord. They will recognize their cross in communion with Christ.'[93] In other words, for Bonhoeffer suffering and the cross do not exemplify the political and social option of Jesus' ministry. Rather, they designate what happens as Christ frees us from our material and worldly attachments and binds us to himself.[94]

However, Bonhoeffer is clear that Christ's call to discipleship, through suffering and by way of the cross, provides the basis for a new Christian community. This call not only leads to a break from existing, worldly community and relationality, it also provides a foundation for a community of a qualitatively different kind.[95] In the second half of *Discipleship*, Bonhoeffer provides a detailed account of this new community. As Hauerwas, McClendon, Nation, Stassen and others have rightly noted, in this account Bonhoeffer emphasizes the visibility and distinctive witness of this new community. In an oft-quoted phrase, he writes that 'the body of Christ takes up physical space here on earth' and that 'anything that takes up space is visible.'[96] Moreover, he insists that Christ's call results in 'a clear separation' between this new community and the world.[97] In other words, Bonhoeffer emphasizes both the church's visibility and its distinctive identity. There are some deep and obvious resonances here with Anabaptist understandings of church.

Less attention, however, has been given to the important ways in which Bonhoeffer subsequently develops and qualifies this initial position.[98] First, Bonhoeffer again insists that Christ's call alone secures the visibility and witness

92. DBWE 4: 85.
93. DBWE 4: 89.
94. Luther writes that 'the only reason they [Christians] must suffer is that they steadfastly adhere to Christ and God's word, enduring this for the sake of Christ'. Luther, 'On the Councils and the Church', *Luther's Works, Volume 41*, 165–7.
95. Bonhoeffer writes: 'There are no longer natural, historical, or experiential unmediated relationships for his disciples.' DBWE 4: 95. After the call to discipleship, all such relationships are mediated in Christ.
96. DBWE 4: 225. See Hauerwas, *Performing the Faith*, 45; Nation, *Bonhoeffer the Assassin?*, 157.
97. DBWE 4: 261.
98. For example, in a recent article Craig Nessan draws on Bonhoeffer to emphasize the holiness of the visible church as the body of Christ. Nessan fails to mention any of

of the church: 'It is not the faith community which separates itself from others, yet this separation necessarily takes place in the call by the Word.'[99] Accordingly, genuine visibility is not a function of human beings adopting one historical-political option among others. True visibility proceeds from Christ's call alone. On this point Bonhoeffer explicitly distances his own position from an Anabaptist (i.e. enthusiast) one:

> The danger is great that in enthusiasts' indifference [*schwärmerischer Gleichgültigkeit*] to this age they will think it their duty now to achieve and make visible the extraordinariness of this new world, separating themselves from the world radically and with no willingness to compromise, in order to force into being what is Christian, what is appropriate to discipleship, what is extraordinary.[100]

Following Bonhoeffer, we are not called on to actively separate ourselves from the world and to create extraordinary communities of witness. Rather, Christ calls us to a more ordinary kind of faithfulness: 'Not the extraordinary, but rather the completely ordinary, everyday, regular, unobtrusive behavior is the sign of genuine obedience and genuine humility.'[101]

In addition, Bonhoeffer insists that the disciples cannot themselves see the distinctive visibility of this new community: 'As a visible church–community, their own identity remains completely invisible to them. They look only to their Lord. He is in heaven, and their life for which they are waiting is in him!'[102] Correlatively, he insists that when those who have been called by Christ look to the Christian community directly, all that they see is 'strife, hardness, weakness and sin'.[103] For Bonhoeffer, the goodness of the church is never directly visible or available to the Christian disciples themselves. This goodness of the church is not for the disciples, but rather for those who are beyond the community: 'they are to see the light of Jesus' disciples shining'.[104]

In a related way, Bonhoeffer claims that the Christian community on its own terms remains a 'visible community of justified sinners'.[105] The church is visible, then, only as a sinful human body, not in terms of its holiness or good works more directly.[106] Bonhoeffer thus explicitly rejects the 'enthusiasts' perfectionism'

Bonhoeffer's careful qualifications of what this visibility entails. See Craig Nessan, 'What if the Church Really Is the Body of Christ?', *Dialog* 51 (2012): 43–52.
99. DBWE 4: 175.
100. DBWE 4: 146.
101. DBWE 4: 147.
102. DBWE 4: 251.
103. DBWE 4: 267.
104. DBWE 4: 149.
105. DBWE 4: 262.
106. For a recent constructive development of this insight see McBride, *The Church for the World*.

whereby 'those who are in God do not sin'.[107] Any righteousness and goodness of the Christian community is in Christ. (Therefore, when Hauerwas claims that 'Bonhoeffer and Yoder unapologetically maintain that we are called to be perfect' – which he glosses as to 'learn to be part of a people who take the time to live without resort to violence' – he underplays this Lutheran emphasis on the continuing presence of sin in the church).[108]

Finally, Bonhoeffer's thoroughgoing emphasis on sin in the church also requires a different eschatology. As we have seen, Yoder tends to stress continuity between 'the present and the promise'.[109] Accordingly, the new Christian community already significantly embodies and anticipates the coming kingdom. While Bonhoeffer agrees that Christ establishes a new community, he emphasizes that it is only with the final judgement that 'Christ himself will reveal to us the good works of which we have been unaware'.[110] In particular, it is only on this final day that Christ will make clear how he was already present in and visible through the church. Christ will make clear how he was present often in spite of – not due to – our human strivings and efforts: 'On that day we will be greatly astonished, and we will recognize that it is not our works which endure here but only the work which God, in God's own time, accomplished through us without our intention and effort.'[111]

Conclusion

What is the broader significance of these differences between Yoder and Bonhoeffer for how we understand and approach Christian ethics? When we recognize these differences – and attend to the aspects of Bonhoeffer's theology that are obfuscated when he is drawn into close proximity with Yoder – what challenges does his theology present for Christian ethics today?

Bonhoeffer's claim that the living Christ calls his disciples directly challenges Christian thinking and action to be oriented to and by this call. This means that genuinely Christian thinking and action remains continually open and attentive to the living Christ, to how Christ calls us and takes form among us in ways we can neither anticipate nor clearly comprehend. There is no Christian ethical thinking or action apart from the call of Christ and human obedience.

On this basis, Bonhoeffer's theology resituates how we understand the role of human agency and activity in ethics. In particular, his theology challenges any

---

107. DBWE 4: 206.
108. Stanley Hauerwas, 'The Sermon on the Mount: Dietrich Bonhoeffer and John Howard Yoder', in *The Sermon on the Mount through the Centuries: From the Early Church to John Paul II*, ed. Jeffrey P. Greenman, Timothy Larsen and Stephen R. Spencer (Grand Rapids: Brazos Press, 2007), 217.
109. Quoted earlier. Yoder, *The Politics of Jesus*, 341.
110. DBWE 4: 279.
111. DBWE 4: 280.

assumption – as in Yoder's language of a Christian option or possibility – that we are responsible for making Christ present in the world or forming Christian community. Bonhoeffer makes it clear that it is Christ who is the primary agent in the Christian community.[112] Christian ethics as a discipline should therefore be more clearly orientated by how Christ is directly present and at work – even when hidden – in our living with God and one another.

This presents a challenge to the language and kinds of concepts that we use in Christian ethics. In particular, Bonhoeffer's theology challenges the use of the language of formative practices, virtues, character, habits and narrative – again, language that is central for Yoder and his followers. For Bonhoeffer, the problem with such language is that it focuses on human agency and activity too directly, rather than keeping the emphasis upon Christ's call and work. It obfuscates the fact that as Christians we are simply to follow after or serve Christ.

One danger of such language is that it downplays the sheer radicality of Christ's call. As we have seen, Bonhoeffer emphasizes a sharp discontinuity or rupture between our lives before and after Christ. In contrast, language of practice or emulation suggests that on some level we are able to direct ourselves towards Christ, or that we have resources for negotiating Christ's call. This potentially mitigates the extent of sin and its effects, on the one hand, and God's work in Christ, on the other.

Finally, Bonhoeffer's theology challenges an understanding of Christian ethics as a particular kind of ethics, the kind done by Christians. As we have seen, Yoder presents Christianity in precisely this way, as a distinctive or particular ethos or politics. For Yoder, the significance of Jesus is that he presents a new sociopolitical option that is visibly different from other options. This calls for a kind of Christian thinking and action that is distinctive within the world. In contrast, Bonhoeffer's theology implies a kind of Christian thinking and action that is both more and less distinct. It is more distinct, in that the living Christ provides the sole foundation for all Christian thinking and action. Christian thinking and action continually depends upon a Christ who stands distinct from and in the world.[113] But Christian thinking and action is less distinct, following Bonhoeffer, precisely in that it is Christ alone – not our own striving or efforts – who secures any visible Christian witness. We ultimately know our thinking and action to be distinctively Christian only in Christ and by means of faith.

---

112. Bonhoeffer more clearly distinguishes between Christ and the church than Yoder and his followers.

113. To be clear, for Bonhoeffer, Christians should be open and attentive to all kinds of human thinking and action. For these to be available to theology and theological ethics, however, they must be (continually) disrupted and interrogated in light of Christ's call. I explore how Bonhoeffer himself does this in more detail elsewhere. See Mawson, *Christ Existing as Community*, especially chapter 2.

In summary, recognizing the deep theological differences between Yoder and Bonhoeffer, and more clearly separating the latter from the former, challenges many contemporary patterns of thinking in contemporary Christian ethics and reaffirms the priority and centrality of Christ's own agency and presence for a genuinely Christian approach.

Chapter 12

THE STUMBLING BLOCK AND THE LYNCHING TREE: READING BONHOEFFER'S 'LECTURES ON CHRISTOLOGY' WITH JAMES CONE

In his 2011 book, *The Cross and the Lynching Tree*, James Cone reflects on how, throughout much of Western Christian history, the cross 'had been detached from the ongoing suffering and oppression of human beings, the crucified people of history'.[1] As he further observes, 'the cross was transformed into a harmless, non-offensive ornament that Christians wear around their neck'.[2] In the context of reflecting on this domestication, Cone invokes Dietrich Bonhoeffer: 'Rather than reminding us of the cross of discipleship, it became a form of "cheap grace" … an easy way to claim salvation without confronting the power of Christ's message and mission.'[3]

Here and elsewhere in his writings, Cone understands Bonhoeffer as providing a precedent and support for the kind of disruptive Christology and discipleship that is central to his own Black theology.[4] Cone finds in Bonhoeffer a rare example of a white theologian who is willing to state truths and take risks for the sake of the gospel. Even when Cone became more critical of some of his other white theological influences,[5] his occasional references to Bonhoeffer remain appreciative.

Cone's consistent appreciation of Bonhoeffer helps to situate some of the resonances and overlaps between their reflections on Christology. In this chapter, I draw attention to these resonances and overlaps, but also to some ways in which I think Cone can be drawn on to extend and deepen Bonhoeffer's Christology. In particular, I will suggest that this is the case for his account of Christ's humiliation

---

1. James Cone, *The Cross and the Lynching Tree*, xiv.
2. Cone, *The Cross and the Lynching Tree*, xiv.
3. Cone, *The Cross and the Lynching Tree*, xiv–xv.
4. For some examples, see James Cone, 'Theology Great Sin: Silence in the Face of White Supremacy', *Black Theology* 2, no. 2 (2004): 139–52.
5. This is especially from *The Spirituals and the Blues* (Maryknoll: Orbis, 1972), in which Cone began relying more directly on Black cultural sources and experience. On this point, see Andrew Prevot, 'Theology and Race: Black and Womanist Traditions in the United States', *Theology* 2, no. 2 (2018): 23–8.

in the final section of his 1933 'Lectures on Christology'. By drawing attention to what crucifixion actually involved, Cone's work can be used to supplement and enrich this area of Bonhoeffer's theology. Simply put, reading Bonhoeffer's 'Lectures on Christology' with James Cone helps us to think 'with Bonhoeffer beyond Bonhoeffer'.[6]

Christ as stumbling block: Bonhoeffer's 'Lectures on Christology'

Bonhoeffer's most detailed and sustained treatment of Christology can be found in his 'Lectures on Christology', which were delivered at Friedrich Wilhelm's University in Berlin in the summer of 1933. Reconstructed from student notes, these lectures were first published in German in 1960, and subsequently translated and published in English in 1966.

One of the threads that runs throughout these lectures is Bonhoeffer's resistance to abstract and speculative thinking about Christ.[7] In the opening section, Bonhoeffer famously prioritizes the 'who' question over the 'how' question.[8] Christological thinking, according to Bonhoeffer, begins with and proceeds as a response to an encounter with the living Christ: 'Who are you, Jesus Christ?'[9] Christology is not simply the attempt to explain or understand how it is that Christ is both fully human and divine.

Bonhoeffer's resistance to abstract thinking is further apparent through his central emphasis on Christ's 'promeity',[10] who Jesus Christ is for us today. In the Christology lectures, he avoids speculating about Christ's divinity or humanity as such, instead choosing to focus on the concrete ways that Christ encounters or is present to us.[11] Bonhoeffer gives particular attention to Christ's presence in the church's preaching and sacraments.[12] That is to say, for Bonhoeffer, Christ

---

6. This phrase comes from a chapter by John W. de Gruchy, 'With Bonhoeffer, Beyond Bonhoeffer: Transmitting Bonhoeffer's Legacy', in *Dietrich Bonhoeffer's Theology Today, A Way between Fundamentalism and Secularism*, ed. Stephen Plant, John W. de Gruchy and Christiane Tietz (München: Guetersloher Verlagshaus, 2009), 403–16.

7. At one point in the lectures, Bonhoeffer states that 'Christ as Word of God in the sense of word spoken to us does not mean Christ as timeless truth, but rather as truth breaking into a concrete moment.' Bonhoeffer, 'Lectures on Christology', DBWE 12: 317.

8. See DBWE 12: 302–8.

9. DBWE 12: 304.

10. Bonhoeffer uses the Latin *pro-me* (for me) and *pro-nobis* (for us) throughout his lectures. Scholars have subsequently referred to 'promeity' to describe this emphasis in Bonhoeffer's theology. See, for example, Philip G. Ziegler, 'Christ for Us' : 25–41.

11. As Bonhoeffer writes, 'it is not only useless to meditate on Christ-in-himself but godless, precisely because Christ is not there in himself, but rather is there for you.' DBWE 12: 314.

12. See DBWE 12: 315–27.

encounters us through these human words and practices.[13] This means that the work of Christology is primarily about reflecting on Christ's presence in these specific and concrete places: 'Only because proclamation and sacraments are carried out in the church can we inquire about Christ.'[14]

Nonetheless, while Christology is about reflecting on Christ's presence in the church, Bonhoeffer maintains that this still requires affirming that he *is* fully human and divine. As he writes, the very 'presence of Jesus Christ compels the statement that Jesus is wholly human, as well as the other statement that Jesus is wholly God – otherwise he would not be present.'[15] On the one hand, if Christ had simply been a human being, then he could be present for us now today only indirectly, as a historical influence or inspiring example.[16] On the other hand, if Christ were divine simply in an abstract or timeless sense, he could not be concretely and personally present to us.

In addition, Bonhoeffer clarifies his understanding of promeity by insisting that Christ's presence for us as human and divine is and remains a 'veiled presence'.[17] He describes this as the 'stumbling block' or 'scandal' at the heart of Christianity (cf. 1 Cor. 1.23).[18] As Bonhoeffer insists, 'it is not the hiddenness of God [in the human Christ] that is the stumbling block but the hiddenness of the God-human'.[19] In other words, the scandal or difficulty of Christology is not that God became human, but rather that this God-human is present to us as the 'humiliated one'.[20] The problem is that Christ as 'the God-human of history is always, already, the God-human who is humiliated, from the manger to the cross'.[21]

Rather than attending to and remaining with Christ as the humiliated one, Christians have instead continually sought to make Christ more acceptable. In a long section on 'Critical Christology or Negative Christology',[22] Bonhoeffer traces various heretical attempts to resolve or move beyond the scandal and offence of Christ's hiddenness. Indeed, he defines heresy itself as simply the attempt to say something about Christ with 'unambiguous directness'.[23]

---

13. On the presence of Christ in preaching, see Lose, 'Bonhoeffer the Preacher', 108–21. On Bonhoeffer on sacramentality, see Christopher Dodson, *The Who Is Given: Dietrich Bonhoeffer's Sacramental Theology and Religionless Christianity* (Lanham: Lexington Books, 2021).

14. DBWE 12: 310.
15. DBWE 12: 312.
16. See DBWE 12: 310–11.
17. DBWE 12: 313.
18. See DBWE 12: 313–14; 323; 358–60.
19. DBWE 12: 313–14.
20. DBWE 12: 274.
21. DBWE 12: 356.
22. DBWE 12: 331–53.
23. DBWE 12: 352.

12. The Stumbling Block and the Lynching Tree

In this section, Bonhoeffer focuses on the heresy of docetism, which he defines as the attempt to speak of or know about Christ as divine apart from his incarnation and humiliated form. Docetism is the attempt to make Christ less offensive by viewing him as 'the appearance of the Godhead in history'.[24] According to this line of thinking, as Bonhoeffer summarizes, 'Christ's humanness is only the garment, the wrapping, the means by which God speaks to humankind, but is not of the essence of God's nature'.[25] Who Christ *really* is, therefore, is other than the Jesus found in the gospels. Drawing on this broad definition, Bonhoeffer also proceeds to discern docetic tendencies in some doctrines of the early church,[26] in modern liberal theology[27] and in Reformed theology.[28]

Against these widespread docetic tendencies in theology, Bonhoeffer insists that we can understand and speak of Christ as God only in terms of his particular humanity or way of being human.[29] He states: 'we believe that Jesus the human being is God, and that he is as *the* human being, not in spite of his humanity or beyond his humanity'.[30] Furthermore, Bonhoeffer makes clear that this belief radically qualifies all Christological speech: 'If we are to describe Jesus as God, we would not speak of his being all-powerful or all-knowing; we would speak of his birth in a manger and of his cross. There is no divine nature as all powerful and ever-present.'[31]

Bonhoeffer begins to develop this *theologia crucis*, or account of Christ's humiliation, in the final part of his lectures: 'Positive Christology'.[32] In this

---

24. DBWE 12: 332.

25. DBWE 12: 332. The end result of this approach, as Bonhoeffer writes, is that 'Jesus as a human being is incidental, as opposed to the substance that is God.' DBWE 12: 335.

26. Bonhoeffer provides the example of the doctrine of 'en-hypostatsia', the early church teaching that Christ's human nature subsists in his divine nature in such a way that the former depends on the latter. While acknowledging that this doctrine emerged as a necessary counter to Apollinarism (which had denied outright that Christ possessed a human mind or individuality), Bonhoeffer contends that in this 'rearguard action by early church dogmatics ... docetism in a refined form ... crept into the early church dogmatics itself'. DBWE 12: 335. In other words, by distinguishing so cleanly between Christ's divine and human natures, this early doctrine left too much room for thinking of Christ's human nature apart from his individuality: 'What is the doctrine of en-hypostasis', Bonhoeffer concludes, 'if not ultimately a concealed form of docetism?' DBWE 12: 335.

27. Bonhoeffer in one place pronounces that 'all liberal theology' after Albrecht Ritschl 'must be understood in the context of a Docetic Christology'. DBWE 12: 337.

28. While Bonhoeffer does not directly identify Reformed theology as docetic, he expresses concerns with Reformed attempts to keep the two natures of Christ cleanly separate, that is, in ways that resonate closely with his reading of docetism. DBWE 12: 345–6.

29. DBWE 12: 355.

30. DBWE 12: 354.

31. DBWE 12: 354.

32. DBWE 12: 353–60.

section, he reiterates the disruptive significance of Christ's presence for us as the humiliated one: 'The God-human who is humiliated is the stumbling block to the pious human being and to the human being, period.'[33] Furthermore, he insists that it is because Christ encounters and confronts us in this way that we are able to have faith: 'Faith exists when I yield myself to God ... even and especially where this goes against all visible appearances.'[34]

Nonetheless, while tantalizing and provocative, I would suggest that Bonhoeffer's brief account of Christ's humiliation and presence as a stumbling block in his lectures remains incomplete. Despite the promise of some of his initial remarks,[35] Christ's particular humanity and existence do not seem to provide much actual content for this *theologia crucis*. Rather than turning to the gospels or attending to the political and bodily realities of Jesus' life and death, he instead locates Christ's humiliation in the fact that Christ 'has taken on sinful flesh'.[36] 'The conditions for his humiliation', he writes, 'are set by the curse, the fall of Adam. In being humiliated, the God-human enters of his own free will into the world of sin.'[37]

By locating Christ's humiliation in the conditions of the fall and human sinfulness at this general level, I would suggest that Bonhoeffer missed an opportunity.[38] At this point in the lectures, he could have provided a more detailed account of how Christ is a stumbling block and scandal *in and through* his life and death as a first-century Jew.[39] Alternatively, Bonhoeffer could have reflected on Christ's humiliation by returning to and developing some earlier comments

---

33. DBWE 12: 358.

34. DBWE 12: 358.

35. Bonhoeffer opens this final section by insisting on the importance of Christ's '*way* of existing as a human being'. DBWE 12: 355.

36. DBWE 12: 356.

37. DBWE 12: 356. In other words, Bonhoeffer locates Christ's humiliation in the logics of sin and salvation: 'His σάρξ is our σάρξ. What is essential about our σάρξ is our vulnerability to temptation, our self-will. Christ took on all the mortifying aspects of being human; otherwise he could not help us in our σάρξ.' DBWE 12: 356.

38. Some of my concerns are expressed in an important article by Gustavo Gutierrez, although he primarily focuses on Bonhoeffer's late theology. While finding much that is promising in Bonhoeffer, Gutierrez ultimately concludes that 'the absence of social analysis [may have] prevented Bonhoeffer from carrying his intuition [of a perspective from beneath] to its mature theological implications'. See Gustavo Gutierrez, 'The Limitations of Modern Theology: On a Letter of Dietrich Bonhoeffer', in *The History of the Poor: Selected Writings*, trans. Robert R. Barr (Maryknoll: Orbis, 1983), 233.

39. Indeed, as Bonhoeffer himself had insisted in a lecture two years earlier, 'God entered history and no human attempt can grasp him beyond this history ... God revealed himself in 'once-ness' from the years from one to thirty in Palestine in Jesus.' Bonhoeffer, 'Concerning the Christian idea of God', DBWE 10: 141.

in the lectures, in which he had briefly aligned Christ with the working classes.[40] Bonhoeffer could have chosen to reflect on how Christ's humiliation connects with and is reflected within the concrete humiliations and struggles of people in his own context.[41]

In the lectures themselves, however, Bonhoeffer pursues neither of these options. What would it look like if we were to read with Bonhoeffer, but to begin to expand on and deepen this area of his Christology?

Jesus on the lynching tree: James Cone's Christology

In his recent *Introducing James H. Cone,* Anthony Reddie has suggested that 'Christology remained his [Cone's] foundational point of departure in how he constructed the initial development of Black theology'.[42] Like Bonhoeffer before him, Cone's theology was profoundly and thoroughly Christo-centric.

One of Cone's early and more systematic reflections on Christology can be found in *A Black Theology of Liberation* (1970).[43] In this work, Cone similarly insists on the importance of attending to Christ in his particular humanity: 'Black theology ... takes seriously the historical Jesus. We want to know who Jesus *was* because we believe that is the only way to assess who he *is*.'[44] On this basis Cone spends significant time in this book working through and reflecting on key moments in the gospel narratives, as well as engaging with modern biblical scholarship.[45] He summarizes his findings: 'To understand the historical Jesus without seeing his identification with the poor as decisive is to misunderstand him and thus distort his historical person.'[46]

---

40. DBWE 12: 306. Bonhoeffer writes earlier in the lecture that Jesus 'stands beside members of the proletariat as a fighter in their ranks against the capitalist enemy'. And he suggests that 'when the proletariat say that Jesus is a good human being, it means more than the bourgeoisie when it says that Jesus is God'. DBWE 12: 306.

41. Bonhoeffer had had significant exposure to African American literature during his Sloan fellowship at Union Theological Seminary in New York in 1930–1. Reggie Williams has provided an overview of the Harlem Renaissance and demonstrated its transformative impact on Bonhoeffer in Reggie Williams, *Bonhoeffer's Black Jesus: Harlem Renaissance Theology and an Ethic of Resistance* (Waco: Baylor University Press, 2014). While this exposure was no doubt influential for Bonhoeffer's theology and development, as Williams has demonstrated, it does not seem to be directly informing the account of Christ's humiliation at the end of the Christology lectures.

42. Anthony Reddie, *Introducing James H. Cone: A Personal Exploration* (London: SCM Press, 2022), 57.

43. James Cone, *A Black Theology of Liberation* (Maryknoll: Orbis, 1970).

44. Cone, *A Black Theology of Liberation*, 201.

45. See Cone, *A Black Theology of Liberation*, 199–212.

46. Cone, *A Black Theology of Liberation*, 203.

In addition, Cone attends closely to the fact that Jesus was a member of a colonized people living under Roman occupation. This sociopolitical context is key for making sense of his ministry, teachings and death. Cone also draws out how this sociopolitical position marked Jesus racially. As he insists in *God of the Oppressed* (1970), 'the particularity of Jesus' person as disclosed in his Jewishness is indispensable for Christological analysis. He was not a "universal" man', Cone continues, 'but a particular Jew who came to fulfill God's will to liberate the oppressed'.[47] Jesus' Jewishness is integral to understanding his humanity and identity.

This leads to Cone's well-known claim that 'Jesus was Black'. 'Taking our cue from the historical Jesus', Cone writes, 'what else, except blackness, could adequately tell us the meaning of his presence?'[48] In other words, Cone claims that Jesus was Black in order to indicate what it actually meant to be a first-century Jew.[49] As Ryan Tafilowski has observed, with this claim Cone 'is stressing the sheer physicality of Jesus's embodied existence, which … was inevitably political because all embodied existence is political'.[50] By describing Jesus as Black, Cone conveys in concrete terms who Jesus was and how he inhabited the world.[51]

Moreover, this claim allows Cone to connect Jesus as a first-century Jew with the present, or to bring together the Jesus of history with the Christ of faith.[52] To use Bonhoeffer's terminology, claiming Jesus as Black draws out to the promeity of Christ, who Jesus Christ is for us today. 'To say that Jesus is Black', as Cone insists, 'means that Black people are God's poor people whom Christ has come

---

47. Cone, *God of the Oppressed*, 109.

48. Cone, *A Theology of Black Liberation*, 213.

49. As Norris writes, 'Christ's blackness, his identification with the oppressed of the world, is based in Jesus' Jewishness, his embodiment as a member of an oppressed religious and ethnic community in Roman-occupied Palestine.' Kristopher Norris, 'James Cone's Legacy for White Christians', *Political Theology* 21, no. 3 (2020): 210.

50. Ryan Tafilowski, 'The Body upon the (Lynching) Tree: The Humanity of Jesus in James Cone and Reinhold Niebuhr', *The Journal of Theological Studies* 20, no. 2 (2020): 773.

51. To be clear, 'blackness' as a way of naming how Jesus inhabited the world is itself contextual. For example, in the context of Aotearoa New Zealand, Te Aroha Rountree has positioned Jesus as 'savage', thereby challenging and disrupting how the Jesus of white missionaries was embedded in a project of 'civilising' Māori and other indigenous peoples. Accordingly, the claim that 'Jesus was savage' conveys in even more concrete terms who Christ is in this context. See Te Aroha Rountree, 'Jesus Christ, Once was a Savage! Selective Memory, Staged Identity, Stolen Places', in *Unsettling Theologies: Memory, Identity and Place*, ed. Brian Kolia and Michael Mawson (Palgrave Macmillan, 2023).

52. As J. Kameron Carter summarizes, Cone 'is critical of any Christology that would unduly sever the relationship between Jesus of history and the Christ of faith. Because the Christ of faith is only knowable through the Jesus of history, separating the Jesus of history from the Christ of faith is a sure sign that abstraction lurks nearby.' J. Kameron Carter, *Race: A Theological Account* (New York: Oxford University Press, 2008), 169.

to liberate.'⁵³ Cone's claim thus expresses in a concrete way where Jesus Christ is to be found in the present. It forges an identity or solidarity between Jesus and contemporary Black existence and struggle.⁵⁴

In addition, Cone's claim that Jesus is Black can be confronting and threatening to those of us who are white. Jesus' blackness disrupts what Kristopher Norris describes as 'the hubris and blindness of white theology's claims to universalism'.⁵⁵ It contests the assumption that Jesus is a universal saviour to whom we all have direct and equal access. To adopt and adapt Bonhoeffer's language, Cone's claim makes clear that for white Christians, Christ is for us only as the 'counter Logos' to whiteness.⁵⁶ Christ's promeity contests and overturns hidden assumptions of universality, neutrality, and impartiality.⁵⁷

Cone deepens this analysis when he positions white theology as broadly docetic. Like Bonhoeffer, he adopts an expansive definition of docetism: as any attempt to diminish or displace Christ's particular humanity and experience.⁵⁸ Cone finds this attempt to be present and recurrent throughout the Western theological tradition. He notes, for example, that 'the Nicaean Fathers showed little interest in Jesus' deeds for the humiliated'. And he suggests that this was precisely 'because most of the discussion took place in the social context of the Church's position as the favoured religion of the Roman state'.⁵⁹

Like Bonhoeffer, Cone also identifies modern liberal theology as broadly docetic. While he makes this identification in a number of places,⁶⁰ it is especially apparent in his reading of Reinhold Niebuhr in *The Cross and the Lynching Tree*.⁶¹ In a recent article, Tafilowski has linked Niebuhr's reticence to take a stand on racial issues to his anaemic Christology: 'Since ... Niebuhr does not take seriously the torture and execution of Jesus of Nazareth's *Jewish flesh* in history, he cannot connect it to the torture and execution of *Black flesh* in history.'⁶² Niebuhr's

---

53. Cone, *God of the Oppressed*, 125.
54. See Reddie, *Introducing James Cone*, 64.
55. Norris, 'James Cone's Legacy for White Christians', 209.
56. Early in the lectures, Bonhoeffer describes Christ as a 'counter Logos' to all human thinking and speaking. Christ as Word confronts and attacks every attempt to fit him within an existing conceptual framework: 'Every possibility of classification must fall short, because the existence of this Logos means the end of my logos.' DBWE 12: 302.
57. As Liam Miller has observed, 'Cone's theology is built on the assertion that there is no universal (or abstract) humanity or community.' Liam Miller, 'James Cone's Constructive Vision of Sin and the Black Lives Matter Movement', *Black Theology* 18, no.1 (2020): 6. See also Cone's comments in *The God of the Oppressed*, 126.
58. Carter notes that 'Cone is acutely attentive to the problem of abstraction in theology. He understands it to be the perennial problem of white theology and Euro-American racism as a whole.' Carter, *Race*, 160.
59. Cone, *God of the Oppressed*, 107.
60. See especially Cone, *God of the Oppressed*, 106–9.
61. Cone, *The Cross and the Lynching Tree*, 30–64.
62. Tafilowski, 'The Body upon the (Lynching) Tree', 760. Emphasis original.

tendency to understand Jesus' ministry and sacrifice in largely symbolic terms, and related failure to attend to Jesus' particular humanity and experience, has consequences for his ethics and politics.

In *The Cross and the Lynching Tree*, Cone therefore develops and presents an alternative to white docetism by pressing into the materiality of the cross. In this book, he describes Jesus' crucifixion as 'a public spectacle accompanied by torture and shame – one of the most humiliating and painful deaths ever devised by human beings'.[63] For Cone, this claim that the messiah or Christ was crucified would have been immediately scandalous to a first-century audience: 'Crucifixion was recognized as the particular form of execution reserved by the Roman Empire for insurrectionists and rebels.'[64] In contemporary terms, Jesus Christ was charged and executed for being a terrorist.

By connecting the cross with the lynching tree,[65] Cone thus helps us to recognize what crucifixion actually involved. Against attempts to understand Jesus' death in symbolic or universal terms,[66] he directs attention to the specific, bodily humiliations and horrors inflicted on Black bodies in the postbellum American South. And Cone allows these realities of lynching to shed light on the cross:

> Both the cross and the lynching tree were symbols of terror, instruments of torture and execution ... Both Jesus and Blacks were publicly humiliated, subjected to the utmost indignity and cruelty. They were stripped, in order to be deprived of dignity, then paraded, mocked and whipped, pierced, derided and spat upon, tortured for hours in the presence of jeering crowds for popular entertainment.[67]

In other words, attending to the concrete realities of lynching helps us to recognize what crucifixion was.[68] As Anthony Reddie succinctly makes this point, it helps us recognize that 'Jesus died like a Black person'.[69]

---

63. Cone, *The Cross and the Lynching Tree*, 1–2.

64. Cone, *The Cross and the Lynching Tree*, 1.

65. It is worth noting that Cone is drawing upon a longer tradition in Black literature and poetry that had linked the cross with the lynching tree, a tradition that Bonhoeffer had some exposure to. See Williams, *Bonhoeffer's Black Jesus*, 53–76.

66. On the tendency of white Christianity to abstraction, see M. Shawn Copeland's *Enfleshing Freedom: Body, Race and Being* (Minneapolis: Fortress Press, 2010), 122–3.

67. Cone, *The Cross and the Lynching Tree*, 31.

68. In a recent collection, Jayme Reaves, David Tombs and Rocio Figueroa have demonstrated that this humiliation should also be labelled as sexual abuse. See Jayme Reaves, David Tombs and Rocio Figueroa, eds, *When Did We See You Naked? Jesus as a Victim of Sexual Abuse* (London: SCM Press, 2021). See in particular the essay in this collection by Mitzi J. Smith, '"He Never Said a Mumbalin Word": A Womanist Perspective of Crucifixion, Sexual Violence, and Sacralised Silence', 46–66.

69. Reddie, *Introducing James Cone*, 69.

Conclusion

What is at stake with some of the broad resonances and important differences between Bonhoeffer's and Cone's approaches to Christology? First, it should be stated directly that the resonances and overlaps between their approaches are significant. Bonhoeffer and Cone share a resistance to abstract and speculative thinking about Christ; they are both critical of some traditional and established understandings of what Christology is. Furthermore, they share an emphasis on Christ's promeity, who Jesus Christ is for us today. In their own ways, they each highlight the disruptive and liberating nature of Christ's presence. Finally, Bonhoeffer and Cone choose to begin and remain with Christ's human suffering and humiliation and they diagnose and resist docetic attempts to separate Christ's divinity from his concrete existence and death.

Nonetheless, on this final issue Cone provides a more concrete and compelling account of Christ's humiliation and the cross. As we have seen, Bonhoeffer in his lectures chooses to locate Christ's humiliation in the curse or sin at a universal level. He understands Christ's 'humiliated state' and the 'stumbling block' as the fact that Christ as the sinless one has freely entered into and embraced a sinful humanity, that is, to the point where he 'is no longer recognizable visibly as the God-human'.[70] Bonhoeffer in this way appears to locate Christ's hiddenness primarily as an epistemological issue. 'What is scandalous', he writes, 'is the lack of historical clarity of this God-human'.[71]

In contrast, Cone gives more direct and sustained attention to the historical realities of crucifixion. He locates Christ's humiliation in the realities of torture and execution in the context of Roman Empire, thereby attending even more closely (than Bonhoeffer) to Christ's bodily existence and death as a particular human being. For Cone, as we have seen, this means that the stumbling block or scandal of Christianity is that Jesus was Black, and that we can encounter Christ today only in relation to Black struggle for liberation. To conclude with Cone's words, 'blackness is the one symbol that cannot be overlooked if we are going to take seriously the Christological significance of Jesus Christ'.[72]

---

70. DBWE 12: 309.
71. DBWE 12: 358.
72. Cone, *A Black Theology of Liberation*, 218.

BIBLIOGRAPHY

'"Alarming but not Unexpected" Increase in Domestic Violence in NSW during Covid 19 Crisis.' *Guardian*, 4 June 2020. www.theguardian.com/society/2020/jun/04/alarming-but-not-unexpected-increase-in-domestic-violence-in-nsw-during-covid-19-crisis. Accessed 16 March 2023.

'Have More than a Billion Animals Perished Nationwide This Bushfire Season? Here Are the Facts.' *ABC News*, 31 January 2020. www.abc.net.au/news/2020-01-31/fact-check-have-bushfires-killed-more-than-a-billion-animals/11912538. Accessed 16 March 2023.

'How Covid 19 Could Set Back Women by a Generation.' *The Guardian*. 28 August 2020. www.theguardian.com/australia-news/audio/2020/aug/28/how-covid-19-could-set-back-women-by-a-generation. Accessed 16 March 2023.

Aquinas, Thomas. *Summa Theologica*. Translated by Fathers of the English Dominican Province. Westminster: Christian Classics, 1981.

Askani, Hans-Christoph. *Das Problem der Übersetzung dargestellt an Franz Rosenzweig*. Tübingen: Mohr Siebeck, 1997.

Ballor, Jordan. 'Christ in Creation: Bonhoeffer's Orders of Preservation and Natural Theology.' *Journal of Religion* 86, no. 1 (2006): 1–22.

Balthasar, Hans Urs von. *Mysterium Paschale*. Translated by Aiden Nichols, O. P. Grand Rapids: Eerdmans, 1996.

Banman, Joel. *Reading in the Presence of Christ: A Study of Dietrich Bonhoeffer's Bibliology and Exegesis*. London: T&T Clark Bloomsbury, 2021.

Barker, Gaylon H. *The Cross of Reality: Luther's* Theologia Crucis *and Bonhoeffer's Christology*. Minneapolis: Fortress Press, 2015.

Barth, Karl. *The Church Dogmatics: III/2*. Edited by G. W. Bromiley and T. F. Torrance. London: T&T Clark, 1960.

Barth, Karl. *The Epistle to the Romans*. Translated by Edwyn C. Hoskyns. 2nd edn. London: Oxford University Press, 1968.

Barth, Karl. *The Göttingen Dogmatics: Instruction in the Christian Religion*. Translated by Geoffrey W. Bromiley. Grand Rapids: Eerdmans, 1991.

Barth, Karl. *The Word of God and Theology*. Translated by Amy Marga. London: T&T Clark, 2011.

Batnitzky, Leora. *Idolatry and Representation: The Philosophy of Franz Rosenzweig Reconsidered*. Princeton: Princeton University Press, 2000.

Benjamin, Mara. *Rosenzweig's Bible: Reinventing Scripture for Jewish Modernity*. Cambridge: Cambridge University Press, 2009.

Bethge, Eberhard. *Dietrich Bonhoeffer: A Biography*. Edited by Victoria Barnett. Rev. edn. Minneapolis: Fortress Press, 2000.

Bird, Michael. *An Anomalous Jew: Paul among Jews, Greeks and Romans*. Grand Rapids: Eerdmans, 2016.

Boer, Martin de. *The Defeat of Death: Apocalpytic Eschatology in 1 Corinthians 15 and Romans 5*. London: T&T Clark, 1988.

Boff, Leonardo. *Trinity and Society*. Translated by Paul Burns. Maryknoll: Orbis, 1988.
Bourdieu, Pierre. *The Logic of Practice*. Translated by Richard Nice. Oxford: Polity Press, 1990.
Braaten, Carl. 'Eschatology and Mission in the Theology of Robert Jenson.' In *Trinity, Time, and Church: A Response to the Theology of Robert W. Jenson*, edited by Colin Gunton, 298–311. Grand Rapids: Eerdmans, 2000.
Brett, Mark G. 'Past and Future of Biblical Studies in Australia.' *Australian Biblical Review* 67 (2019): 85–97.
Brett, Mark G., and Naomi Wolfe. 'Sovereignty: Indigenous Counter-Examples.' *The International Journal of Public Theology* 14, no. 1 (2020): 24–40.
Brock, Brian. 'Bonhoeffer and the Bible in Christian Ethics: Psalm 119, the Mandates and Ethics as a Way.' *Studies in Christian Ethics* 18, no. 3 (2005): 7–29.
Brock, Brian. *Singing the Ethos of God: On the Place of Christian Ethics in Scripture*. Grand Rapids: Eerdmans, 2007.
Brock, Brian. *Wondrously Wounded: Theology, Disability and the Body of Christ*. Waco: Baylor University Press, 2019.
Brock, Brian, and Michael Mawson, eds. *The Freedom of a Christian Ethicist: The Future of a Reformation Legacy*. London: T&T Clark Bloomsbury, 2016.
Brock, Brian, and Bernd Wannenwetsch. *The Malady of the Christian Body: A Theological Exposition of Paul's First Letter to the Corinthians*. Volume 1. Eugene: Cascade, 2016.
Buber, Martin, *I and Thou*. Translated by Walter Kaufmann. Edinburgh: T&T Clark, 1970.
Buber, Martin. '*Leitwort* Style in Pentateuch Narrative.' In *Scripture and Translation*, translated by Lawrence Rosenwald with Everett Fox, 114–28. Bloomington: Indiana University Press, 1993.
Buber, Martin, and Franz Rosenzweig. *Die Schrift*. Stuttgart: Deutsche Bibelgesellschaft, 1993.
Buber, Martin, and Franz Rosenzweig. *Scripture and Translation*. Translated by Lawrence Rosenwald with Everett Fox. Bloomington: Indiana University Press, 1993.
Butler, Judith. 'A Bad Writer Bites Back.' *The New York Times*, 20 March 1999.
Campbell, Douglas. *The Deliverance of God: An Apocalyptic Rereading of Justification in Paul*. Grand Rapids: Eerdmans, 2009.
Carter, J. Kameron. *Race: A Theological Account*. Oxford: Oxford University Press, 2008.
Cavanaugh, William. *Torture and the Eucharist: Theology, Politics, and the Body of Christ*. Oxford: Blackwell, 1998.
Chapman, Jr. G. Clarke. 'Hope and the Ethics of Formation: Moltmann as Interpreter of Bonhoeffer.' *Studies in Religion/Sciences Religieuses* 12, no. 4 (1983): 449–60.
Clark, Adam C. 'The Creator Sovereign in Christ: Dietrich Bonhoeffer and Protestant Natural Law Retrieval.' PhD Dissertation. University of Notre Dame, 2017.
Clark, Adam C., and Michael Mawson, eds. *Ontology and Ethics: Bonhoeffer and Contemporary Scholarship*. Eugene: Pickwick Publications, 2013.
Coakley, Sarah. '*Kenōsis* and Subversion: On the Repression of "Vulnerability" in Christian Feminist Writing.' In *Powers and Submissions: Spirituality, Philosophy and Gender*, 3–39. Oxford: Blackwell, 2002.
Cone, James. *A Black Theology of Liberation*. Maryknoll: Orbis, 1970.
Cone, James. *The Cross and the Lynching Tree*. Maryknoll: Orbis, 2011.
Cone, James. *The Spirituals and the Blues: An Interpretation*. Maryknoll: Orbis, 1972.

Cone, James. 'Theology's Great Sin: Silence in the Face of White Supremacy.' *Black Theology* 2, no. 2 (2004): 139–52.
Congdon, David. 'Bonhoeffer and Barth: Toward an Apocalyptic Rapprochement.' *International Journal of Systematic Theology* 15, no. 2 (2013): 172–95.
Connor, William F. 'The Natural Life of Man and Its Laws: Conscience and Reason in the Theology of Dietrich Bonhoeffer.' PhD Dissertation. Vanderbilt University, 1973.
Copeland, M. Shawn. *Enfleshing Freedom: Body, Race and Being*. Minneapolis: Fortress Press, 2010.
Cramer, David, Jenny Howell, Jonathan Tran and Paul Martens. 'Scandalizing John Howard Yoder.' *The Other Journal*, 2014. https://theotherjournal.com/2014/07/scandalizing-john-howard-yoder/.
Davis, Joshua B., and Douglas Harink, eds. *Apocalyptic and the Future of Theology: With and Beyond J. Louis Martyn*. Eugene: Cascade, 2012.
De Gruchy, John. 'With Bonhoeffer, beyond Bonhoeffer: Transmitting Bonhoeffer's Legacy.' In *Dietrich Bonhoeffer's Theology Today, A Way between Fundamentalism and Secularism*, edited by S. Plant, J. W. de Gruchy and C. Tietz, 403–16. München: Guetersloher Verlagshaus, 2009.
DeJonge, Michael P. *Bonhoeffer's Theological Formation: Berlin, Barth, and Protestant Theology*. Oxford: Oxford University Press, 2012.
DeJonge, Michael P. *Bonhoeffer's Reception of Luther*. Oxford: Oxford University Press, 2017.
DeJonge, Michael P. 'Non-Lutheran Influences, Scholarly Impasses, and Spiritual Influences: A Response to Mawson, Harvey and Plant.' *Modern Theology* 35, no. 2 (2019): 374–6.
DeJonge, Michael P. 'Respecting Rights and Fulfilling Duties: Bonhoeffer's *Formed Life* in Bioethical Perspective.' In *Bonhoeffer and the Biosciences: An Initial Exploration*, edited by Ralph K. Wüstenberg, Stefan Heuser and Ester Hornung, 109–22. Pieterlen: Peter Lang, 2010.
DeJonge, Michael P., and Clifford J. Green, eds. *The Bonhoeffer Reader*. Minneapolis: Fortress Press, 2013.
Deverell, Garry Worete. *Gondwana Theology: A Trawloolway Man Reflects on Christian Faith*. Sydney: Morning Star Publishing, 2018.
Devlin, Hannah. 'Ageing Process May Be Reversible, Scientists Claim', *Guardian*, 16 December 2016.https://www.theguardian.com/science/2016/dec/15/ageing-process-may-be-reversible-scientists-claim. Accessed 16 March 2023.
Dodson, Chris. *The God Who Is Given: Bonhoeffer's Sacramentality and Religionless Christianity*. Langham: Lexington, 2021.
Eastman, Susan. *Recovering Paul's Mother Tongue: Language and Theology in Galatians*. Grand Rapids: Eerdmans, 2007.
Emerton, David. *God's Church-Community: The Ecclesiology of Dietrich Bonhoeffer*. London: T&T Clark Bloomsbury, 2020.
Emery, Gilles. 'The Immutability of the God of Love and the Problem of Language Concerning the "Suffering God".' In *Divine Impassibility and the Mystery of Human Suffering*, edited by James F. Keating and Joseph Thomas White, 27–76. Grand Rapids: Eerdmans, 2009.
Emilsen, William, ed. *An Informed Faith: The Uniting Church at the Beginning of the 21st Century*. Sydney: Morning Star Publishing, 2014.
Erickson, Robert P. *Theologians under Hitler*. New Haven: Yale University Press, 1985.

Fabrycky, Laura M. *Keys to Bonhoeffer's Haus: Exploring the World and Wisdom of Dietrich Bonhoeffer*. Minneapolis: Fortress Press, 2020.
Farrow, Douglas. 'Person and Nature: The Necessity–Freedom Dialectic in John Zizioulas.' In *The Theology of John Zizioulas: Personhood and the Church*, edited by Douglas Knight, 87–104. Burlington: Ashgate, 2007.
Feil, Ernst. *The Theology of Dietrich Bonhoeffer*. Translated by Martin Rumscheidt. Minneapolis: Fortress Press, 1985.
Feuerbach, Ludwig. *The Essence of Christianity*. Translated by George Eliot. Mineola: Dover, 2008.
Feuerbach, Ludwig. *The Essence of Faith according to Martin Luther*. Translated by Melvin Cherno. London: Harper and Row, 1967.
Forde, Gerhard. *On Being a Theologian of the Cross: Reflections on Luther's Heidelberg Disputation, 1518*. Grand Rapids: Eerdmans, 1997.
Fiddes, Paul. *The Creative Suffering of God*. Oxford: Oxford University Press, 1988.
Flett, John G. 'Communion as Propaganda: Reinhard Hütter and the Missionary Witness of the "Church as Public".' *Scottish Journal of Theology* 62, no. 4 (2009): 457–76.
Francabandera, Brandin. 'Reading beneath the Cross: Dietrich Bonhoeffer's Doctrine of Scripture as *Theologia Crucis*.' PhD Dissertation. University of Aberdeen, 2022.
Frick, Peter. *Understanding Bonhoeffer*. Tübingen: Mohr Siebeck, 2017.
Galot, Jean. *Dieu Souffre-t-il?* Paris: P. Lethielleux, 1976.
Gaventa, Beverly. *When in Romans: An Invitation to Linger with the Gospel according to Paul*. Grand Rapids: Baker, 2016.
Glatzer, Nahum. 'Editor's Postscript.' In Martin Buber, *On the Bible: Eighteen Studies*, 233–40. Syracuse: Syracuse University Press, 2000.
Grabill, Stephen J. *Rediscovering the Natural Law in Reformed Theological Ethics*. Grand Rapids: Eerdmans, 2006.
Green, Clifford J. *Bonhoeffer: A Theology of Sociality*. Grand Rapids: Eerdmans, 1972.
Grenz, Stanley. *The Social God and Relational Self: A Trinitarian Theology of the* Imago Dei. Louisville: Westminster John Knox, 2002.
Gunton, Colin. *The One, the Three and the Many: God, Creation and the Culture of Modernity*. Cambridge: Cambridge University Press, 1993.
Gunton, Colin. 'Until He Comes: Towards an Eschatology of Church Membership.' *International Journal of Systematic Theology* 3 (2001): 187–200.
Guðmundsdóttir, Arnfríður. *Meeting God on the Cross: Christ, the Cross and the Feminist Critique*. Oxford: Oxford University Press, 2011.
Gutiérrez, Gustavo. 'The Limitations of Modern Theology: On a Letter of Dietrich Bonhoeffer.' In *The Power of the Poor in History: Selected Writings*, translated by Robert R. Barr, 222–44. London: SCM, 1983.
Halbach, Ross E. *Bonhoeffer and the Racialized Church*. Waco: Baylor University Press, 2020.
Hall, Amy Laura. *Laughing at the Devil: Seeing the World with Julian of Norwich*. Durham: Duke University Press, 2018.
Hamilton, Clive. *Defiant Earth: The Fate of Humans in the Anthropocene*. Sydney: Allen and Unwin, 2017.
Hamilton, Nadine. *Dietrich Bonhoeffers Hermeneutik Der Responsivitat: Ein Kapital Schriftlehre im Anschluss an 'Schopfung und Fall'*. Göttingen: Vandenhoeck & Ruprecht, 2016.
Harink, Douglas. *Paul among the Postliberals: Pauline Theology beyond Christendom and Modernity*. Eugene: Wipf & Stock, 2003.

Harnack, Adolf von. *Marcion: The Gospel of the Alien God*. Translated John E. Steely and Lyle D. Bierma. Grand Rapids: Baker Books, 1995.

Harvey, Barry. *Can These Bones Live? A Catholic Baptist Engagement with Ecclesiology, Hermeneutics, and Social Theory*. Grand Rapids: Brazos Press, 2008.

Haslam, Molly. *A Constructive Theology of Intellectual Disability: Human Being as Mutuality and Response*. New York: Fordham University Press, 2012.

Hauerwas, Stanley. 'On Being a Church Capable of Addressing a World at War: A Pacifist Response to the United Bishops' Pastoral *In Defense of Creation* (1988).' In *The Hauerwas Reader*, edited by John Berkman and Michael Cartwright, 436–48. Durham: Duke University Press, 2001.

Hauerwas, Stanley. *The Peaceable Kingdom: A Primer in Christian Ethics*. Notre Dame: University of Notre Dame Press, 1983.

Hauerwas, Stanley. *Performing the Faith: Bonhoeffer and the Practice of Non-violence*. Grand Rapids: Brazos Press, 2004.

Hauerwas, Stanley. 'The Sermon on the Mount: Dietrich Bonhoeffer and John Howard Yoder.' In *The Sermon on the Mount through the Centuries: From the Early Church to John Paul II*, edited by Jeffrey P. Greenman, Timothy Larsen and Stephen R. Spencer, 207–22. Grand Rapids: Brazos Press, 2007.

Havea, Jione. *Jonah: An Earth Bible Commentary*. London: T&T Clark Bloomsbury, 2020.

Havea, Jione, ed. *Theologies from the Pacific*. London: Palgrave, 2021.

Haynes, Stephen. *The Bonhoeffer Legacy: Post-Holocaust Perspectives*. Minneapolis: Fortress Press, 2006.

Hays, Richard B. 'Review of J. Louis Martyn, *Galatians: A New Translation*.' *Journal of Biblical Literature* 119, no. 2 (2000): 373–9.

Hedley, Douglas. 'Review of John Milbank, Catherine Pitstock and Graham Ward, ed., *Radical Orthodoxy: A New Theology*.' *The Journal of Theological Studies* 51, no. 1 (2000): 405–8.

Herskowitz, Daniel. 'Franz Rosenzweig and Karl Barth: A Chapter in the Jewish Reception of Dialectical Theology.' *Journal of Religion* 97, no. 1 (2017): 79–100.

Healy, Nicholas M. 'Practices and the New Ecclesiology: Misplaced Concreteness?' *International Journal of Systematic Theology* 5, no. 3 (2003): 287–308.

Hegel, G. W. F. *Lectures on the Philosophy of Religion: One-Volume Edition, The Lectures of 1827*, edited by Peter Hodgson. Berkeley: University of California Press, 1988.

Hegel, G. W. F. *Phenomenology of Spirit*. Translated by A. V. Miller. Oxford: Oxford, 1977.

Hegel, G. W. F. 'The Positivity of Christian Religions.' In *On Christianity: Early Theological Writings*, translated by T. M. Knox, 67–180. Philadelphia: University of Pennsylvania Press, 1971.

Heuvel, Steven van den. *Bonhoeffer's Christocentric Theology and Fundamental Debates in Environmental Ethics*. Eugene: Pickwick Publications, 2017.

Herschel, Susannah. *The Aryan Jesus: Christian Theologians and the Bible in Nazi Germany*. Princeton: Princeton University Press, 2008.

Hinlicky, Paul. *Paths Not Taken: Fates of Theology from Luther through Leibniz*. Grand Rapids: Eerdmans, 2009.

Hockenos, Matthew. 'Bonhoeffer and the Church Struggle'. In *The Oxford Handbook of Dietrich Bonhoeffer*, edited by Michael Mawson and Philip G. Ziegler, 52-64. Oxford: Oxford University Press, 2019.

Höhne, David. *Spirit and Sonship: Colin Gunton's Theology of Particularity and the Holy Spirit*. Farnham: Ashgate, 2010.

Holmes, Christopher, R. J. 'Bonhoeffer and Reformed Christology: Towards a Trinitarian Supplement.' *Theology Today* 71, no. 1 (2014): 28–42.

Holmes Christopher R. J. 'The Holy Spirit'. In *The Oxford Handbook of Dietrich Bonhoeffer*, edited by Michael Mawson and Philip G. Ziegler, 168–78. Oxford: Oxford University Press, 2019.

Hryniuk, Michael. *Theology, Disability and Spiritual Transformation: Learning from the Community of L'Arche*. Amherst: Cambria Press, 2010.

Hunsinger, George. 'Robert Jenson's Systematic Theology: A Review Essay.' *Scottish Journal of Theology* 55, no. 2 (2002): 161–200.

Huyssteen, J. Wentzel van. *Alone in the World: Human Uniqueness in Science and Theology*. Grand Rapids: Eerdmans, 2006.

Hütter, Reinhard. *Suffering Divine Things: Theology as Church Practice*. Grand Rapids: Eerdmans, 2000.

Ivereigh, Austen. 'Sant'Egidio: Prophets of the Poor and of Peace.' In *Small Christian Communities Today: Capturing the Movement*, edited by Joseph G. Healy and Jeanne Hinton, 170–6. Maryknoll: Orbis, 2006.

Jenkins, Willis. *Ecologies of Grace: Environmental Ethics and Christian Theology*. Oxford: Oxford University Press, 2013.

Jenkins, Willis. *The Future of Ethics: Sustainability, Social Justice, and Religious Creativity*. Washington: Georgetown University Press, 2013.

Jennings, Willie James. *The Christian Imagination: Theology and the Origins of Race*. New Haven: Yale University Press, 2010.

Jenson, Robert W. 'Christ as Culture 1: Christ as Polity.' *International Journal of Systematic Theology* 5, no. 3 (2003): 323–9.

Jenson, Robert W. 'The Church as *Communio*.' In *The Catholicity of the Reformation*, edited by Carl E. Braaten and Robert W. Jenson, 1–12. Grand Rapids: Eerdmans, 1996.

Jenson, Robert W. *Systematic Theology, Volume 1: The Triune God*. Oxford: Oxford University Press, 2001.

Jenson, Robert W. *Systematic Theology 2: The Works of God*. New York: Oxford University Press, 1999.

Jodon, Cole. *Discipleship and Unity: Bonhoeffer's Ecumenical Theology*. Langham: Lexington, 2022.

Johnson, Elizabeth: *She Who Is: The Mystery of God in Feminist Theological Discourse*. New York: Crossroad Publishing, 1992.

Jones, Kimberly. 'How Can We Win? Speech at Black Lives Matter Protest in Atlanta.' YouTube, June 2020. https://www.youtube.com/watch?v=llci8MVh8J4.

Jüngel, Eberhard. *God's Being Is in Becoming: The Trinitarian Being of God in the Theology of Karl Barth*. Translated by John Webster. Edinburgh: T&T Clark, 2001.

Kaa, Hirini. *Te Hāhi Mihinare: The Māori Anglican Church*. Wellington: Bridget Williams Books, 2020.

Kaltwasser, Cambria. 'Karl Barth on Death'. In *The Wiley Blackwell Companion to Karl Barth*, edited by George Hunsinger and Keith Johnson, 217–29. Oxford: Wiley Blackwell, 2020.

Ketchell, Misha. 'I Once Thought Catholic Humanist Jean Vanier a Hero. Now I'm Wrestling with His Coercive Legacy'. *The Conversation*, 1 May 2020, https://theconversation.com/i-once-thought-catholic-humanist-jean-vanier-a-hero-now-im-wrestling-with-his-coercive-legacy-135794. Accessed 16 March 2023.

Kilby, Karen. 'Perichoresis and Projection: Problems with Social Doctrines of the Trinity.' *New Blackfriars* 81 (2000): 432–5.

Kim, Hyun Joo. *Bearing Sin as Church Community: Bonhoeffer's Hamartiology*. London: T&T Clark Bloomsbury, 2022.
Kitamori, Kazoh: *Theology of the Pain of God*. London: SCM Press, 1966.
Kline, Peter. 'Dietrich Bonhoeffer: Faith as Unsovereign Attention.' *Anglican Focus*, April 2019. https://anglicanfocus.org.au/2019/04/05/dietrich-bonhoeffer-faith-as-unsovereign-attention/.
Kolia, Brian. '*Maota Tau Ave*: Towards an Australian-Samoan Diasporic Understanding of Wisdom in Ecclesiastes.' PhD Dissertation, University of Divinity, 2021.
Krötke, Wolf. 'Dietrich Bonhoeffer and Martin Luther.' In *Bonhoeffer's Intellectual Formation*, edited by Peter Frick, 53–82. Tübingen: Mohr Siebeck, 2008.
Kuske, Martin. *The Old Testament as the Book of Christ: An Appraisal of Bonhoeffer's Interpretation*. Translated by S. T. Kimbrough, Jr. Philadelphia: The Westminster Press, 1976.
LaCugna, Catherine Mowry. *God for Us: The Trinity and the Christian Life*. New York: HarperCollins, 2000.
Laffin, Michael. *The Promise of Martin Luther's Political Theology: Freeing Luther from the Modern Political Narrative*. London: T&T Clark Bloomsbury, 2016.
Levinas, Emmanuel. *Totality and Infinity: An Essay on Exteriority*. Translated by Alphonso Lingis. Pittsburgh: Dusquene Univeristy Press, 1969.
Lim, Chin Ming Stephen. *Contextual Biblical Hermeneutics as Multicentric Dialogue: Towards a Singaporean Reading of Daniel*. Leiden: Brill, 2020.
Lim, Chin Ming Stephen. 'The Impe(/a)rative of Dialogue in Asian Hermeneutics within the Modern/Colonial World System: Renegotiating Biblical Pasts for Planetary Futures.' *Biblical Interpretation* 25 (2017): 663–78.
Lindbeck, George. *The Nature of Doctrine*. Louisville: Westminster John Knox, 1984.
Linton, Simi. *Claiming Disability: Knowledge and Identity*. New York: New York University Press, 1998.
Looper, Joel. *Bonhoeffer's America: A Land without Reformation*. Waco: Baylor University Press, 2021.
Lose, David J. 'Bonhoeffer the Preacher.' In *The Oxford Handbook of Dietrich Bonhoeffer*, edited by Michael Mawson and Philip G. Ziegler, 108–20. Oxford: Oxford University Press, 2019.
Lovin, Robin. *Christian Faith and Public Choices: The Social Ethics of Barth, Brunner and Bonhoeffer*. Minneapolis: Fortress Press, 1984.
Lowe, Walter. *Theology and Difference*. Bloomington: Indiana University Press, 1993.
Luther, Martin. *Luther's Works, Volume 26: Lectures on Galatians Chapters 1–4*. Edited by Jaroslav Pelikan and Walter A. Hansen. Saint Louis: Concordia Publishing House, 1963.
Luther, Martin. 'The Freedom of a Christian.' In *Luther's Works, Volume 31: Career of the Reformer I, 1517–1520*, edited by Harold J. Grimm, 343–77. Philadelphia: Fortress Press, 1957.
Luther, Martin. 'Heidelberg Disputation.' In *Luther's Works, Volume 31: Career of the Reformer I, 1517–1520*, trans. Helmut T. Lehmann, edited by Harold J. Grimm, 39–70. Philadelphia: Fortress Press, 1957.
Luther, Martin. 'On the Councils of the Church.' In *Luther's Works, Volume 41: Church and Ministry III*, edited by Eric W. Gritsch, 3–178. Minneapolis: Fortress Press, 1966.
Luther, Martin. 'Predigten des Jahres 1531.' In *Luthers Werke: Kritische Gesammtausgabe*, 34/1. Weimar: Hermann Bölaus Nachfolger, 1908.

Luther, Martin. 'Sermon on the Man Born Blind, John 9:1-38, 17 March 1518.' In *Luther's Works, Volume 51: Sermons*, edited by John W. Doberstein, 35–43. Philadelphia: Fortress Press, 1959.

Luther, Martin. 'That These Words of Christ, "This Is My Body," Etc. Still Stand Firm against the Fanatics.' In *Luther's Works, Volume 37: Word and Sacrament III*, edited and translated by R. H. Fischer, 3–150. Minneapolis: Fortress Press, 1961.

McBride, Jennifer. *The Church for the World: A Theology of Public Witness*. New York: Oxford University Press, 2011.

McClendon, James. *Systematic Theology, Volume 1: Ethics*. Nashville: Abingdon Press, 2002.

McCormack, Bruce. *Karl Barth's Critically Realistic Dialectical Theology: Its Genesis and Development 1909–1936*. New York: Oxford University Press, 1995.

McLaughlin, Timothy. 'Where the Virus Is Cover for Authoritarianism.' *The Atlantic*, 25 August 2020.

McKenny, Gerald. *Biotechnology, Human Nature, and Christian Ethics*. Cambridge: Cambridge University Press, 2018.

McKenny, Gerald. 'Biotechnology and the Normative Signifcance of Human Nature: A Contribution from Theological Anthropology.' *Studies in Christian Ethics* 26, no. 1 (2013): 18–36.

MacIntyre, Alasdair. *After Virtue: A Study in Moral Theory*. Notre Dame: University of Notre Dame Press, 1981.

MacIntyre, Alasdair. *Dependent Rational Animals: Why Human Beings Need the Virtues*. Chicago: Open Court, 1999.

MacIntyre, Alasdair. *Three Rival Versions of Moral Inquiry: Encyclopaedia, Genealogy and Tradition*. Notre Dame: University of Notre Dame Press, 1990.

MacIntyre, Alasdair. *Whose Justice? Which Rationality?* Notre Dame: Notre Dame University Press, 1988.

Mascall, E. L. *Whatever Happened to the Human Mind?* London: SPCK, 1980.

Martyn, J. Louis. *Galatians: A New Translation with Introduction and Commentary*. New Haven: Yale University Press, 1997.

Mattes, Mark. 'An Analysis and Assessment of Robert Jenson's Systematic Theology.' *Lutheran Quarterly* 14, no. 4 (2000): 463–94.

Mawson, Michael. *Christ Existing as Community: Bonhoeffer's Ecclesiology*. Oxford: Oxford University Press, 2018.

Mawson, Michael. 'Review of David S. Robinson's *Christ and Revelatory Community*.' *Scottish Journal of Theology* 73, no. 2 (2020): 182–3.

Mawson, Michael. 'Speaking of God: Unruly God-Talk with Julian of Norwich.' In *Doing Theology in the New Normal: Global Perspectives*, edited by Jione Havea, 196–208. London: SCM Press, 2021.

Mawson, Michael, and Justin Duckworth. 'Building Prophetic Community in Aotearoa.' In *Small Christian Communities Today: Capturing the Movement*, edited by Joseph G. Healy and Jeanne Hinton, 148–56. Maryknoll: Orbis, 2006.

Mawson, Michael, and Philip G. Ziegler, eds. *Christ, Church and World: Bonhoeffer's Theology and Ethics*. London: T&T Clark Bloomsbury, 2016.

Mawson, Michael, and Philip G. Ziegler, eds. *The Oxford Handbook of Dietrich Bonhoeffer*. Oxford: Oxford University Press, 2019.

Maxey, James A., and Ernst Wendland. *Translating Scripture for Sound and Performance: Biblical Performance Criticism*. Eugene: Wipf & Stock, 2012.

Meilaender, Gilbert. *Bioethics: A Primer for Christians*. Grand Rapids: Eerdmans, 2005.
Mercedes, Anna. *Power For: Feminism and Christ's Self-Giving*. London: T&T Clark Bloomsbury, 2011.
Mercer, Phil. 'Australia Seeks International Help as Flood Crisis Worsens.' *VOA News*, 15 November 2022. www.voanews.com/a/australia-seeks-international-help-as-flood-cri sis-worsens/6834792.html.
Merleau-Ponty, Maurice. *Phenomenology of Perception*. Translated by Colin Smith. New York: Routledge, 2002.
Milbank, John. *Theology and Social Theory: Beyond Secular Reason*. Oxford: Blackwell, 1990.
Milbank, John, Catherine Pitstock and Graham Ward, eds. *Radical Orthodoxy: A New Theology* London: Routledge, 1999.
Miller, Liam. 'James Cone's Constructive Vision of Sin and the Black Lives Matter Movement.' *Black Theology* 18, no. 1 (2020): 4–22.
Mjaaland, Marius Timmann. *The Hidden God: Luther, Philosophy and Political Theology*. Bloomington: Indiana University Press, 2016.
Moltmann, Jürgen. *A Broad Place: An Autobiography*. Translated by Margaret Kohl. Minneapolis: Fortress Press, 2009.
Moltmann, Jürgen. *The Crucified God: The Cross of Christ as the Foundation and Criticism of Christian Theology*. Translated by R. A. Wilson and John Bowden. Minneapolis: Fortress Press, 1993.
Moltmann, Jürgen. *Ethics of Hope*. Translated by Margaret Kohl. Minneapolis: Fortress Press, 2012.
Moltmann, Jürgen. *Theology of Hope: On the Ground and Implications of a Christian Eschatology*. Translated by James W. Leitch. London: SCM, 1964.
Moltmann, Jürgen. *The Trinity and the Kingdom. The Doctrine of God*. Translated by Margaret Kohl. San Francisco: Harper & Row Publishers, 1981.
Moses, Sarah. *Ethics and the Elderly: The Challenge of Long-Term Care*. Maryknoll: Orbis, 2015.
Moyn, Samuel. *The Origins of the Other: Emmanuel Levinas between Revelation and Ethics*. Ithaca: Cornell University Press, 2005.
Moyse, Ashley. *Reading Karl Barth, Interrupting Moral Technique, Transforming Biomedical Ethics*. London: Palgrave MacMillan, 2015.
Mumford, James. *Ethics at the Beginning of Life*. Oxford: Oxford University Press, 2013.
Nation, Mark Thiessen. *Discipleship in a World Full of Nazis: Recovering the True Legacy of Dietrich Bonhoeffer*. Eugene: Cascade, 2022.
Nation, Mark Thiessen. 'Discipleship in a World Full of Nazis: Dietrich Bonhoeffer's Polyphonic Pacifism as Social Ethics.' In *The Wisdom of the Cross: Essays in Honor of John Howard Yoder*, edited by Stanley Hauerwas, Chris K. Huebner, Harry J. Huebner and Mark Thiessen Nation. Grand Rapids: Eerdmans, 1999.
Nation, Mark Thiessen. 'The First Word Christians Have to Say about Violence Is "Church": On Bonhoeffer, Baptists and Becoming a Peace Church.' In *Faithfulness & Fortitude: In Conversation with the Theological Ethics of Stanley Hauerwas*, edited by Mark Thiessen Nation and Samuel Wells. Edinburgh: T&T Clark, 2000.
Nation, Mark, Anthony G. Siegrist and Daniel P. Umbel. *Bonhoeffer the Assassin: Challenging the Myth, Recovering His Call to Peacemaking*. Grand Rapids: Baker Academic, 2013.
Nessan, Craig. 'What if the Church Really Is the Body of Christ?' *Dialog* 51 (2012): 43–52.

Ngien, Dennis. 'Chalcedonian Christology and Beyond: Luther's Understanding of the *Communicatio Idiomatum*.' *Heythrop Journal* 45, no. 1 (2004): 54–68.
Norris, Kristopher. 'James Cone's Legacy for White Christians.' *Political Theology* 21, no. 3 (2020): 207–24.
Norris, Jr., Richard A., trans. and ed. *The Christological Controversy: Sources of Early Christian Thought*. Philadelphia: Fortress Press, 1980.
O'Connell, Mark. *To Be a Machine: Adventures among Cyborgs, Utopians, Hackers, and the Futurists Solving the Modest Problem of Death*. London: Granta, 2017.
O'Donovan, Oliver. *Resurrection and Moral Order: An Outline for Evangelical Ethics*. Grand Rapids: Eerdmans, 1986.
O'Regan, Cyril. *The Heterodox Hegel*. New York: SUNY, 1994.
Pangritz, Andreas. *Karl Barth in the Theology of Dietrich Bonhoeffer*. Translated by Martin Rumscheidt. Grand Rapids: Eerdmans, 2000.
Pattel-Gray, Anne. *The Great White Flood: Racism in Australia*. Atlanta: Scholar's Press, 1998.
Peppiatt, Lucy. *Imago Dei*. Eugene: Cascade, 2022.
Peterson, Erik. *Theological Tractates*. Translated by Michael Hollerich. Stanford: Stanford University Press, 2012.
Pinnock, Clark. *Most Moved Mover: A Theology of God's Openness*. Grand Rapids: Baker and Paternoster, 2000.
Plant, Stephen J. *Taking Stock of Bonhoeffer: Essays in Biblical Interpretation and Scripture*. Farnham: Ashgate, 2014.
Pope, Stephen. 'Reason and Natural Law.' In *The Oxford Handbook of Theological Ethics*, edited by Gilbert Meilaender and William Werpehowski, 148–67. Oxford: Oxford University Press, 2007.
Porter, Jean. 'Tradition in the Recent Work of Alasdair MacIntyre.' In *Alasdair MacIntyre*, edited by Mark C. Murphy, 38–69. Cambridge: Cambridge University Press, 2003.
Prevot, Andrew. 'Theology and Race: Black and Womanist Traditions in the United States.' *Theology* 2, no. 2 (2018): 1–79.
Pribbenow, Brad. *Prayerbook of Christ: Dietrich Bonhoeffer's Christological Interpretation of the Psalms*. Lanham: Rowman and Littlefield, 2018.
Radner, Ephraim. *A Brutal Unity: The Spiritual Politics of the Christian Church*. Waco: Baylor University Press, 2012.
Rayson, Dianne. *Bonhoeffer and Climate Change: Theology and Ethics for the Anthropocene*. Langham, Lexington, 2021.
Rashover, Randi. *Revelation and Theopolitics: Barth, Rosenzweig and the Politics of Praise*. London: T&T Clark, 2005.
Reaves, Jayme, David Tombs and Rocio Figueroa, eds. *When Did We See You Naked? Jesus as a Victim of Sexual Abuse*. London: SCM Press, 2001.
Reddie, Anthony. *Introducing James H. Cone: A Personal Exploration*. London: SCM Press, 2022.
Reinders, Hans. *Disability, Providence and Ethics*. Waco: Baylor University Press, 2014.
Reinders, Hans. *The Future of the Disabled in Liberal Societies*. Notre Dame: University of Notre Dame Press, 2000.
Reinders, Hans. *Receiving the Gift of Friendship: Profound Disability, Theological Anthropology and Ethics*. Grand Rapids: Eerdmans, 2008.
Reynolds, Thomas. *Vulnerable Communion: A Theology of Disability and Hospitality*. Grand Rapids: Brazos Press, 2008.

Ridenour, Autumn. *Sabbath Rest as Vocation: Aging Toward Death*. London: T&T Clark Bloomsbury, 2018.
Ringma, Charles. *Seize the Day with Dietrich Bonhoeffer*. Carol Stream: Nav Press, 2000.
Robinson, David S. *Christ and Revelatory Community in Bonhoeffer's Reception of Hegel*. Tübingen: Mohr Siebeck, 2018.
Rosner, Jennifer M. *Healing the Schism: Barth, Rosenzweig, and the New Jewish-Christian Encounter*. Minneapolis: Fortress Press, 2005.
Rosenwald, Lawrence. 'On the Reception of Buber and Rosenzweig's Bible.' *Prooftexts: A Journal of Jewish Literary History* 14, no. 2 (1994): 141–65.
Rosenzweig, Franz. 'Scripture and Luther.' In *Scripture and Translation*, edited by Martin Buber and Franz Rosenzweig, 47–69. Bloomington: Indiana University Press, 1994.
Rosenzweig, Franz. 'Scripture and Word.' In *Scripture and Translation*, edited by Martin Buber and Franz Rosenzweig, 40–6. Bloomington: Indiana University Press, 1994.
Ross, Jameson. *Bonhoeffer as Biblical Interpreter: Reading Scripture in 1930s Germany*. London: T&T Clark Bloomsbury, 2021.
Rountree, Te Aroha. ' "Jesus Christ, once Was a Savage!" Selective Memory, Staged Identity, Stolen Places.' In *Unsettling Theologies: Memory, Identity and Place*, edited by Brian Kolia and Michael Mawson. London: Palgrave MacMillan, 2023.
Sanders, E. P. *Jesus and Judaism*. London: SCM Press, 1985.
Sanders, E. P. *Paul and Palestinian Judaism: A Comparison of Patterns of Religion*. Minneapolis: Fortress Press, 1977.
Sanders, John. *The God Who Risks: A Theology of Divine Providence*. Downers Grove: IVP Academic, 2009.
Sher, Leo. 'The Impact of the COVID-19 Pandemic on Suicide Rates.' *An International Journal of Medicine* 113, no. 10 (2020): 707–12, https://doi.org/10.1093/qjmed/hcaa202.
Schlingensiepen, Ferdinand. *Dietrich Bonhoeffer: 1906–1945*. Translated by Isabel Best. London: T&T Clark, 2010.
Schraer, Rachel. 'Depression Doubles during Coronavirus Pandemic.' BBC, 18 August 2020. https://www.bbc.com/news/health-53820425. Accessed 16 March 2023.
Singer, Peter. *Practical Ethics*. 2nd edn. Cambridge: Cambridge University Press, 1993.
Slot, Edward van'. *Negativism of Revelation? Barth and Bonhoeffer on Faith and Actualism*. Tübingen: Mohr Siebeck, 2015.
Smith, Mitzi J. ' "He Never Said a Mumbalin Word": A Womanist Perspective of Crucifixion, Sexual Violence, and Sacralised Silence.' In *When Did We See You Naked? Jesus as a Victim of Sexual Abuse*, edited by Jayme R. Reaves, David Tombs and Rocio Figueroa, 46–66. London: SCM Press, 2001.
Smith, Ted. *The New Measures: A Theological History of Democratic Practice*. Cambridge: Cambridge University Press, 2007.
Smith, Ted. 'Theories of Practice.' In *The Wiley-Blackwell Companion to Practical Theology*, edited by Bonnie J. Miller-McLemore, 246–50. Oxford: Wiley Blackwell, 2013.
Smythe, Shannon Nicole. *Forensic Apocalpytic Theology: Karl Barth and the Doctrine of Divine Justification*. Minneapolis: Fortress Press, 2016.
Sölle, Dorothee. *Suffering*. Translated by Everett Kalin. Minneapolis: Fortress Press, 1984.
Song, Robert. 'Review of Gerald Mckenny's *Biotechnology, Human Nature and Christian Ethics*.' *Theology* 123, no. 1 (2020): 46–7.
Song, Robert. 'Technological Immortalization and Original Mortality: Karl Barth on the Celebration of Finitude.' In *Immortal God, Immortal Life: Theological Investigations into*

the Concept of Technology, edited by Philip G. Ziegler, 187–209. London: T&T Clark Bloomsbury, 2016.

Soosten, Joachim von. *Die Sozialität der Kirche: Die Theologie and Theorie der Kirche in Dietrich Bonhoeffers 'Sanctorum Communio'*. Munich: Chr. Kaiser, 1992.

Spanring, Paul. *Dietrich Bonhoeffer and Arnold Köster: Two Distinct Voices in the Midst of Germany's Third Reich Turmoil*. Eugene: Pickwick, 2013.

Stassen, Glen. *A Thicker Jesus: Incarnational Discipleship in a Secular Age*. Louisville: Westminster John Knox, 2012.

Swinton, John. *Dementia: Living in the Memories of God*. Grand Rapids: Eerdmans, 2012.

Swinton, John. 'Who Is the God We Worship? Theologies of Disability; Challenges and New Possibilities.' *International Journal of Practical Theology* 14, no.2 (2011): 273–307

Tafilowski, Ryan. 'The Body upon the (Lynching) Tree: The Humanity of Jesus in James Cone and Reinhold Niebuhr.' *The Journal of Theological Studies* 20, no. 2 (2020): 756–77.

Tanner, Kathryn. *Christ the Key*. Cambridge: Cambridge University Press, 2009.

Tanner, Kathryn. 'Trinity, Christology, and Community.' In *Christology and Ethics*, edited by F. LeRon Shults and Brent Waters, 56–74. Grand Rapids: Eerdmans, 2010.

Taylor, Derek W. *Reading Scripture as the Church: Bonhoeffer's Hermeneutic of Discipleship*. Downers Grove: IVP Academic, 2020.

Thompson, Geoff. *Disturbing Much, Disturbing Many: Theology Provoked by the Basis of Union*. Eugene: Wipf & Stock, 2016.

Thompson, Geoff. *A Genuinely Theological Church: Ministry, Theology and the Uniting Church*. Sydney: Morning Star Publishing, 2018.

Thunberg, Greta. 'Speech at UN Climate Action Summit.' YouTube, 23 September 2019. www.youtube.com/watch?v=KAJsdgTPJpU.

Tietz, Christiane. *Theologian of Resistance: The Life and Thought of Dietrich Bonhoeffer*. Minneapolis: Fortress Press, 2016.

Tödt, Heinz Eduard. *Authentic Faith: Bonhoeffer's Theological Ethics in Context*. Grand Rapids: Eerdmans, 2007.

Tonstad, Linn Marie. '(Un)wise Theologians: Systematic Theology in the University.' *International Journal of Systematic Theology* 22, no. 4 (2020): 494–511.

Tooley, Michael. *Abortion and Infanticide*. Oxford: Clarendon, 1983.

Tranter, Samuel. *Oliver O'Donovan's Moral Theology*. London: T&T Clark Bloomsbury, 2020.

Ulrich, Hans. 'The Form of Ethical Life.' In *The Oxford Handbook of Dietrich Bonhoeffer*, edited by Michael Mawson and Philip G. Ziegler, 289–305. Oxford: Oxford University Press, 2019.

Ulrich, Hans. 'Stations on the Way to Freedom: The Presence of God – The Freedom of the Disciples.' In *Who Am I? Bonhoeffer's Theology through His Poetry*, edited by Bernd Wannenwetsch, 147–74. London: T&T Clark, 2009.

Vaka'uta, Nāsili. *Reading Ezra 9-10 Tu'a-wise Rethinking Biblical Interpretation in Oceania*. Atlanta: SBL Press, 2011.

Van der Westhuizen, Henco, ed. *Letters to a Young Theologian*. Minneapolis: Fortress Press, 2022.

Verhagen, Koert *Being and Action* Coram Deo: *Bonhoeffer and the Retrieval of Justification's Social Import*. London: T&T Clark Bloomsbury, 2021.

Vischer, Wilhelm. *The Witness of the Old Testament to Christ*. Translated by A. B. Crabtree. London: Lutterworth Press, 1949.

Volf, Miroslav. *Exclusion and Embrace: Theological Exploration of Identity, Otherness and Reconciliation*. Nashville: Abingdon Press, 1994.

Vosloo, Robert. 'Body and Health in the Light of the Theology of Dietrich Bonhoeffer.' *Religion and Theology* 13, no. 1 (2006): 23–7.

Walker, Peter, and Jonathan Cole. *Theology on a Defiant Earth: Seeking Hope in the Anthropocene*. Lanham: Lexington, 2022.

Wannenwetsch, Bernd. 'Angels with Clipped Wings: The Disabled as Key to the Recognition of Personhood.' In *Theology, Disability and the New Genetics: Why Science Needs the Church*, edited by John Swinton and Brian Brock, 182–200. London: T&T Clark, 2007.

Wannenwetsch, Bernd. 'Christians and Pagans: Towards a Trans-Religious Second Naiveté or How to Be a Christological Creature.' In *Who Am I? Bonhoeffer's Theology through His Poetry*, edited by Bernd Wannenwetsch, 175–96. London: T&T Clark Bloomsbury, 2009.

Wannenwetsch, Bernd. 'My Strength Is Made Perfect in Weakness: Bonhoeffer and the War over Disabled Life.' In *Disability in the Christian Tradition: A Reader*, edited by Brian Brock and John Swinton, 354–60. Grand Rapids: Eerdmans, 2012.

Wannenwetsch, Bernd. ' "Responsible Living" or "Responsible Self"? Bonhoefferian Reflections on a Vexed Moral Notion.' *Studies in Christian Ethics* 18, no. 3 (2005): 125–40.

Weber, Max. 'Politics as Vocation.' In *Weber: Selections in Translation*, edited by W. G. Runciman and translated by Eric Matthews, 212–25. Cambridge: Cambridge University Press, 1978.

Webster, John. 'Reading the Bible: The Example of Barth and Bonhoeffer.' In *Word and Church: Essays in Christian Dogmatics*, 87–112. London: T&T Clark, 2001.

Webster, John. 'The Self-Organizing Power of the Gospel.' In *Word and Church: Essays in Christian Dogmatics*, 191–210. Edinburgh: T&T Clark, 2001.

Weinandy, Thomas. *Does God Suffer?* Edinburgh: T&T Clark, 2000.

Wells, Samuel. *God's Companions: Reimagining Christian Ethics*. Oxford: Wiley-Blackwell, 2006.

Whitehead, A. N., and David Ray Griffin, eds. *Process and Reality: An Essay in Cosmology*. New York: The Free Press, 1978.

White, Graham. 'Luther's Views on Language.' *Journal of Theology and Literature* 3, no. 2 (1989): 188–218.

Williams, Reggie. *Bonhoeffer's Black Jesus: Harlem Renaissance Theology and an Ethic of Resistance*. Waco: Baylor University Press, 2014.

Williams, Rowan. *The Edge of Words: God and the Habits of Language*. London: Bloomsbury, 2014.

Wilson-Kastner, Patricia. *Faith, Feminism and the Christ*. Philadelphia: Fortress Press, 1983.

Winter, Sean. 'Present-ing the Word: The Use and Abuse of Bonhoeffer on the Bible.' *The Bonhoeffer Legacy: The Australasian Journal of Bonhoeffer Studies* 2, no. 2 (2014): 17–35.

Winter, Sean. 'Word and World: Dietrich Bonhoeffer and Biblical Interpretation Today.' *Pacifica: Australasian Theological Studies* 25, no. 2 (2012): 161–75.

Wood, Donald. '*This* Ability: Barth on the Concrete Freedom of Human Life.' In *Disability in the Christian Tradition: A Reader*, edited by Brian Brock and John Swinton, 391–426. Grand Rapids: Eerdmans, 2012.

Wright, N. T. *Jesus and the Victory of God*. London: SPCK, 1996.
Wright, N. T. *Paul and His Recent Interpreters*. London: SPCK, 2015.
Wright, N. T. *Paul and the Faithfulness of God*. Minneapolis: Fortress Press, 2013.
Wüstenberg, Ralf, Stefan Heuser and Ester Hornung, eds. *Bonhoeffer and the Biosciences: An Initial Exploration*. Pieterlen: Peter Lang, 2010.
Wüstenberg, Ralf K., and Jens Zimmermann, eds. *God Speaks to Us: Bonhoeffer's Biblical Hermeneutics*. Frankfurt: Peter Lang, 2013.
Yeago, David. 'The Church as Polity? The Lutheran Context of Robert W. Jenson's Ecclesiology.' In *Trinity, Time, and Church: A Response to the Theology of Robert W. Jenson*, edited by Colin Gunton, 208–14. Grand Rapids: Eerdmans, 2000.
Yoder, John Howard. *Body Politics: Five Practices of the Community before the Watching World*. Harrisonburg: Herald Press, 2001.
Yoder, John Howard. 'The Christological Presuppositions of Discipleship.' In *Being Human, Becoming Human: Dietrich Bonhoeffer and Social Thought*, edited by Jens Zimmermann and Brian Gregor. Eugene: Pickwick Publications, 2010.
Yoder, John Howard. *The Original Revolution: Essays on Christian Pacifism*. Waterloo: Herald Press, 1971.
Yoder, John Howard. 'Light to the Nations.' *Concerns* 9 (1961): 14–18.
Yoder, John Howard. *The Politics of Jesus*. 2nd edn. Grand Rapids: Eerdmans, 1994.
Yong, Amos. *Theology and Down Syndrome: Reimagining Disability in Late Modernity*. Waco: Baylor University Press, 2007.
Yong, Ed. 'How the Virus Defeated America.' *The Atlantic*, 4 August 2020.
Ziegler, Philip G. 'Christ for Us Today – Promeity in the Theologies of Bonhoeffer and Kierkegaard.' *International Journal of Systematic Theology* 15, no. 1 (2013): 25–41.
Ziegler, Philip G. 'Dietrich Bonhoeffer—An Ethics of God's Apocalpyse?' *Modern Theology* 23, no. 4 (2007), 579–94.
Ziegler, Philip G. 'God.' In *The Oxford Handbook of Dietrich Bonhoeffer*, edited by Michael Mawson and Philip G. Ziegler, 137–49. Oxford: Oxford University Press, 2019.
Ziegler, Philip G. *Militant Grace: The Apocalyptic Turn and the Future of Christian Theology*. Grand Rapids: Baker Academic, 2018.
Ziegler, Philip G. 'A Response.' *International Journal of Systematic Theology* 22, no.3 (2020): 327–35.
Zimmermann, Jens. 'Reading the Book of the Church: Bonhoeffer's Christological Hermeneutics.' *Modern Theology*, 28, no. 4 (2012): 763–80.
Zimmermann, Jens. 'Recovering the Natural for Politics: Bonhoeffer and the Natural Law Tradition.' In *Dietrich Bonhoeffer, Theology and Political Resistance*, edited by Lori Brandt Hale and W. David Hall, 27–48. Lanham: Lexington, 2020.
Zizioulas, John. *Being as Communion: Studies in Personhood and the Church*. London: Darton, Longman, and Todd, 1985.
Zizioulas, John. 'On Being a Person: Towards an Ontology of Personhood.' In *Persons, Divine and Human*, edited by Christoph Schwöbel and Colin E. Gunton, 33–46. Edinburgh: T&T Clark, 1992.

INDEX

Act and Being 37, 68
Adam 85, 87, 100, 102, 114–16, 176
agency 38, 41, 77, 133, 143, 169, 170–1
anabaptist 8, 62–3, 153–4, 161–2, 167–8
anthropology 8, 48, 73–81, 83–4, 86, 88–90, 93–4, 96, 110, 132, 158, 163–4
apocalyptic 8, 37–41, 46, 48, 159–60
Augustine 2, 10, 91, 138
Australia ix, 5, 6, 11, 14, 15
authority 47, 49, 134, 139–41, 148, 156
Aquinas, Thomas 2, 51, 75

Barth, Karl 8, 13, 16, 21, 24–6, 28, 32, 34–5, 37, 39–40, 41, 43, 62, 68, 92–100, 107–13, 115–16, 119, 125, 142–4
Church Dogmatics 94, 110–13, 116
Bethel Confession 25, 27–8
Bible (*see also* scripture) 10, 16, 21–35, 37, 40–7, 56, 126, 156
Black Lives Matter 12, 16, 179
Black theology 9, 173, 177
body (*see also* embodiment) 24, 30, 38, 47–8, 66, 76, 82, 95, 98, 104, 106, 115, 135, 137, 139, 147, 152, 161, 167–8, 178–80
Brett, Mark 6, 14–15
Brock, Brian ix–x, 4, 16, 29–31, 42, 76, 85, 96–7
Buber, Martin 43–7, 77
Butler, Judith 13–14

Carter, J. Kameron 178–9
Chalcedon 121–3, 129, 131
Christology (*see also* Jesus Christ) 9, 32, 42, 53, 56–7, 61, 70, 81, 92–3, 115, 121, 123, 126, 129, 131, 134, 141, 161–2, 172–5, 177–9, 181
church (*see also* ecclesiology) 2, 4–6, 8, 10, 12–15, 21–2, 26, 28, 35, 37, 45, 52, 67, 79, 82, 85, 124, 128, 135–60, 163, 165, 167–70, 173–5, 179

climate change 7, 11, 13, 16
community 1–5, 8, 13, 15, 33, 35, 42–7, 68, 80–1, 87–9, 102, 113, 117, 129, 135–55, 157–62, 167–70, 178–9
Cone, James 9, 18, 53, 172–3, 177–81
Confessing Church 10, 22, 67, 136
confession (of sin) 149, 151, 169
confessional (context) 62–3, 68–9
'Contemporizing New Testament Texts' 22–3, 25, 27–8, 30, 32, 34, 41–2, 55–6, 123
coram Deo 40, 48, 86, 132, 166
creation 31, 38, 51, 63, 80, 87, 92, 98, 103, 106–7, 110, 119, 123, 147
Creation and Fall 8, 16, 22, 28, 31, 73, 83–5, 87, 100, 102
crisis 6–7, 10–11, 17, 141
cross (*see also* crucifixion) 8, 15–18, 28, 32–4, 50–9, 86, 115, 119–20, 123–4, 128–31, 133–4, 153–4, 156–61, 167, 172–81
crucifixion (*see also* cross) 9, 124, 130–1, 156, 157, 160, 167, 173, 180–1

death 25, 32, 38, 53, 56–7, 102, 110, 114–16, 124, 126–7, 129, 130–1, 158, 160, 166, 176, 178, 180–1
DeJonge, Michael 5, 8, 40, 54, 61–3, 65–9, 104, 123
de Gruchy, John 61, 173
disability x, 8, 48, 73–7, 80, 82–5, 88–9, 96–7
Discipleship 1, 22, 25, 27, 49–50, 54, 56, 67, 128, 153–5, 162, 164–5, 167
discipleship 6, 8, 21, 49–50, 58, 67, 128, 153–5, 158, 160–8, 172
divine passibility 119–20, 123–4, 128, 133
divine suffering *see* suffering
docetism 175, 179–81

earth 11, 13, 16, 26, 31, 85, 155, 157, 167
ecclesiology (*see also* church) 3, 5, 35, 68, 135–6, 138, 140, 143–4, 151
embodied, embodiment (*see also* body) 64, 66, 73, 76, 82–3, 86, 88, 90, 111, 116, 139, 145, 151, 158, 166, 169, 178
empire *see* Roman Empire
ethics, ethical ix, 3–7, 13–14, 16, 31, 34, 37, 42, 46–9, 64–8, 73–91, 93, 97–105, 110–11, 131–6, 150, 153–8, 161–2, 165, 169–71, 177, 180
Ethics 2, 8, 51, 58–9, 69, 83–4, 86–8, 97, 100–1, 105, 115, 165
eschatology 38, 40, 131, 136–8, 160, 169
euthanasia 97, 105
evangelism 50, 58–9

faith 6–7, 17, 26–7, 32, 40, 50–1, 55–8, 60, 68, 79, 89, 98, 105, 124–5, 128, 131, 135, 149–50, 152–4, 162, 165–8, 170, 176, 178
feminist theology 15–16, 54, 79, 119
Finkenwalde 10, 22–3, 25, 35, 55
Floyd, George 12
formation 6, 10, 14, 24, 40, 123, 132, 155, 164–5
freedom 4, 12, 42, 49, 51–2, 54, 56–8, 82, 84–6, 96, 100–1, 105–6, 110, 131, 137, 148
    divine 39, 41, 123, 130, 144, 150
friendship 74, 76, 78–83, 88–9, 123, 159

glory 50–4, 104, 124
goodness 50, 52, 85, 96, 100, 106–7, 116, 168–9
grace 13, 29, 38–40, 48, 51, 53, 57, 59, 67, 75, 85, 87, 89, 91, 94, 101, 112–16, 152, 159, 163, 165, 172
Green, Clifford 5, 61, 145
Gunton, Colin 79, 81, 136–8, 145

habitus 65–9
Halbach, Ross ix, 5, 15
Harnack, Adolf von 28
Harlem 177
Hegel, G. W. F. 3, 68, 138, 146, 148, 158
hermeneutics 6, 8, 17, 21, 23, 30, 62, 65–6, 136

hiddenness (of God) 26, 33, 53, 56, 113, 124, 170, 174, 179, 181
historical-critical method 26–7
history 24–6, 41, 51, 100, 122, 130–1, 140–2, 147, 160, 162, 172, 174–6, 179
Hitler, Adolf 10, 28, 126
Holy Spirit 8, 80, 82, 93–4, 96, 129–32, 135–45, 147–52, 163
Holmes, Christopher 123, 145
hope 1, 7, 17, 18, 32, 50, 55–7, 59, 68, 110, 112, 116, 120, 130–1, 152
human beings 11, 15, 25–6, 38, 41, 47, 50, 52–3, 73–82, 84–9, 92–8, 100–6, 109–16, 125, 129, 132–3, 146, 158–9, 162–3, 165–6, 168, 172, 180
human nature 8, 73–6, 80–5, 91–100, 104, 106–8, 110–11, 121–3, 129, 139, 145, 175
Hütter, Reinhart 8, 135–6, 141–6, 148–51

idealism 1, 3, 55, 122, 146
imago Dei 75–80, 84–5, 93–4, 99, 100
incarnation 28, 99, 129, 143, 161–2, 175
indigenous theologies 6, 178

Jenkins, Willis 13, 64, 66
Jennings, Willie James 13
Jenson, Robert x, 8, 119, 135–42, 145–6, 148–51
Jesus Christ (*see also* Christology) 1, 17, 25–6, 28–30, 32–4, 51–4, 56–7, 59, 86, 93–4, 96, 99, 101, 103, 112–13, 121–3, 125–7, 129, 132, 139, 141, 153–71, 173–81
Jews, Jewish 8, 28, 37, 39, 43, 45–6, 113, 157, 161, 176, 178–9
Julian of Norwich 6, 17
justification (doctrine) 38–40, 59, 101, 125, 158–9, 166

Kant, Immanuel 104, 143
kenosis 15

LaCugna, Catherine 79, 82, 119
'Lectures on Christology' 9, 53, 56–7, 121, 123, 131, 134, 161–2, 173–7, 181
liberal theology 4, 155, 175, 179
Life Together 1, 22, 33, 58, 87
logos 122, 179

Luther, Martin 2, 4, 8, 10, 16, 24–5, 32, 44–5, 47, 50–9, 61, 63, 66–70, 86, 123–4, 127–9, 131, 136–8, 139, 142–3, 146, 152, 165, 167
Lutheranism 4, 8, 32, 49, 54, 57–8, 61–3, 65–9, 136–7, 140, 169
lynching 7, 18, 53, 172, 177–80

MacIntyre, Alasdair 63–6, 69, 77
materiality (*see also* substance) 8, 30, 37, 41, 55, 180
meditation 22, 26, 28, 31, 34–6, 42, 122–3, 144
metaphysics 6, 34–5, 80, 83, 89, 125
McBride, Jennifer ix, 15, 168
McClendon, James 135, 153, 162, 167
McKenny, Gerald ix, 2, 8
Mjaaland, Marius 47, 53, 91–7, 99, 103–4, 106–8, 110–11, 113
Milbank, John 13, 136, 139
mission 50, 58–9, 78, 83, 137–8, 144, 172
missionary 6, 143, 178
Moltmann, Jürgen 8, 79, 119–21, 124, 128–33
moral, morality 16, 34–5, 64, 87, 98, 103, 105, 110, 125, 140

Nation, Mark Thiessen 61, 153–4, 162, 167
National Socialism (*incl* Nazi) 5, 10, 28, 62, 97, 102, 136, 153–4
'Natural Life' 2, 8, 91–2, 97–108, 115
natural rights 73–4, 91, 97–8, 103–6, 108
nature *see* human nature
New Zealand ix, 1, 14, 178
Niebuhr, Reinhold 178–89

obedience 42, 130, 164–5, 168–9
ontology 4, 38, 80–1

penultimate 51, 98, 101, 106–7, 165
power 12, 15, 53–6, 58, 105, 123, 125–7, 137, 139, 151, 158, 172, 175
practices 33, 42, 47–8, 65–6, 74, 88, 135–6, 141–5, 149–53, 156, 170, 174
prayer 1, 13, 26, 33–5, 59, 144
preaching 34–5, 42–3, 45, 47, 149, 173–4
promeity 132, 161, 173–4, 178–9, 181

Protestant 2, 4, 39–40, 45, 67, 98–9, 119, 142, 148–9, 155
Psalms 21–2, 26, 28, 33, 55

race 5, 13, 178–80
racism 6, 12–13, 97, 179
Rayson, Dianne ix, 7
reality 1, 4, 32, 38–9, 43, 48–51, 53–5, 57, 59, 86, 101, 112–13, 120, 123, 133, 137–8, 146, 148, 156, 161, 163
reason 2, 75–7, 80, 95, 98–9, 103–6, 122, 133, 136, 141, 164
Reddie, Anthony 177, 179, 180
Reformed 62–3, 67–8, 98, 122, 123, 175
Reinders, Hans 73–4, 76–85, 89
relationship 4, 6, 8, 14, 28, 40, 43, 47–8, 62–3, 66–9, 77, 80, 83–4, 87–90, 92, 100–1, 111–12, 116, 126–9, 135, 145–6, 156, 158, 162, 164, 167, 178
relationality 77–8, 83–4, 87–9, 95, 108, 112, 142, 167
religion 3, 13, 25, 34, 39, 125, 127, 158, 179
religionless 5, 29, 125, 126, 128, 174
responsibility 37, 47–8, 84, 86, 89, 90, 156
resurrection 25, 27, 87, 96, 103, 107
revelation 4, 24–8, 32, 37–41, 43, 46, 51–3, 55–6, 68, 78, 85, 96, 99, 112, 122–3, 125, 146–8
rights *see* natural rights
Roman Empire 9, 180–1
Rosenzweig, Franz 8, 37, 40, 43–8

sacrament 5, 81, 137, 139, 141–2, 149, 150, 173–4
Sanctorum Communio 3, 35, 68, 145–7
Sanders, E. P. 38, 119, 157
scripture (*see also* Bible) 8, 10, 14–17, 21–37, 40–8, 53–7, 114, 128, 144, 159, 162–3
sexual abuse 78, 154, 180
substance (*see also* materiality) 8, 30–2, 34–5, 37, 41–3, 46–8
suffering 8, 15, 17, 32–3, 49–50, 53–9, 119–21, 127–34, 141–4, 155–6, 167, 172, 181
  divine 8, 15, 17, 49, 53–9, 119, 120–1, 124–34, 141–4
  human 8, 17, 32–3, 49–50, 52–9, 120, 127–34, 141–4, 155–6, 167, 172, 181

status confessionis 10, 12
Swinton, John ix, 4, 73–4, 76, 80, 85, 96–7, 144

Tanner, Kathryn 81, 92–7, 99, 107
Tegel prison 23, 29, 34, 56
telos 81, 86, 138–43, 151
theologia crucis 32, 50, 52–4, 58, 128–33, 175–6
Tietz, Christiane 3, 5, 173
transformation 80, 82–3, 87–8, 94, 96, 107
Trinity 73, 79–85, 89, 93, 119–20, 123, 129–32, 136–8

Ulrich, Hans 4, 30, 49–52, 54, 56–7, 101
ultimate 51, 98, 101–2, 107, 125, 165

Verhagen, Koert 40, 166

vicarious representation action (*Stellvertretung*) 84, 86
vulnerability 5, 8, 16, 176

weakness 49–50, 53–8, 60, 97, 121, 126–8, 168
Webster, John 4, 21, 34, 119, 141
Williams, Reggie 177, 180
worldliness 58, 125, 127–9
Wright, N. T. 38–9, 156

Yoder, John Howard 8, 68, 135, 153–63, 165–7, 169–71
Yong, Amos 73, 76–7

Ziegler, Philip ix, 4, 22, 24, 38–40, 42, 53, 101, 110, 132, 145, 173
Zizioulas, John 79–83, 85, 88, 141–2

www.ingramcontent.com/pod-product-compliance
Lightning Source LLC
Chambersburg PA
CBHW051523230426
43668CB00012B/1715